John Lewis-Stempel is an award-winning writer predominantly known for his books on nature and history. He lives in Herefordshire, on the very edge of England before it runs into Wales, and within a stone's throw (with a decent gust of wind) from where his family farmed in the 1300s. His many books include the bestselling *Six Weeks*, *The War Behind the Wire* and *Meadowland*, winner of the Wainwright Book Prize for nature writing. His books have been published in languages as diverse as Brazilian Portuguese and Japanese, and are available on all continents apart from Antarctica. He is married with two children and also farms. At present he writes for *Country Life*, and in 2016 he was named a Columnist of the Year by the British Society of Magazine Editors.

@JLewisStempel

*By John Lewis-Stempel*

Fatherhood: An Anthology

The Autobiography of the British Soldier

England: The Autobiography

The Wild Life

The Wildlife Garden

Foraging: The Essential Guide

Six Weeks: The Short and Gallant Life of the
British Officer in the First World War

The War Behind the Wire: Life, Death and Heroism Amongst
British Prisoners of War, 1914–18

Meadowland: The Private Life of an English Field

The Running Hare: The Secret Life of Farmland

Where Poppies Blow: The British Soldier, Nature, the Great War

# WHERE POPPIES BLOW

## THE BRITISH SOLDIER, NATURE, THE GREAT WAR

JOHN LEWIS-STEMPEL

WEIDENFELD & NICOLSON

A W&N PAPERPACK

First published in Great Britain in 2016
This paperback edition first published in 2017
by Weidenfeld & Nicolson
an imprint of The Orion Publishing Group Ltd
Carmelite House, 50 Victoria Embankment
London EC4Y 0DZ

An Hachette UK Company

1 3 5 7 9 10 8 6 4 2

A CIP catalogue record for this book
is available from the British Library.

ISBN 978-1-78022-491-6

Typeset by Input Data Services Ltd, Bridgwater, Somerset

Printed and bound by CPI Group (UK) Ltd, Croydon, CR0 4YY

MIX
Paper from
responsible sources
FSC® C104740

www.orionbooks.co.uk

*Et in Arcadia ego*

# CONTENTS

# ACKNOWLEDGEMENTS

My profound thanks are due to Charlotte Zeepvat, Sally Kirkwood, Luci Gosling, David Underdown, Alison Tindale (@Backyard Larder), James Grant Repshire, staff of the London Library, staff of the Imperial War Museum, Andy Arnold, Edmund King, Steve Clifford, Matthew Ball, Sevenoaks Memorial Project @7Oaksmemorial, Stephen Cooper, Anna Stenning, David Underwood, @roadtowar1914, Ed Hutchings, Ben Clark, Paul Murphy, Julian Beech, Helen Richardson, Jessica Purdue.

My agent Julian Alexander and my publisher Alan Samson gave understanding, inspiration and logistical support above and beyond the call of duty. My daughter, Freda, provided superlative map-reading and photographic skills on a recce of the Western Front. My son, Tris, was a genius raider of medical archives. My wife, Penny, was muse, critic, support, and it would never have been done without her. Again.

The book is for Freda, Penny and Tristram. Of course. And for every British soldier, sailor and airman who fought for King and Countryside. Of course.

# LIST OF ILLUSTRATIONS

# AUGUST, 1914

How still this quiet cornfield is to-night!
By an intenser glow the evening falls,
Bringing, not darkness, but a deeper light;
Among the stocks a partridge covey calls.

The windows glitter on the distant hill;
Beyond the hedge the sheep-bells in the fold
Stumble on sudden music and are still;
The forlorn pinewoods droop above the wold.

An endless quiet valley reaches out
Past the blue hills into the evening sky;
Over the stubble, cawing goes a rout
Of rooks from harvest, flagging as they fly.

So beautiful it is, I never saw
So great a beauty on these English fields,
Touched by the twilight's coming into awe,
Ripe to the soul and rich with summer's yields.

These homes, this valley spread below me here,
The rooks, the tilted stacks, the beasts in pen,
Have been the heartfelt things, past-speaking dear
To unknown generations of dead men,

Who, century after century, held these farms,
And, looking out to watch the changing sky,
Heard, as we hear, the rumours and alarms
Of war at hand and danger pressing nigh.

And knew, as we know, that the message meant
The breaking off of ties, the loss of friends,
Death, like a miser getting in his rent,
And no new stones laid where the trackway ends.

The harvest not yet won, the empty bin,
The friendly horses taken from the stalls,
The fallow on the hill not yet brought in,
The cracks unplastered in the leaking walls.

Yet heard the news, and went discouraged home,
And brooded by the fire with heavy mind,
With such dumb loving of the Berkshire loam
As breaks the dumb hearts of the English kind,

Then sadly rose and left the well-loved Downs,
And so by ship to sea, and knew no more
The fields of home, the byres, the market towns,
Nor the dear outline of the English shore,

But knew the misery of the soaking trench,
The freezing in the rigging, the despair
In the revolting second of the wrench
When the blind soul is flung upon the air,

And died (uncouthly, most) in foreign lands
For some idea but dimly understood
Of an English city never built by hands
Which love of England prompted and made good.

If there be any life beyond the grave,
It must be near the men and things we love,
Some power of quick suggestion how to save,
Touching the living soul as from above.

An influence from the Earth from those dead hearts
So passionate once, so deep, so truly kind,
That in the living child the spirit starts,
Feeling companioned still, not left behind.

Surely above these fields a spirit broods,
A sense of many watchers muttering near
Of the lone Downland with the forlorn woods
Loved to the death, inestimably dear.

A muttering from beyond the veils of Death
From long-dead men, to whom this quiet scene
Came among blinding tears with the last breath,
The dying soldier's vision of his queen.

All the unspoken worship of those lives
Spent in forgotten wars at other calls
Glimmers upon these fields where evening drives
Beauty like breath, so gently darkness falls.

Darkness that makes the meadows holier still,
The elm-trees sadden in the hedge, a sigh
Moves in the beech-clump on the haunted hill,
The rising planets deepen in the sky,

And silence broods like spirit on the brae,
A glimmering moon begins, the moonlight runs
Over the grasses of the ancient way
Rutted this morning by the passing guns.

*John Masefield, Red Cross orderly, 1915*

# NOTE ON TERMINOLOGY
# IN THE TEXT

Where individuals are identified by rank, the rank stated is that held by the individual at the time. Where battalions are identified, I have generally rendered 2nd Battalion Royal Welch Fusiliers as 2/Royal Welch Fusiliers and so on.

# PREFACE

I have written books on nature, and books on the Great War. In the following pages the two rivers meet . . .

Sometimes the mind of the Great War soldier is open and familiar to us; sometimes it is opaque and strange, and we are reminded that we are separated from him by a century of change. When the First World War combatant (and post-war politician) Anthony Eden titled the memoir of his early life *Another World* he was precisely on the mark.

Few today would go to war for the fields, woods, brooks of Britain. Or, rather, what is left of them. We have become de-natured and über-urban. Contrast us with the men of 1914–18; a single paragraph from E.B. Osborn's 1919 collective biography of gilded young who fell in the Great War, *The New Elizabethans*, will do:

> Foreign critics, however, fail to understand how the Englishman's profound patriotism finds its best expression in what are really acts of Nature-worship – worship of the various and benign Nature that inhabits this fair and fortunate island.

In our divining of the reasons why men volunteered to fight in 1914, one motive is persistently blind to us, which was their wish to preserve inviolate, to borrow Osborn's words, rural Britain's 'fair sights and sounds and perfumed airs'. For the generation of 1914–18 love of country meant, as often as not, love of countryside.

Nature mattered in 1914–18. What is the emblem of the Great War? A wildflower. A Flanders poppy.

If nature inspired men to volunteer, the Briton on service on the Western Front lived inside nature. There was no escape from nature a century ago. In the trenches, soldiers actually habited the bowels of the earth, in direct and myriad contact with all flora and fauna of Flanders and the Somme. Nature was all around, in every one of Its/His/Her guises. There could only be heightened awareness of nature when at war.

The ability of nature to endure, despite the bullets and blood, gave men a psychological, spiritual, religious uplift. The unconquerability of nature provided the reassurance that life itself would go on, that there was after all a purpose and meaning to things.

Nature was palliative too. Second Lieutenant Paul Nash, Hampshire Regiment, wrote to his wife about the war, and the profound and collective trauma it caused. But the result? 'An ancient and enduring idea emerged – that Nature could heal.'

Instinctively, soldiers kept companion animals (domesticated nature) in the trenches, by making pets of the wild or stray animals they found. Those who worked with the army's dogs and horses of war duly promoted their charges from dumb animals to friends and, honour of honours, 'comrades'. The army grasped how useful birds were in keeping the spirits up: ambulance trains were fitted with canary cages, so the birds could sing to wounded troops in transit to hospital.

A deeply pastoral people, despite (actually, because of) two centuries of industrialisation, the British on the frontline recreated many of the same countryside hobbies at the front as they enjoyed at home: they went bird-watching, they fished village ponds and flooded shell holes, they hunted hares with beagles, they shot pheasants for the pot, they planted flower gardens in the trenches and vegetable gardens in their billets.

It is a myth universally recognised that the Great War was an unrelieved mud and blood show. The nouns 'horror' and 'trenches' have become as eternally conjoined as 'horse' and 'carriage'. Yet the front could be beautiful. One soldier, Private J.W. Graystone of 10/East Yorkshire Regiment, wrote of his camp at Authie on the Somme:

> The woods looked simply glorious in the morning sun, and all nature was at its best. Fancy a war on in surroundings like this. It seems unthinkable.

In Spring 1918, Arnold Monk-Jones, a young subaltern, was stationed at Ronville on the Western Front. He recorded in his journal:

> Going to and from work at Fenchy tonight I heard both Cuckoo and Nightingale; it is a most delightful walk along the Arras-Douai road between the railway and the Scarpe Watery Wood, though within half a mile of the front line, is almost intact and is as beautiful a spot as one would strike anywhere . . . There are some strange contrasts in this existence.

There were. The Great War was fecund in its antimonies. Some relationships between man and fauna/flora were friendly and pleasant, others were hateful and vile. The front was rife with rats, loathsome insects and bacteria. The 1914–18 war was the first act in the Age of Industrialised Slaughter; it was simultaneously the last act of Ancient, Pre-antibiotic Warfare. Disease, especially beyond the Western Front, had its dark victories.

In this New/Old War men reached for idioms from nature as explanation. So, for Captain Francis Hitchcock enemy planes were 'angry hornets', while Private Ivor Gurney, seemingly unimpressed (like many a foot soldier) by the achievements of the RFC, dismissed British aeroplanes as 'harmless gnats'. Guardsman Stephen Graham considered an aeroplane flying low over a wood akin to 'an owl staring for mice'. Lieutenant Edward Thomas thought the artillery shells at Beauvrains at night were 'like starlings returning 20 or 30 a minute'. Of the First World War's neologisms, nature consistently provided part of the etymological stem, thus 'warbirds', 'dog-fight', 'gas cloud'.

The dead of the Great War ended up buried in nature, a circle completed. The missing rotted unretrieved into foreign ground, the luckier were buried in war cemeteries, deliberately designed to look like British gardens, or formalised nature.

Lieutenant Ewart Mackintosh MC, 5/Seaforth Highlanders, wondered in the poem 'Beaumont-Hamel':

Dead men at Beaumont
Do you dream at all
When the leaves of summer
Ripen to their fall?
Will you walk the heather,
Feel the Northern weather,
Wind and sun together,
Hear the grouse-cock call?

Even heaven, the British soldier hoped, was British Rural.

Poetry is significant in the following pages, though little comes from the familiar bran-bucket of the semi-official 'War Poets', those canonised for their 'correct' politics, meaning anti-war, by academe. I once analysed the major themes of 200 soldier poets from the Great War – hardly scientific, though instructive enough. Pity was well-nigh absent, affinity with nature was everywhere, as metaphor, as subject. In the poem 'Into Battle' by Captain Julian Grenfell, the soldiers' soldier-poet, combat finally becomes revealed as the natural warrior state of man.

For the British soldier in the First World War, nature was always a matter of life and death.

# CHAPTER I

# For King and Countryside

*The Natural History of the British*

'Literally for this'

*Private Edward Thomas, Artists Rifles, on being asked why he had volunteered for service in the army. In the same moment he said these words he scooped up a handful of English earth.*

What's in a name? If that name is Adlestrop then the answer is the quintessence of England on the very eve of the First World War.

It was on 24 June 1914 that Edward Thomas, a self-confessed hack writer ('I hate my work'), took a train from Paddington to Gloucestershire. He was accompanied by his wife, Helen. The temperature was 80 degrees in the shade. Thomas wrote in his diary:

Then we stopped at Adlestrop, thro the willows cd be heard a chain of blackbirds' songs at 12.45 & one thrush & no man seen, only the hiss of engine letting off steam. Stopping outside Campden by banks of long grass willow herb & meadowsweet, extraordinary silence between two periods of travel – looking out on grey dry stones between metals & the shiny metals & over it all the elms willows & long grass one man clears his throat – and a greater rustic silence. No house in view. Stop only for a minute till signal is up.[1]

His famous poem 'Adlestrop' came two years later, with its perfect crystallised evocation of that last summer of peace; the brightness of birdsong, the tranquillity and the beauty of the Cotswold country-side with its 'meadowsweet, and haycocks dry'.

'Adlestrop' would become one of the nation's favourite poems, although Thomas himself would not live to see its success. As Lieu-tenant Edward Thomas, Royal Garrison Artillery, he was killed in action on the Western Front in April 1917.

Edward Thomas died at Arras for Adlestrop.

Thomas was never much of a jingo, never a Boche-hater, versing about the causes of the 1914 conflagration:

This is no case of petty right or wrong
That politicians or philosophers
Can judge. I hate not Germans, nor grow hot
With love of Englishmen, to please newspapers . . .[2]

Thomas considered his true countrymen to be the birds. Or the trees. When someone queried the meaning of his poem 'Aspens', describing the whispering trees beside the crossroad in the village of Steep he replied, 'I am the aspen'. Already thirty-six when the war broke out, Edward Thomas had no statutory obligation to fight. He volunteered to fight in the Great War less for King and Country, more for King and Countryside.

Adlestrop summated the rural England of 1914; Edward Thomas himself embodied the Englishman's attitude to that self-same countryside.

*

When Edward Thomas's train stopped at Adlestrop in June 1914, only weeks before the deluge, he and Helen were on their way to Dymock in Gloucestershire, where a sort of unofficial poets' colony had been founded. What united these poets was a pared verse style and an eye for the everyday (rather than the ornamented epic beloved of high Victorians) and an intense love of nature much in the manner of the earlier Wordsworthian Romantics. The Dymock poets were 'Georgians', writing new verse for the new age of King George V. 'The Old Vicarage, Grantchester', penned by Rupert Brooke, the shining satellite of the Dymock circle, in Berlin's Café des Westens in 1912, was the Georgian's flower-filled model eulogy to nature.[3]

There was a strong element of 'back to the land' among the Georgians, a throwing over of city for countryside. When Brooke visited Lascelles Abercrombie at his Dymock home, The Gallows, he rhapsodised that the cottage 'is the most beautiful you can imagine: black beamed & rose covered. And a porch where one drinks great mugs of cider, & looks at fields of poppies in the corn. A life that makes London a foolish affair.'

Thomas himself spent much of his time at Dymock walking the fields, slopes, deep lanes and woods of the Vale of Leadon, usually in the company of the American poet Robert Frost, who, like Abercrombie was a Dymock sun. (Frost was constantly amused by Thomas's havering over direction on their 'talks-walking'; his famous 'The Road Not Taken' is as much a joke on Thomas as it is an existential statement.)

On 26 August 1914 Thomas went walking in the night with Frost; Thomas noted in his journal:

A sky of dark rough horizontal masses in N.W. with a 1/3 moon bright and almost orange low down clear of cloud and I thought of men eastward seeing it at the same moment. It seems foolish to have loved England up to now without knowing it could perhaps be ravaged and I could and perhaps would do nothing to prevent it.[4]

The war was on, and Thomas was calculating the value of the land beneath his feet.[5] But he was not yet decided. As the weeks passed Thomas's conscience pained him; on 24 February 1915 he wrote of an owl's cry 'telling me plain what I escaped/And others could not' – that is, enlistment. He was commissioned to write a book, *This England*, a sort of patriotic travelogue; part of the research was more perambulating of the Gloucestershire/Herefordshire border. It was enough:

> Something, I felt, had to be done before I could look again composedly at English landscape, at the elms and poplars about the houses, at the purple-headed wood-betony with two pairs of dark leaves on a stiff stem, who stood sentinel among the grasses or bracken by hedge-side or wood's-edge.[6]

On 19 July 1915 Thomas reported to 17 Duke's Road, London, to be attested Private 4229 in 28/The London Regiment (Artists Rifles). When one dismayed writer friend, Eleanor Farjeon, pressed him on why he had volunteered, this was the moment when he said, 'Literally, for this'.

Edward Thomas volunteered not once but twice. Realising that map-reading in the Artists Rifles was not sufficient he applied for officer training. Again the countryside was the prompt. Thomas himself is surely the narrator in 'As the Team's Head Brass', he who goes from flippancy to comprehension that the horse ploughing scene in England, his England, requires someone to *fight* for it. The ploughman asks bystander Thomas the fundamental question 'Have you been out?' He can only answer 'No', and the negative is inadequate as he watches 'the clods crumble and topple over/ After the ploughshare and the stumbling team'.[7]

Thomas was commissioned a subaltern in the Royal Garrison Artillery on 23 November 1916.

*

Perhaps the love of Thomas and the Georgians for the countryside is the sort of naive sentimentality one might expect from middle-class urban poets? Certainly the canard that love of nature is restricted to metropolitans – who, it is assumed, know nothing of the hardships of rural employment, or the bloody cruelties of nature – is one that flies again and again.

There was nothing unusual in Thomas's love for rural England, or indeed his desire to don khaki and fight for it. He was always exemplar, not exception. Soldiers' letters from Flanders, France and Gallipoli are full of longings for strolls in flowery meadows, for roses-round-the-door cottage homes (the abiding popular symbol of pastoral purity in contrast to the corrupt, encroaching city[8]), the dawn chorus under a British springtime sky.

Frederick William Harvey, known to all as Will, was a farmer's son from Minsterworth, who enlisted as a private in 1/5th Battalion of the Gloucestershire Regiment at the outbreak of war. At the front Harvey co-founded one of the first trench journals, the *5th Gloucester Gazette*, in which he tried out poetry for himself. Or, more accurately, he used poetry to exorcise his heartache for his own countryside:

> I hear the heart within me cry:
> 'I'm homesick for my hills again –
> My hills again!
> Cotswold or Malvern, sun or rain!
> My hills again!'[9]

Will Harvey was a farm boy who turned to poetry, not a poet who turned to farming. As Lieutenant F.W. Harvey DCM he was captured during a solo reconnaissance of the German front lines on 17 August 1916 and spent the rest of the war in various prisoner of war camps. Imprisonment, at least, gave Harvey time to indulge his new passion for writing verse, in which one theme would recur over and over again: the Gloucestershire countryside. The titles of Harvey's wartime poetry collections say it all: *A Gloucestershire Lad at Home and Abroad*, and *Gloucestershire Friends, Poems from a German Prison Camp*.

If anything Will Harvey's childhood friend, Ivor Gurney, suffered a more profound identification with landscape. Gurney, the son of a literal tailor of Gloucester, spent so much time at Redlands, the Harvey farm, he was virtually family. Gurney joined the county regiment in 1915 to become a soldier 'of a sort'. As 3895 Private Ivor Bertie Gurney, he believed that his military duty was predicated on his intense relationship with the hills around the Severn; 'hills, not only hills, but friends of mine and kindly'.[10] He asked the Severn meadows to 'not forget me quite'.[11] Gurney's love for the countryside was almost physical.

For Harvey, as for Gurney, as for other countrymen, war service was exile from a landscape that was part of their being, from which they were *uprooted* by service.

Whether from countryside or city, love of nature was the British condition, which manifested itself in everything from the national hobby of gardening to the folk-influenced music of classical composers such as George Butterworth and Ralph Vaughan Williams. (What did Vaughan Williams write in the first week of war? 'The Lark Ascending', the very musical embodiment of pastoralism and patriotism, the same pastoralism and patriotism that would inspire Vaughan Williams, despite being at forty-two over age, to volunteer to serve.) The British led the world in the keeping of pets, animal welfare legislation and a regard for birds so marked by 1910 that *Punch* declared their feeding to be a national pastime, with the dockers and clerks of London included.[12]

Something of British nature-love is explained by the nation's torn-from-the-rural-womb early industrialisation, which left a psychic wound in the mind of the new town-dwellers. (The injury was so abysmal that urban Britons recreated the countryside in their back gardens; the lawn is nothing but the country meadow brought, as salve, into *urbia*. With the pot-plant, notably the aspidistra, Victorian

Britons eventually brought the countryside *into* the home; the more industry, with its satanic mills and smoking chimneys, despoiled the countryside, the more the British valued nature.) Yet, the nature-love was antique, as well as acute and trans-class. British nature-love preceded the Industrial Revolution, as the most cursory reading of Geoffrey Chaucer's fourteenth century poem 'The Parlement of Fowles' confirms.[13]

The people of Britain in 1914 were connected to nature wherever they dwelt. Nature was not 'other', separate, a thing apart. Transport, in the shape of the railways, bicycles and (for the rich) the car enabled Edwardian–Georgian city dwellers to explore the countryside. And what they found was a place of bottomless peace and bountiful nature.

An odd celebrity proof of the wonder of the countryside in the first decades of the twentieth century occurred on 9 June 1910 in the little village of Itchen Abbas in Hampshire, when the British Foreign Secretary, Sir Edward Grey, and former US President Theodore Roosevelt went for a 'bird walk'.

Sir Edward Grey is known to everyone because of a single, immortal quotation. Looking out of his office window at dusk on 3 August 1914 and towards St James's Park, he remarked to his friend J.A. Spender: 'The lamps are going out all over Europe. We shall not see them lit again in our lifetime.'

Grey was always looking out of the window. He was a devout ornithologist, hence his invitation to Roosevelt to accompany him on a twelve mile walk in the New Forest. Grey recalled that they were 'lost to the world' for hours. They saw forty separate species of bird, heard the song of twenty. Grey later wrote *The Charm of Birds*, first published in 1927, the core message of which was that watching and listening to birds could bring solace and regeneration to the world-weary.

The charm of the Edwardian–Georgian countryside is that it was full of birdsong. It was countryside worth fighting for. On the embarkation train to Southampton, before crossing the Rubicon channel to

the Western Front, Second Lieutenant Ford Madox Hueffer, 9/Welsh
Regiment, watched the countryside roll by:

> And I thought:
> 'In two days' time we enter the Unknown,
> But this is what we die for . . . As we ought . . .'
> For it is for the sake of the wolds and the wealds
> That we die,
> And for the sake of the quiet fields . . .

For 'beautiful and green and comely' England, Hueffer was perfectly
prepared to endure 'the swift, sharp torture of dying'.[14]

Lance Corporal Francis Ledwidge was a working-class, die-hard
Irish nationalist in the King's service with the Royal Inniskilling
Fusiliers. And yet in 1915:

> Coming from Southampton in the train, looking on England's
> beautiful valleys all white with spring, I thought indeed its free-
> dom was worth all the blood I have seen flow. No wonder England
> has so many ardent patriots. I would be one myself did I not pre-
> sume to be an Irish patriot.[15]

Ledwidge was killed in action in Flanders in July 1917. He had taken
up arms 'for the fields along the Boyne and the birds and the blue sky
over them'.[16]

But it was not just the Edwardian New Forest or the countryside
that musicked with bird song. So did the cities, which were less kept,
less kempt, less concreted, smaller than now. Thus, the countryside
was in closer reach. When young Edward Thomas went exploring
on Wandsworth Common in London it was a wilderness. The spill-
age of grain from horses' nosebags and its survival in their dung on
every street of every conurbation was food for flocks of sparrows and
finches. So abundant was the house sparrow in London's East End
that it became the district's unofficial emblem. (Today, the sparrows

have all but gone from London having declined by the order of 99 per cent.)

An Edwardian childhood was conducted outdoors as much as it was within the confines of the house. This was the era when every doctor and moral reformer prescribed lashings of fresh air. Cecil Bullivant's ubiquitous vade mecum for boyhood, *Every Boy's Book of Hobbies*, suggested among its pastimes 'Birds' Egg Collecting', 'The Collecting of Butterflies and Moths', 'The Making of a Botanical Collection', 'Out and About with a Geological Hammer', 'How to Make an Aviary', 'Bee-Keeping', 'Pigeons'. Edward Thomas's boyhood hobbies included keeping pigeons, and at school he wrote in his algebra book, 'I love birds more than books'. The boy next to him laughed, but only at his execrable Latin.[17]

In the cities of Britain in 1914 animals were everywhere. There were pigs in backyards, linnets in cages, and despite the rise of the internal combustion engine horses were the main mode of transport. There were 25 million horses in the UK, 300,000 horses in London. Families from Birmingham and London went on hop-picking holidays in Herefordshire and Kent.

Whether visiting or inhabiting, people commonly referred to the British countryside as 'God's Own Country'. This passing compliment to the beauty of the Weald of Kent, the South Downs, the Lakes, the rolling red plough-land of Herefordshire, hid a rarely reflected truth; the British love of nature contained a distinct religiosity. Lacking both full doctrine and ritual, Anglicanism was born with a vacuum in its centre; and religion abhors a vacuum. Partly the vacuum was filled with ethical humanism, partly with nature-love. Within two centuries of Henry VIII pulling England out of the Church of Rome, God and nature had become so conflated in the British mind that they were one and the same. In *Centuries of Meditations* by the theologian Thomas Traherne (*c.* 1636–74) the countryside he adores is not the handiwork of God, it *is* God, His flesh: 'How do we know, but the world is that body; which the Deity has assumed to Manifest His Beauty.'[18] Victorian England sponsored 'Earth Lore for Children' primers for Anglican/nature faith, while adults had John Keble's *The Christian Year*, a combination of pastoral poem and Anglican breviary.

Inside Anglicanism, the majority faith of Britain, there was a type of pantheism.

*

When the British viewed the countryside around them they saw nature, they saw God. They also beheld the labour of their forefathers.

At the front in France, Lieutenant Christian Carver, Royal Field Artillery, wrote home:

> I always feel that I am fighting for England, for English fields, lanes, trees, English atmospheres, and good days in England – and all that is synonymous for liberty.[19]

Some 75 per cent of Edwardian Britain was farmland, the result of agri-*culture* over centuries. The landscape was manufactured; it was man-made from nature. The countryside, to borrow the phrase of Red Cross orderly and Poet Laureate John Masefield, was the 'past speaking dear'.

For the British, their landscape was their identity, their heritage. British patriotism, unlike the patriotism of other countries, was not based on race, but shared values (Carver's 'liberty') and love of countryside. Germany, by contrast, was a country of black forests, whose people's patriotism was anchored in a belief in *Blut*.

When Carver headed his list of beloved British pastoral features with 'fields', he wrote for many who served in the Great War. Meadows with 'haycocks dry' and arable acres ploughed by 'the stumbling team' dominated in their nostalgia, rather than remote fells or estuary wastes, although these places had their admirers.[20]

Lieutenant Carver, like Edward Thomas and Rupert Brooke, would die for English scenes.

When the soldiers of Britain went to war they took a pre-existing and intense love and knowledge of nature with them. Of course, whether nature-love was urban false sentiment or organic rooted-ness or patriotism hardly mattered. The love existed, that is what mattered.

*

OED *Nostalgia: G. nostos* return home + *algos* pain

The nostalgia for the countryside of 'England', as Britain was uni-versally known in those far off days, began as soon as men entered service, which was the first step away to war. Thomas himself wrote 'Adlestrop' in 1916. The difference between the diary entry and the poem is telling; the distance of time, of two years of war, has made the scene at the Cotswold halt more luminous, more precious. In the poem Thomas himself acknowledges he cannot return to Adlestrop; it has disappeared into the haze of the past, just as birdsong dwindles away in summer heat:

And for that minute a blackbird sang
Close by, and round him, mistier . . .

For Lieutenant Edward Thomas, 'all roads now lead to France', as they did for four million British soldiers, among them Lieutenant Robert Nichols, Royal Artillery. Nichols was barely off the boat in France before he was struck by chronic homesickness. He took to poetry, which would become the soldier's medium, to explain his longing:

NOW that I am ta'en away
And may not see another day
What is it to my eye appears?
What sound rings in my stricken ears?
Not even the voice of any friend
Or eyes beloved-world-without-end,
But scenes and sounds of the country-side

In far England across the tide:
An upland field when spring's begun,
Mellow beneath the evening sun . . .
A circle of loose and lichened wall
Over which seven red pines fall . . .
An orchard of wizen blossoming trees
Wherein the nesting chaffinches
Begin again the self-same song
All the late April day-time long . . .
Paths that lead a shelving course
Between the chalk scarp and the gorse
By English downs; and oh! too well
I hear the hidden, clanking bell
Of wandering sheep . . . I see the brown
Twilight of the huge, empty down
Soon blotted out! for now a lane
Glitters with warmth of May-time rain.
And on a shooting briar I see
A yellow bird who sings to me.

O yellow-hammer, once I heard
Thy yaffle when no other bird
Could to my sunk heart comfort bring;
But now I could not have thee sing
So sharp thy note is with the pain
Of England I may not see again![21]

*

'Certainly I have never lived so close to nature before or since.'
                    *Corporal Fred Hodges, Lancashire Regiment, 1918*

Few Edwardians travelled abroad. For the majority of soldiers of the
Great War, military service gave them their first taste of foreign parts.

Even France was exotic, with its *estaminets* and its poplar-lined roads.

Of course, the one truly novel place to be posted was the underground world; *Subterranea*. During the Great War the front line soldier lived inside the earth, in trenches or chambers excavated in their side ('dugouts' or 'funk holes'), for days, even weeks, at a time. Charles Douie, a young subaltern with the Dorsets at Usna Redoubt, near La Boisselle, noted the soldiers there inhabited 'noisome holes burrowed out of the earth, as primitive man had lived in forgotten ages'.[22] It is small wonder that when one wartime officer, Lieutenant J.R.R. Tolkien, later turned to writing epic medieval fiction he had his 'Hobbits' living in earthen dwellings, replicas of the dugouts in the trenches he had once slept and sheltered in.[23]

With telling frequency soldiers in the trenches likened themselves to rabbits, with all the hypogean strangeness and all the vulnerability that species suggests. Captain Ivar Campbell, Argyll and Sutherland Highlanders, wrote home from his Flanders trench:

You perceive ... men infinitely small, running, affrightened rabbits, from the upheaval of the shells, nerve-wracked, deafened; clinging to earth, hiding eyes, whispering 'O God, O God!'[24]

In the Great War men lived closer to nature than they had done for centuries, millennia even. The defences of civilisation were gone. 'Trench life,' wrote Lieutenant Siegfried Sassoon of the Royal Welch Fusiliers, 'was an existence saturated by the external senses; and although our actions were domineered by military discipline, our animal instincts were always uppermost.'[25] When he looked at his diary, he realised that it contained 'lists of birds and flowers, snatches of emotion and experience' but people were 'scarcely mentioned'.

As is the way with nature, living in her bosom was Heaven and Hell. Nature is always contradictory, always blackberry and barb.

Men got uplift from the sights and sounds of some birds, animals and wild flowers. As the battle of the Somme deliquesced into

November mud Captain Sidney Rogerson, on encountering a mole, thought it 'one of Nature's miracles that this blind, slow creature could have survived in ground so pounded and upturned', and took heart from the tiny mammal's survival.[26] Other manifestations caused discomfort, depression, disease, even death. Just one trench disease, nephritis, accounted for 5 per cent of all medical admissions on the Western Front.

When the boys came home, they brought their diseases with them. Spanish flu (caused by the H1N1 virus), originated in China, spread to western Europe with American troops, and for the British probably had its epicentre in the training and distribution bases in the Pas-de-Calais, especially Étaples.[27] The triumphant Tommies on returning to Britain in 1918 took the virus with them. The kiss they gave their wives, mothers, children was the kiss of death.

In the trenches, one way or another, nature mattered.

*

Those who live, as perforce we were compelled to live, exposed to sun, rain, and wind, surrounded by natural forces, in the constant presence of death, are conscious of a mystery in the heart of things, some identity of man with that which gave him birth, nourishes him, and in due time receives him again.

*Lieutenant Charles Douie, Dorsetshire Regiment, The Weary Road.*

In this last ancient war, the soldier's calendar was still dictated by nature; the Somme battle started in the traditional campaigning season, summer, and petered out in winter snow; Passchendaele, the 'Big Push' of 1917 sunk in autumn mud. There was no escaping nature.

Stationed on the Somme, Charles Douie saw a link between time of day and death; the evening of the day was the evening of life:

Evening came and the broad fields of Picardy, now almost ripe for harvest were emblazoned by the setting sun with an unforgettable splendour. The evening was in harmony with the thought of many of us, for whom this could not but be the last 'March'.[28]

The harvest on the Somme in 1916 would be of men, cut down like greening wheat, their blood to grow another crop, that of white crosses. Douie believed that the men of his regiment were the 'flower of the shire' of Dorset.

In the trenches, in spring and summer, soldiers were literally 'up with the lark'. The migration of birds and the blooming of flowers, the spring greening of trees and the frosts of winter were the natural markers of time passing. One reason for First World War soldiers' liking of Laurence Binyon's poem 'For the Fallen' was that it echoed the natural rhythm of the trench-day; 'At the going down of the sun and in the morning/ We will remember them'. Many soldiers too would have recognised the truth of Sir Edward Grey's observation:

In those dark days I found some support in the steady progress unchanged of the beauty of the seasons. Every year, as spring came back unfailing and unfaltering, the leaves came out with the same tender green, the birds sang, the flowers came up and opened, and I felt that a great power of Nature for beauty was not affected by the war. It was like a great sanctuary into which we could go and find refuge.[29]

Private Norman Ellison at Wailly, where the spring 'burst upon us with amazing suddenness' with the arrival of swallows, warblers and nightingales, wrote:

I cannot recollect any spring that thrilled me more. One felt that man might destroy himself and his civilisation through the incredible stupidity of war, but the annual re-birth of nature would continue. Here was something assured and permanent: an established truth in a world of constantly alternating values.[30]

For the soldier in the trenches, the turn of the seasons was about more than the passing of time; it was about the immutability of nature. A soldier's life, more even than a Foreign Secretary's life, is one of uncertainty. Win or lose? Live or die? Here or there? In nature soldiers looked for, and found, the eternalities and the verities. Recently married, and anxious both about the war and separation from his wife, Second Lieutenant Max Plowman gained solace from the stars:

> What joy it is to know that you [his wife] in England and I out here at least can look upon the same beauty in the sky. We've the stars to share.[31]

Douie, for one, averred that trench life, with its exposure to the elements and the imminence of death, returned man to his essential natural state, whereas:

> In the life of cities man is protected from the play of natural forces; and death, when it comes, has a suggestion of the unnatural by virtue of its unfamiliarity. But those whose daily lot is to witness the processes of Nature, the awakening and renewing of life in the miracle of dawn, the coming of rest and sleep in the glory of the setting sun, have a greater opportunity of seeing life and death in their true perspective, a fuller appreciation of the place of man in Nature.[32]

*

It could be a lovely war.

Second Lieutenant Alexander Douglas Gillespie, known to all as Douglas, was vaguely ashamed to inform his parents in a letter written in May 1915 from a Flanders trench:

> There is no use pretending that I am soldiering at the minute, and I don't deserve anybody's sympathy . . . The weather is still perfect;

our trenches and breastworks are brown and bare and dusty, and the sand-bags are getting bleached with sun, but everything else is green. The meadow behind is yellow with buttercups and dandelions; there's a large patch of yellow mustard out between the lines, and a forest of leeks and cabbages.[33]

He had just had 'as good a lunch as I ever want to get' (curried beef, boiled rice, rhubarb, plum cake, washed down with red wine and soda) and they hadn't had a man hit since entering the line.

On the Western Front there were sections of the British front which would stretch from the Channel to the Somme river, where local truces or victories obtained and the main stress was the noise of the frogs at night. Corporal A.H. Roberts, Gloucestershire Regiment, confided to his diary on 7 May 1918 that he was 'fed up' with being at Ruminghem: 'Thousands of frogs round here and the croaking noise they make all night is just awful.'

Captain Francis Hitchcock, Leinster Regiment, led a work party out on the night of 6 June 1915:

Every now and then shrapnel would burst over us to break the stillness of the night. Otherwise the only sounds were in the sighing of the poplars and the everlasting croaking of the frogs . . . [34]

Soldiers could get lost in nature on the Western Front. On a day off in July 1916 twenty-two-year-old Captain Arthur Adams, Cambridgeshire Regiment, intentionally took a walk away from the battle zone 'without any object save to see as much as possible of the beauty of God's world'. He went to nature for respite, for tonic.

Born in Edinburgh, son of an editor of *Country Life*, Stephen Graham had been the Russian correspondent for *The Times* before enlistment. His war memoir, *A Private in the Guards*, raised a great commotion for its account of the conditions at the army's Little Sparta training camp, Caterham. Of his service in France in 1917 with the Scots Guards, Private Graham recalled:

I had been sent to a neighbouring headquarters with a message, and at noon I sat for a while beside a high hawthorn on a daisy-covered bank. The war ceased to exist; only beauty was infinitely high and broad above and infinitely deep within. Birds again sang in the heavens and in the heart after a long sad silence, as it seemed.[35]

There was always relief in unwrecked land: billeted in a Flanders village somehow by-passed by the war, Second Lieutenant George Atkinson and his men went solemnly to look 'at a large green field without a single shell-hole in it'; the meadow seemed an enchanting 'fairyland'. Private W.H.A. Groom found few pleasures in army life and wrote a memoir, *Poor Bloody Infantry*, detailed with his dislikes. Nonetheless, when out of the front line, 'amongst the trees, grass and wild life of the countryside there was an affinity with nature'.[36] For a city boy such as Hull's Private J.W. Graystone, full exposure to nature could be intoxicating and life-changing.

How free Nature is and what a call it makes to us in the Army! It makes us feel more and more how much we shall appreciate life when the war is over. No more being cooped up in smoky towns, spending our time in frivolous pleasures. Out into the country for us, but no army.[37]

Although before the war he 'didn't know much about birds' he soon learned to pick out the song of thrushes, larks and robins and the plaintive call of the cuckoo. 'Nature is wonderful.' Private Graystone had volunteered in August 1914 and, while proud of 10/East Yorkshire Regiment's growing military prowess, chafed at the petty restrictions of army life. The freedom seemingly offered by nature versus the 'enslavement' of the army was always pointed.

The relationship with nature was reciprocal. In the trenches, men gave back to nature, often to their own inconvenience, sometimes to the detriment of their own safety. At Gallipoli Sergeant Bernard

W. Gill, Royal Army Medical Corps (RAMC), witnessed a skylark suffer a shrapnel wound; some men nearby took it in and fed it 'heartily on biscuit crumbs made moist with water'. In a few days the wing was healed, and the bird released.[38] Captain J.C. Dunn, RAMC, in spring 1916 'avoided treading on little frogs in Cambrin trenches' despite the busy burden of being the medical officer for 2/Royal Welch Fusiliers.

The destruction of nature on the Western Front, its reduction to timberless mudland with shell holes full of gas and rain, evoked pity and pain. Over and over, the soldier poets recollected the British landscape ('home') as antidote and counterpoint to the horror of war. In entering the ravaged town of Laventie, with its churned mud and 'stricken' houses, Lieutenant The Hon. Edward Tennant, Grenadier Guards, noticed a miraculously intact garden. The mere sight of it transported him back to English 'meadows with their glittering streams, and silver scurrying dace/ Home what a perfect place!'[39]

Many saw the destruction of the France–Flanders countryside as the wicked, guilty hand of man; equally, many saw in nature's regeneration of the self-same countryside the work of God or some universal 'Spirit', no matter how imprecisely conceived or described. Nature inspired because it was elemental, eternal, unvanquished. Even when war descended in all its artillery fury, nature was quick to reclaim and re-beautify, as Second Lieutenant Stephen Hewett, Royal Warwickshire Regiment, explained to his parents:

The trenches which in February were grim and featureless tunnels of gloom, without colour or form, are already over-arched and embowered with green. You may walk from the ruins of a cottage, half hidden in springing green, and up to the Front line trenches through a labyrinth of Devonshire lanes.[40]

*

The Somme. Today the name tolls like a funeral bell, but in July 1915 when the British took over the front line from Arras to the

Somme river they thought they had taken possession of Arcadia.

Flanders in northern Belgium never truly appealed to the British, except maybe the men of Kent who felt affinity with the hop yards. Flanders was always cramped by the multiplicity of its peasant homesteads, their monotonous single-storey redbrick houses, the midden in the yard. Looking out of the train window en route to the Ypres sector all Douglas Gillespie could see was 'the usual landscape of Northern France – farm buildings and long rows of lanky poplars with magpies' nests in them'.[41]

No one is more interested in reading landscape than a soldier because his life may depend on it. Landscape needs to be safety in defence, opportunity in attack.

Flanders was flat, and flattened the mood of the soldiery. The hills were so few that everyone knew their names, and if a soldier stood on the top of Kemmel Hill, a mere 500 feet above sea level, he could see the Flanders Plain stretching around him for miles. Hill 60 was only by a stretch of linguistics any sort of tump, since it consisted of spoil from the adjacent railway cutting. (Spectral traces of the mutilations of fighting make Hill 60 a moving place to visit on a Western Front pilgrimage to this day.) In Flanders, a molehill gave vantage and advantage, and was the objective of grand military plans.

And the relentlessly flat, low-lying Flanders was wet. Flanders was riven with dank and with dykes, and the Belgian king's decision to open the sea-locks at Nieuport on the Channel in 1914, in a forlorn attempt to stall the German advance, had created a vast salt marsh on the uppermost portion of the battlefield. Never one to lament or find a glass half-empty, Lieutenant Charles Douie was forced to concede that a Flanders' twilight was 'unmitigated gloom':

The appearance of the countryside suggested that it has been raining since the beginning of time.[42]

Into the German line in Flanders bulged the British 'Salient' around Ypres, where the army's resolve to hold its ground was tested to destruction. By the time Second Lieutenant George Atkinson reached Flanders in 1918, the Salient had taken on the aspect of Armageddon:

> Away on the left we could distinguish the ruins of Ypres shining faintly in the evening sun, and smoking under a desultory bombardment. Closer to us was the brick pile and swamp once known as Dickebusch, and in front, a few hundred yards away, the bulk of Kemmel Hill towered above us. Two months ago I saw it covered with beautiful woods and peaceful rest camps; now it is a bare, brown pile of earth, and only a few shattered tree-stumps in the shell-holes remain to mock the memory of its verdant beauty. The whole of Kemmel Hill and the valley and the ravines in front are one solid mass of shell-holes. The earth has been turned and turned again by shell-fire, and the holes lie so close together that they are not distinguishable as such. The ground in many places is paved with shrapnel balls and jagged lumps of steel – in ten square yards you could pick up several hundredweight.[43]

Men called it Hell. Even the earth seemed dead. Modern war's weaponry, the shells and the chemical gases, did its damnedest in the Salient.

The Somme was different, and not just because when the British entered the zone in 1915 it was untouched by war's devastations, or that it offered fresh hope after the stalemate of battle in the Ypres area.

The countryside of the Somme, with its rolling chalk downland, its open fields with their knuckles of white flint, its big sky, its spreckling of copses which floated on the horizon, was intrinsically beautiful. A 'modern Garden of Gethsemane', no less, was Lieutenant Geoffrey Dearmer's opinion of the parish of Gommecourt in the Somme *département*.

The clear flowing river which gave its name to the region had its own magic. Soldiers loved to swim and bathe in the Somme in spring and summer, to swim and wash away the dirt and the cares. Lieutenant Richard Talbot Kelly recalled:

> The joy of endless water, clean, clear, fresh water in which we could lie and bathe and at the same time enjoy quietness and peace, was a miraculous thing.[44]

Private E.W. Parker, a London builder's son who joined Kitchener's army at seventeen, and started his army life as a Hussar before transferring to the Durham Light Infantry, entered the Somme plain in 1916:

> In these idyllic surroundings we were happy. Golden fields rippling in the wind healed the sight of our eyes, and the green depths of the woodland shadows, like soft music, quietened the tortured nerves of our bodies. We awoke in our barns at sunrise to hear, not the angry crashes of the morning strafe, but the forgotten songs of birds.[45]

Parker and his mates sunbathed by a stream, and went swimming in its waters so pure that the boys could see 'the sharp flints soon to leave long scratches on our knees'.

Men were struck too by the Somme's similarity with the last piece of England most of them had seen, the South Downs and the New Forest, as their embarkation train had pounded to the port of Southampton. Private David Jones, 1/Royal Welch Fusiliers, reached for poetry to explain the resemblance:

> The gentle slopes are green to remind you
> Of South English places, only far wider and flatter spread and
> Grooved and harrowed criss-cross whitely . . .[46]

In his letters to his mother, Lieutenant Harold Rayner, 9/Devonshire Regiment, always referred to the Somme as 'the Downs'. The 'Downs' of Picardy moved Rayner into an ecstasy – there is no other word for it – about nature, about England, as he explained to his mother on 1 May 1916:

> It was as I breasted a rise of ground that I suddenly met god Pan by a cluster of dandelions, and then the scales fell from my eyes, and I saw the 'Numina coci' – the nymphs and fauns were in possession and the Downs were full of enchantment, and May magic lurked in the banks and the trees hanging on them, and in the hill-shapes and the springing crops whose vivid green was tinged with yellow, which made them singularly rich in tone, and contrasted with the almost mauve fallow land. Uncultivated stretches of turf were starred with dandelions so thick as almost to merit the name of 'Fields of cloth of gold', while in one place there were patches of daisies so white that they looked like sheets laid on the ground to dry. The leaves on most of the trees were out, the tender new green of early summer, so full of charm and suggestive of graceful presences. There swept over me the keen, almost wild quasi-pagan worship of Nature . . .

Rayner added that the sensations evoked by nature on the Somme had hitherto given him 'a consuming desire to be at home', but 'for the first time French scenes satisfied me'.[47] The Somme produced the same intensity of nature-worship as England did; the Somme was not merely an aid to nostalgia. In the Somme, the British found a second home. One reason the Somme would come to haunt the collective memory of the British soldiery is that its despoliation seemed like original and native sin.

*

*Et in Arcadia ego.* By war's strange cruelty, the very Somme landscape the British loved killed them, because its chalk and flint geology enabled the Germans to dig trenches and bunkers virtually impervious to British artillery shells – even 1,627,824 of them during that meteorologically marvellous summer of 1916. Some German dugouts on the Somme were sixty feet deep. Inside them the Germans were stone cold safe.

The deciduous copses and woods of the Somme, in which British soldiers took shade from the Picardian sun, were simultaneously the earth and timber protectors of German soldiers. Woods were nature's fortresses.[48]

The British 1916 Ordnance Survey maps suggest a count of 44 woods and 15 copses on the Somme battlefield, with Mametz Wood, extending to 186 acres of lime, oak, hornbeam, hazel and beech, the largest. High Wood was known for the sweet chestnuts used to make pitchforks; after September 1916 it became renowned as a graveyard. It is estimated that 10,000 British and German soldiers still lie un-recovered within the bounds of High Wood. Some of the Somme's sylvan extents had open grassy 'rides' – broad pathways for horse riding and for game shooting, especially of woodcock; the same rides also gave excellent lines of fire for the grey-clad German defenders.

And so the khaki casualties piled up at Mametz Wood and High Wood, names which to this day resound with the tragedy of it all. Those injured at Mametz Wood, amid the 'straggle tangled oak and flayed sheeny beech-bole, and fragile/Birch', included Private David Jones, wounded in the leg and cut in the mind. His immense prose-poem 'In Parenthesis' is at once personal catharsis, memorial for the Welsh nation, whose volunteer soldiers were blooded there, and sane warning to historians. For the men of 1914–18 the war was a great thing in their lives, but not the only thing in their lives. The war was bounded by brackets. It was an experience in parenthesis.

In the death zone of the Somme, which at its widest was ten to twenty kilometres across, a fat brown gash in the landscape, dev-astation could be apocalyptic; on the road between Albert and the Somme four villages essentially disappeared. Writing from the Somme in March 1917, Lieutenant Christian Carver told his brother:

We live in that desolate belt, extending from the Ancre to the Somme, some five miles in depth, where no trees remain to make a show of green in the coming spring, and the chateaux and churches are pounded to mounds of red and white dust ... By way of relieving the monotony we have just chivvied a wild boar. God knows where he came from or why. Perhaps to visit the home of his childhood – in which case he will be disappointed.[49]

Christian Carver died of wounds on 23 July 1917, aged twenty.

The murderous activities of men never quite managed to vanquish the Edenic splendour and wildlife of the Somme. Lieutenant Stormont Gibbs, whose battalion of the Suffolks was at the absolute end of the British line, the banks of the Somme itself, in winter 1916 wrote:

There was a full moon and a clean starry sky. As wars have a job to spoil rivers it seemed an exceedingly beautiful place. I spent much of the first night outside soaking in the glory of the moonlight on the water. It was very peaceful, with an occasional distant explosion just to heighten the romance by recalling that in contrast to the beauty of nature there were two lines of men stretching hundreds of miles in each direction waiting to be told to kill each other. And here flowed the Somme sublimely indifferent to it all.[50]

The war artist William Orpen visited the Somme six months after 415,000 men had been killed there:

I had left it mud, nothing but water, shell-holes and mud – the most gloomy abomination of desolation the mind could imagine; and now, in the summer of 1917, no words could express the beauty of it. The dreary, dismal mud was baken white and pure – dazzling white. Red poppies, and a blue flower, great masses of them, stretched for miles and miles. The sky was dark blue, and the whole air up to a height of 40 feet, thick with white butterflies.[51]

*

When Edward Thomas transferred to the Western Front in early 1917, there were one and a half million other Britons there in soldier's khaki and nurse's white. In contemplating the Western Front, the mind fixes on the 450-mile snake-line of the trenches from the Channel to Switzerland, but the British occupied a Pale of temporary settlement which stretched back from no man's land to Le Havre. Effectively, this tranche of France was a Colony of Britain.

In the Colony, the man who once declared that birds were 'more important to me than books' birdwatched to the end. Almost the last entry in Thomas's diary, a small 3in x 5¾in Walker's pocketbook (cost: 2s), was made at Arras on 7 April 1917, two days before his death:

> Up at 6 to O.P. [Observation Post] A cold bright day of continuous shelling N. Vitasse and Telegraph Hill. Infantry all over the place in open preparing Prussian way with boards for wounded. Hardly any shells into Beaurains. Larks, partridges, hedge-sparrows, magpies by O.P. A great burst in red brick building in N. Vitasse stood up like a birch tree or a fountain, Back at 7.30 in peace. Then at 8.30 a continuous roar of artillery.[52]

There were a few scribbled laconic notes, among them the prophetic: 'And no more singing for the bird . . .'

Thomas was killed by a whimsical shell blast as he stepped outside his observation post to light his pipe.

Lieutenant Edward Thomas thought the greatest gift he could leave his children Bronwyn, Merfyn and Myfanwy was the British countryside. It was a gift to us all.

# Interstice 1

## Birds of the Battlefield, Western Front 1914–18

Birds seen on the British front line*, Nieuport to the Somme, as compiled from the field notes of Captain Arthur de C. Sowerby, Captain W. Medlicott, Captain A.W. Boyd. Medlicott personally saw 106 species in Pas-de-Calais in the period March–August 1917.

### Order Acciptres (Eagles, hawks, etc.)

Common buzzard (*Buteo buteo*)
Goshawk (*Accipiter gentilis*)
Hobby (*Falco subbuteo*)
Kestrel (*Falco tinnunculus*) Common
Kite (*Milvus milvus*)
Marsh harrier (*Circus aeruginosus*)

* Defined here as the strip between no man's land and the reserve trenches.

Merlin (*Falco c., oesalon*)
Montagu's harrier (*Circus pygargus*)
Peregrine falcon (*Falco peregrinus*)
Sparrowhawk (*Accipiter nisus*)

## Order Anseres (Ducks, geese, and swans)

Mallard (*Anas platyrhyncha*)
Shoveler (*Spatula clypeata*)

## Order Columbae (Pigeons and doves)

Turtle dove (*Streptopelia turtur*)
Wood pigeon (*Columba palumbus*) Common

## Order Fulicariae (Rails and coots)

Coot (*Fulica atra*)
Corncrakes (*Crex crex*) Common in the Somme
Dabchicks (*Podiceps ruficollis*)
Moorhen (*Gallinula chloropus*)

## Order Gallinae

Partridge (*Perdix perdix*) Common
Pheasant (*Phasianus colchicus*)
Quail (*Coturnix coturnix*) Common in the Somme
Red-legged partridge (*Alectoris rufa*)

## Order Herodiones

Grey heron (*Ardea cinerea*)

## Order Limicolae (Waders)

Common sandpiper (*Actitis hypoleucos*)
Curlew (*Numenius arquata*)
Golden plover (*Charadrius apicarius*)
Stone curlew (*Burhinus oedicnemus*)
Woodcock (*Scolopax rusticola*)

## Order Passeres (Perching birds)

Blackbird (*Turdus merula*)
Blackcap (*Sylvia atricapilla*)
Black redstart (*Phoenicurus o. gibraltariensis*)
Blue tit (*Parus caeruleus*)
Blue-headed wagtail (*Motacilla flava*)
Brambling (*Fringilla montifringilla*)
Carrion crow (*Corvus corone*) Not common
Chaffinch (*Fringilla coelebs*) Common
Chiffchaff (*Phylloscopus collybita*)
Cirl bunting (*Emberiza cirlus*)
Coal tit (*Periparus ater*)
Common whitethroat (*Sylvia communis*) Common
Corn bunting (*Emberiza calandra*)
Crested lark (*Galerida cristata*) Common
Garden warbler (*Sylvia borin*)
Golden oriole (*Oriolus oriolus*)
Goldfinch (*Carduelis carduelis*)

Grasshopper warbler (*Locustella naevia*)

Great grey shrike (*Lanius excubitor*)

Great tit (*Parus major*)

Greenfinch (*Chloris chloris*) Common

Grey wagtail (*Motacilla boarula*)

Hawfinch (*Coccothraustes coccothraustes*)

Hedge sparrow (*Prunella modularis*)

Hooded crow (*Corvus cornix*) Common

House sparrow (*Passer domesticus*) Common

Icterine warbler (*Hippolais icterina*)

Jackdaw (*Coloeus monedula*)

Jay (*Garrulus glandarius*)

Lesser whitethroat (*Sylvia curruca*)

Linnet (*Acanthis cannabina*) Common

Long-tailed tit (*Aegithalos c. europoaeus*)

Magpie (*Pica pica*) Common

Marsh warbler (*Acrocephalus palustris*)

Meadow pipit (*Anthus pratensis*)

Melodious warbler (*Hippolais polyglotta*)

Nightingale (*Luscinia megarhynchos*)

Nuthatch (Sitta europaea)

Pied wagtail (*Motacilla lugubris*)

Red-backed shrike (*Lanius collurio*)

Reed bunting (*Emberiza schoeniclus*)

Robin (*Erithacus rubecula*)

Rook (*Corvus frugilegus*) Not common

Skylark (*Alauda arvensis*) Common

Song thrush (*Turdus musicus*)

Starling (*Sturnus vulgaris*) Common

Stonechat (*Saxicola t. rubicola*)

Tree pipit (*Anthus trivialis*)

Tree sparrow (*Passer montanus*) Common

Treecreeper (*Certhia familiaris*)

Wheatear (*Oenanthe oenanthe*)

Whinchat (*Saxicola rubetra*)
White wagtail (*Motacilla alba*)
Wood lark (*Lullula arborea*)
Woodchat shrike (*Lanius senator*)
Wren (*Troglodytes troglodytes*)
Yellow wagtail (*Motacilla rail*)
Yellowhammer (*Emberiza citrinella*) Common

## Order Picariae

Cuckoo (*Cuculus canorus*)
Great spotted woodpecker (*Dryobates major*)
Green woodpecker (*Picus viridis*)
Kingfisher (*Alcedo ispida*)
Lesser spotted woodpecker (*Dryobates minor*)
Nightjar (*Caprimulgus europaeus*)
Sand martin (*Riparia riparia*)
Swallow (*Hirundo rustica*)
Swift (*Apus apus*)
Wryneck (*Jynx torquilla*)

## Order Striges (Owls)

Barn owl (*Tyto alba*)
Little owl (*Athene noctua*)
Tawny owl (*Strix aluco*)

## CHAPTER II

# And the Birds Are Beautiful Still

*Avifauna and Men on the Western Front*

'Funny about that bird. Made me feel quite braced up. Sort of
made me think about my garden of an evening – walking round
in me slippers after supper, smoking me pipe.'

*Lieutenant Trotter in R.C. Sherriff's autobiographical play*
Journey's End, *Act 2, Sc. 1*

On a dreary Flanders day in 1917, Lieutenant Edwin Campion
Vaughan and his platoon of Royal Warwickshires began their trudge
out of the line, when they encountered a dead pigeon in the communication trench.

In silent unanimity, they gently picked up the pigeon and buried
it: 'railing his grave with little sticks and chains of sedge grass, and in
his coverlet of pimpernels we erected a tiny white cross'.[1]

Neither Vaughan nor his men were overly sentimental. Vaughan's
batman had carted, in a mud-plastered sandbag, a cooked wild rabbit
for his officer to eat as a triumphal prize on capturing Springfield

pill-box on Langemarck Ridge. They were time-served soldiers.

The poignant funeral laid on for the pigeon by Vaughan's platoon of 1/8th Royal Warwickshires is loaded with symbolism and meaning. There is pity for an innocent victim of war, amplified by the pigeon's genetic closeness to the dove, the bird of peace and Christianity. The pigeon may even have been a messenger for men, an army carrier pigeon, and in a sense 'one of us' and due the accordant rituals. But it is not difficult to discern in the Warwicks' collective oblation the quality of gratitude. Kindnesses to birds were legion; on the first day of the Somme British soldiers carried shell-shocked partridges to safety; in the same battle an officer of a London regiment guarded a plover's nest for half an hour to prevent eggs being trampled by troops passing up to the front line.

Birds had a special place in the hearts and minds of men on the Western Front. When one Scottish miner turned soldier (and presumably no fey, Wordsworthian-wannabe) told his local newspaper 'If it weren't for the birds, what a hell it would be' he spoke for millions.

One of the great trials for soldiers on the Western Front was ennui, plain and simple. For all of the misconception of the Great War as unrelieved combat, the truth was that the Great War was much like any other war: 90 per cent tedium, 10 per cent action. The personal diary of Private G.W. Broadhead, kept against army regulations (but a Tommy would not be a Tommy if he did not bend rules) makes for dull but edifyingly truthful reading. He was in the trenches with 18/West Yorkshire Regiment at Neuve Chapelle in October 1916:[2]

29/10: Nothing much doing in the line but repair work.
30/10: Nothing special going on except the usual shelling. Weather still keeping beautiful.
31/10: Nothing exceptional happened except the usual shelling etc.[3]

Fritz's for-form's-sake shelling was known as 'the daily hate'.

In the walled world of the trenches birds broke the blank boredom, whether it was from observing their antics, or spotting different species. Almost every front line chore, from sentry duty to bringing up supplies, could be improved by the presence of 'feathered friends'. Teenager Second Lieutenant Arnold Monk-Jones, at Arras in June 1918, was delighted to write in his diary:

> While doing a reconnaissance of Blangy Support wire with Ratcliffe this morning, I found a partridge's nest of which I had been told by Willie. It is just at the N. end of the wire 20 or 30 yards from London Avenue. It contained 21 eggs, a trifle smaller than I had expected somehow, I measured them, however I found them about 1.3 inches long. They were packed very closely in a deepish cup hollowed into a tuft of grass, a very pretty sight.[4]

There was pleasure too in simple bird song. Denis Barnett, a subaltern in the Leinsters, wrote to his mother from the trenches in 1915: 'It is lovely sitting in the sun, listening to the cock chaffinches and yellowhammers tuning up.'[5]

Barnett, born 1895, had spent his youth 'among the lanes and heaths of Berkshire', which gave him 'a passionate love for the countryside', declared his memorial volume, published by his grieving parents. He was killed in action at Hooge, a bullet through his guts; the medical officer recorded that Barnett 'stuck his wound splendidly'.

'Birding' was probably the most popular single hobby among officers on the front line; in June 1916 *Country Life*, along with *Tatler*, an in-house journal of the British upper class, reported that egg collecting was a veritable vogue in the trenches, whatever the state of the weather. Or the war. Captain John Jeffries, an officer with the Durham Light Infantry was pleased to be invited to lunch with General Chetwode; Jeffries was less pleased to find that the post luncheon entertainment was a bird-nesting expedition, and more dismayed still when the area to be explored was a shell-strewn wilderness a mere three-quarters of a mile from the front line and comfortably within shelling distance. The birders found a nightingale's nest with six eggs, along with the nests of a chaffinch, a blackbird and a mistle thrush.

Ornithological, sporting and country magazines were packed to the end papers with learned articles and letters by birdwatchers on active service. Captain Arthur de C. Sowerby wrote to the RSPB's magazine:

> Many of the readers of British Birds will agree with me when I say it is gratifying to find that in spite of the turmoil and stress of war, bird lovers have been able to devote part of their time, at least, to the study of bird life, even in the fighting zones.[6]

With a suitably English modesty, Major Walter Maitland Congreve MC, who was a Regular soldier and a member of the British Ornithologists' Union, apologised for the brevity of his notes in *Ibis*, writing that they 'rely for their interest on the fact that they were taken in a theatre of war under unusual conditions'.

The Western Front was curiously good birdwatching country. After all, an enormous corridor of it, as much as a mile across, was composed of 'no man's land' where, as the name indicated, humans feared to tread. In a letter home to his beloved wife Maude, Captain Charlie May of the Manchesters described the front in frosty March 1916:

> Just over the brink of the parapet one catches a glimpse of jagged earthenware, the remains of a rum jar, or the battered lid, rising oyster fashion, from a discarded jam tin. That is No Man's Land, a portion of the earth where Tommy can with impunity gratify his natural tendency to untidiness by flinging to it all that endless rubbish which a battalion mysteriously accumulates even in the short span of a day.
>
> Only birds live out there – apparently as happily as ever. A lark trills blithefully somewhere up in the heavens above even as I

write, his note throbbing as though 'twould burst his throat, full of the joy of the dawning and the promise of spring.[7]

*The English Review* confirmed in March 1918: 'No-man's-land proved an attractive place, in spite of the noise and all the dangers of artillery fire, for thousands of birds to nest and rear their young.'

Since for long periods of the war long stretches of the front were verdant idylls rather than shell-blasted mudlands, the barbed wire enclosed pristine meadows and cornucopian arable fields. No man's land was, effectively, a bird reserve with a barbed wire perimeter. Some bird species discovered man's barbed wire to be as beneficent as nature's brambles in providing protective cover. Captain Walter Medlicott, born in 1879 and longer in the tooth than most wearing khaki, noted that 'Whinchats and Common Whitethroats rejoiced in the wire entanglements and rough grass which grew long amongst them'. Of the 106 species Medlicott ticked off in the Pas-de-Calais between March and August 1917, most of them were nesting 'within four or five miles of our front line trenches'.[8] One soldier observer near Péronne counted nearly sixty different varieties within a two-mile radius.[9] By common consent, the great avian winner of abandoned farmland was the common partridge (*Perdix perdix*), partly because the lack of harvest enabled undisturbed breeding, partly because the French prohibited game shooting from the first year of the war onwards. The corncrake and the yellowhammer also thrived where and when it was all quiet on the Western Front.

When fighting came, and destruction with it, bird numbers and species tended to reduce. Lieutenant Christian Carver was amazed at the heron living beside him in the mire of the Somme in March 1917, adding in his letter to his brother: 'It is the last place *I* would choose.' Casting his eyes over the post-apocalyptic battlefield of Devil's Wood on the Somme, all Lieutenant-Colonel Rowland Feilding, 6/Connaught Rangers, could spot among the ruins and weeds were magpies flitting 'silently about the waste'.[10]

Magpies were *the* birds of desolation. Subject of British folklore for centuries, *Pica pica* had associations with both the Devil and the Grim Reaper; the oldest version of the famous magpie nursery rhyme, dating to about 1750, begins:

One for sorrow, two for joy
Three for a wedding, four for death . . .

When soldiers crossed the Channel, they took the folkloric beliefs of home with them, as surely as they did nature-worship. Superstitions about birds and animals lived on into the machine age; the Great War soldier was superstitious to the nth degree.[11] When Captain Robert Graves saw a tame magpie ('German, we guessed') hop in the trench at Bazentin, he said 'That's one for sorrow'.[12] There was indeed sorrow for the Royal Welch Fusiliers at High Wood, including for Graves himself, who received a chest wound so serious that the colonel, wrongly believing there to be no hope, reported him dead of wounds.

The bird of sorrow had a good war. In the studied opinion of Captain Sowerby, zoologist and explorer before taking the King's shilling for service in the Chinese Labour Corps (he could speak the language), the magpie and the hooded crow were 'the commonest birds of the devastated areas' in France. They were the emblematic birds of the ruins.

There were other avian winners amid the destruction aside from *Pica pica*; Sowerby singled out the kestrel, 'doubtless attracted to these desolate wastes by the small rodents, field-voles, harvest mice and the like, which appear to have greatly increased in numbers'. The reduction by artillery of agricultural land to quagmire may have appalled soldiers and French farmers alike, yet for waders such as snipe it offered thousands of acres of new habitat. Looking out from his observation post at Arras towards the German lines 2000 yards away, Lieutenant Edward Thomas noted in his diary another bird to benefit from man's mayhem: 'The shelling must have slaughtered many jackdaws but have made home for many more'.[13]

Thomas, who had arrived in France in January 1917 with 244 Siege

Battery, puzzled over the lack of thrushes as much as he did the deployment of his guns; he was saddened in particular by the absence of blackbird song. Like other perching birds, blackbirds suffered from the eradication of trees and shrubs brought by shelling, while the winter of 1916–17, one of the harshest of the twentieth century, wiped out as many as three-quarters of western Europe's insect eating birds.

Edward Thomas's war diary was a proper naturalist's diary, full of precise observations and imaginative wonderings. 'Does a mole ever get hit by a shell?' he pondered on 25 April 1917. Shells indisputably hit men, Thomas among them. When the telegram announcing Thomas's death arrived at his home in Steep, his daughter Myfanwy, knowing his love for birds, was embroidering a wild duck on a postcard to send him.

Thomas's body was recovered for burial. The less fortunate of war's dead lay on the surface of the earth, providing a direct meal for carrion-scavenging birds (thus the ubiquity of magpies and hooded crows) and an indirect food source for others; while rats fed on the decomposing dead, kestrels fed on the rodents, often in prodigious numbers. During guard duty on the Somme, Private Norman Ellison once 'counted thirty-one kestrels hovering over a large field of corn stubble all at the same time. Of course everywhere is swarming with rats and mice.'

One officer wrote to *The Times*, always a willing recipient of nature news from the front:

> When I was up in the trenches recently I saw numerous Owls; they used to flap about among the trenches at night, quite regardless of shells and snipers, getting a fine harvest of rats and mice, with which the trenches literally swarm. They were the big brown Owls. They always disappeared two hours before dawn; I never could make out where to, but I suppose to woods behind the lines.[14]

And because of the rotting corpses of men and horses there were flies everywhere. With some discretion, *Country Life* pointed out that the front's 'abnormal quantity of insects doubtless formed an attraction to insectivorous birds, and this was particularly noticed as regards Swallows, Martins, and Swifts'.[15] What a mass of swallows feeding on corpse-flies actually looked like was recorded, unforgettably, by Lieutenant Ford Madox Hueffer in his semi-autobiographical novel *Parade's End*, where the hero, Captain Christopher Tietjens, walks a recently vacated battlefield:

> He went down with long strides, the tops of the thistles brushing his hips. Obviously the thistles contained things that attracted flies. They are apt to after a famous victory. So myriads of swallows pursued him, swirling round and round him, their wings touching; for a matter of twenty yards all round and their wings brushing him and the tops of the thistles.[16]

In the Colony across the Channel the world turned upside down. For the British the swallow was solely and traditionally the glad bird of summer; in the Colony the swallow became an eater of corpse-flies.

So, there were birds everywhere in the war zone, whether devastated fly-blown ruins or Elysian fields untrod by men.

Birdspotters everywhere too. In quantity and quality, the Western Front was the most birdwatched war zone in history. It was a rare soldier who did not betray some interest in battlefield avifauna, and among the millions of men in khaki there were some very serious ornithologists indeed. Sowerby was a Fellow of the Zoological Society, while Captain Arnold W. Boyd, 7/Lancashire Fusiliers and Major W. Maitland Congreve, Royal Engineers, were both members of the British Ornithologists' Union; all wrote up detailed notes on birds of the Flanders and Somme battlefield, their observations tallying almost exactly.[17] Post-war, Boyd would go on to become assistant editor of *British Birds*, contribute to the *Guardian*'s 'Country Diary' column and revise Thomas Coward's *The Birds of the British Isles and Their Eggs* for a new edition.[18]

By modern mores, though, the scientific methods of some of the expert birders of the Western Front leave something to be desired. The fame of Captain Collingwood Ingram RFC rests on his post-war reputation as an authority on Japanese flowering cherries (hence his nickname 'Cherry') but before 1914 he was known as an accomplished field ornithologist and bird artist. Ingram saw no problem in shooting birds to confirm their identification. One entry in his wartime diary of service runs: 'Later I shot a marsh tit for my collection'; on another day he 'obtains' a crested lark. Cherry Ingram used a small bore .410 shotgun disguised as a walking stick for such enterprises. Of course, in those far off days birds were more plentiful and nature was undiminished by shoot-to-identify.

Second Lieutenant C.C. Baring assiduously kept a birding diary when in France and Flanders. As a teenager, Baring had won the RSPB's Silver Medal in the Public Schools Competition. His diary for mid 1917 is indicative of the range of birds a fighting man might see on the Flanders section of the front, in combat and at rest:

April. [1917] – Out in rest at last, after an 'over the top with the best of luck.'

11th. – The first Swallow has turned up, and in the lane behind the farm we are billeted in is a Blackbird's nest with one egg.

23rd. – The House-Martins, Chiffchaffs, and a few Willow-Wrens are here.

26th. – This afternoon I watched a small Warbler hopping about in the creeper out-side the farmhouse. From its note and general appearance I am convinced it was an Icterine Warbler.

28th. – To-day I saw a fine cock Wheatear; it was probably still on migration.

May 5th. – This morning I put up a hen Meadow Pipit from her nest, while doubling across a field on 'open warfare' manoeuvres. It had five eggs in it.

7th. – All the Magpie and Carrion Crows nests which I have found so far in at all accessible positions have been robbed. The Meadow Pipit has deserted, I am sorry to say. There are five or six Sandpipers passing up and down the river here. They are very shy and I have not been able to get a good look at them. I am almost sure they are not Common Sandpipers, as their note seems to me quite different. Along the same river there are a number of small bushes in which several pairs of White-throats have begun to build their nests. If one is lucky one can see a Kingfisher flash by in all the glory of its breeding-season plumage.

8th. – I have located the Kingfisher's home quite by chance. I put the hen bird off the nest of fish-bones, on which reposed seven pearly white eggs. She was just beginning to sit, and the eggs had lost the beautiful pink glow that suffuses them when newly laid. I found nests of the Robin, Yellow-hammer, Hedge-Sparrow, Wren, Linnet, and Garden-Warbler containing eggs; Nightingales are fairly plentiful in suitable spots, but I have found no nest as yet.

June. – An end to rest and peace; we have moved up to the ill-fated 'Salient.' We are in a once-famous town, now sadly smashed about. There is a fine tower still left standing. At least five pairs of Kestrels nest in it, besides Jackdaws, Pigeons, and Starlings, so there is everlasting war in the air round it; how they all fit in together I can't think. The air seems full of screaming Swifts. They don't seem to mind the tower being shelled, but rejoice in the additional nesting-places the ruins afford. Last night on patrol I ran into a flock of Redshanks in 'No man's land,' which is a marsh in this part of the line. Fortunately for us they did not scream out and only displayed a certain vague restlessness. One full-throated alarm call, and we should have had a dozen Hun lights at us. – We are in a place where the front line is in the middle of a wood, now a mere ghost of itself. But a pair of Nightingales still haunt it, and Chaffinches, Hedge-Sparrows, Blackbirds, and Whitethroats are singing everywhere. Last night I heard a Great Reed-Warbler singing beside a lake I had to pass. Its song dominated the whole night as the

Nightingale's does, but of course it is not quite so melodious.

This morning I had a most delightful adventure. I stumbled across a ruined chalet surrounded by most beautiful grounds, which were full of syringa bushes in full bloom, while Golden Orioles called from the tall trees or flashed by in the sunshine.

Later. – We are in the middle of the offensive, the shelling is almost incessant, and there is very little cover. Naturally there are not many birds up here now. I have seen several Sparrows suffering from 'shell shock.' A most beautiful cock Pied Wagtail haunts a large shell-hole full of water near one of my posts. Besides these a few Swifts and Swallows occasionally come over.[19]

Cecil Baring, Queen's Own (Royal West Kent Regiment) died of wounds in March 1918. He was twenty. His brothers Arthur, Charles and Reginald also fell.

Despite being a mere twenty miles or so from England, the Colony had its particular and unusual species. There were birds in Baring's diary to amaze British birders, led by the nightingale, which in Britain was restricted in breeding range to the south and east. On the Western Front in 1914–18 the nightingale was recorded as 'Very common' by Captain Boyd. So spellbound was J.C. Faraday in July 1917 that he rushed off a letter to *The Times*:

You will have a terrific tearing and roaring noise of artillery and shot in the dead of night; then there will be a temporary cessation of the duel, with great quietness, when lo! And behold and hear! Hearken to his song! Out came the nightingales, right about the guns . . . And another kind of love music is introduced to our ears and souls, which does us good. Think! It makes you think – and beautiful thoughts come along to relieve you from the devilment of war and the men who cause it . . .[20]

Someone who found 'beautiful thoughts' produced by the nightingale's music was Siegfried Sassoon. Sassoon was at an army school in France thirty miles from the front, in late spring 1916:

> With half an hour to spare after breakfast, I strolled up the hill and smoked my pipe under a quick-set hedge. Loosening my belt I looked at a chestnut tree in full leaf and listened to the perfect performance of a nightingale. Such things seemed miraculous after the desolation of the trenches. Never before had I been so intensely aware of what it meant to be young and healthy in fine weather at the outset of summer.[21]

Private Ellison, who came from nightingale-less Liverpool, was far from impressed, however, when he encountered *Luscinia megarhynchos* at Wailly:

> Quite recently a nightingale has arrived in our neighbourhood. As a northerner I ought to be charmed with its singing, but I am much disappointed. This bird certainly gets out a few sweet trills occasionally, but most of its song consists of hoarse gurglings and burblings as if his throat was confoundedly sore. The corncrake has also made himself heard – his hoarse rattle blends beautifully with the machine-guns![22]

He would have sympathised with Lieutenant Richard Talbot Kelly, 52nd Brigade, Royal Field Artillery at St Yves Wood at Ploegsteert ('Plugstreet' in the argot of the British infantryman) whose sleep was banished because of 'the singing of the scores of nightingales'.[23]

Contra Faraday and Sassoon, for most soldiers melancholia was the sentiment brought about by listening to the evensong of the nightingale. This was understandable: the bird's Latin name *Luscinia* is from *luctus* = lamentation and *cano* = sing, in recognition of the sorrowful tone of its tune. (In British Romantic literature the nightingale had often taken the guise of 'Philomel', alluding to the classical myth of Philomel, ravished and then de-tongued by her brother-in-law, Tereus, King of Thrace, and only saved from death by the gods turning her into a nightingale.) Listening to a nightingale outside his Flanders billet, Second Lieutenant Douglas Gillespie was sent into a morose reflection John Keats would have understood:

> Presently a misty moon came up, and a nightingale began to sing. I have only heard him once before, in the day-time, near Farly Mount, at Winchester; but, of course, I knew him at once, and it was strange to stand there and listen, for the song seemed to come all the more sweetly and clearly in the quiet intervals between the bursts of firing. There was something infinitely sweet and sad about it, as if the countryside were singing gently to itself, in the midst of all our noise and confusion and muddy work; so that you felt the nightingale's song was the only real thing which would remain when all the rest was long past and forgotten. It is such an old song too, handed on from nightingale to nightingale through the summer nights of so many innumerable years . . .[24]

Philip Gosse's problems with the nightingale were altogether more down to earth. One of the dangers of being a birder in uniform was that a birder in very senior uniform might turn up expecting the full ornithological tour. Captain Gosse was on duty as a medical officer at the RAMC hospital in Coupigny in the Lens coalfield when General Babington turned up for an inspection:

> When the inspection was finished he called me up and asked if I had any birds' nests to show him. I told him I had and off we went, the General and his aide-de-camp Lord Wodehouse, led by myself. What the General had thought about his inspection of the hospital I do not know, but he was certainly pleased with his second inspection.[25]

Gosse showed him the nests of blackcaps, hedge sparrows, blackbirds, song thrushes, cirl buntings. The general himself found a goldfinches' nest with five eggs in it. They also heard a goldcrest, a serin finch, an icterine warbler and, right on cue, 'our one and only night-ingale woke up in the shrubbery and obliged with a few sweet notes'. Babington was a highly popular general and Gosse 'felt grateful to all my small friends for behaving so handsomely at the general's visit'. Birds were a boon to Gosse for the entire duration of his service, as he explained in the introduction to his memoirs:

> Some of my readers may find fault with me for having compar-atively so little to say about the 'horrors' of war and so much about beasts and birds. The title might well have been 'A Solace of Birds' for without the birds I dare not think how I should have got through the war at all.[26]

If the nightingale was a novelty for many soldier-birdwatchers, the absolute holy grail of Western Front twitching was the golden oriole.

With its fluting call the Eurasian golden oriole (*Oriolus oriolus*) is merely adequate as a chorister, having tone without variety. One officer–birdwatcher wrote home:

> The Oriole's whistle has a very human sound, rich and full, but his repertoire is meagre. He starts with a splendid note, which can be heard 400 yards off, but it is all over after half-a-dozen bars.[27]

The bird's beauty is all corporeal. The male with its bright yellow body and black wings is an almost paradisiacal spectacle; the female, with her greenish-yellow upper body and olive wings, is stunning, though less so than the male. A summer visitor from Africa the golden oriole, like the nightingale, is more common in France than Britain. To the joy of Major W. Maitland Congreve stationed near Péronne, 'Every wood of any size at all had at least one pair nesting in it and they were found occasionally in quite open spinneys'.

No soldier who encountered a golden oriole failed to marvel at its livery. A correspondent for *Country Life* who signed himself 'C.W.R.K.' and served 'somewhere in Flanders' was scanning the

German trenches when he heard the short liquid call of a bird, and it suddenly dawned 'that this song was none other than that of the golden oriole – a bird that had been eagerly looked for at home, and never discovered'. To see a golden oriole was, C.W.R.K. considered, worth a risk and he crept with a press-ganged friend to the shell-blasted wood where the golden oriole was singing. Every now and then rifle bullets cracked into the trees above. 'For a time, though, the war is forgotten.' He discovered, as many others have before and since, that the bright yellow oriole is oddly difficult to see:

> Our eyes are straining to pick him out among the foliage which harmonizes so well with his plumage. He must be near the top. Yes; there he sits with his wonderful yellow breast, slender beak and short tail. All unconscious he sang on, oblivious of one pair of eyes that gazed in admiration, or of a second pair that also gazed, but whose owner wondered why a mere bird should excite such enthusiasm, even though the bird be a golden oriole.

But the brilliance of the golden oriole is not limited to its plumage. The golden oriole's nest is an architectural marvel, which hangs suspended from two forks of a horizontal branch. One pair of orioles near Péronne, according to Congreve, had lined their nest with wool from an abandoned mattress, thus putting to good use the detritus caused by man's violence. C.W.R.K., in order to peep into the golden oriole's nest in the Flanders copse, went to extraordinary endeavours, firstly finding a long larch pole, then fashioning and attaching a hook to its end. Then:

> Once more I climb the tree and, after a very great deal of difficulty, manage to fix the hook in a fork of the coveted branch. Now to pull it over. Nearer and nearer the nest swings. A little higher I climb and, exerting all my strength, I manage to jamb the larch pole into a fork of the branch on which I stand. To strap it there is the next

thing to do, and having done so, I found that the interior of the nest can just be seen. There are four glorious eggs.[28]

For all of the startling exoticism of the golden oriole, the bird synonymous with the Western Front was a drab little farmland thing. Then again, the skylark was ubiquitous; it was also easily identifiable from its habit of rising up to Heaven's Gate while pouring out song. Major W. Maitland Congreve in his 'Ornithological and Oological Notes from the River Somme Valley at its Mouth and near Peronne' concluded that *Alauda arvensis* was 'A common breeding species'. Sergeant H.H. Munro (better known as Scottish short story writer 'Saki') noted how the skylark had:

> stuck tenaciously to the meadows and crop-lands that have been seamed and bisected with trenches and honeycombed with shell-holes. In the chill, misty hour of gloom that precedes a rainy dawn, when nothing seemed alive except a few wary waterlogged sentries and many scuttling rats, the lark would suddenly dash skyward and pour forth a song of ecstatic jubilation that sounded horribly forced and insincere. It seemed scarcely possible that the bird could carry its insouciance to the length of attempting to rear a brood in that desolate wreckage of shattered clods and gaping shell-holes, but once, having occasion to throw myself down with some abruptness on my face, I found myself nearly on the top of a brood of young larks. Two of them had already been hit by something, and were in a rather battered condition, but the survivors seemed as tranquil and comfortable as the average nestling.[29]

The skylark's refusal ('brave' was the adjective usually attached) to quit its habitat because of warring man caused widespread admiration. The bird even stayed put on day one of the Somme, the never to be forgotten 1 July 1916, the bloodiest day in British military history, with its 58,000 British casualties (one third of them fatalities). The attack was launched on a thirty kilometre front, between Arras and Albert. Siegfried Sassoon, Royal Welch Fusiliers, at Fricourt, scribbled in his diary:

> Since 6.30 there has been Hell let loose. The air vibrates with the incessant din – the whole earth shakes and rocks and throbs – it is one continuous roar . . . Inferno-inferno-bang-smash.[30]

Despite the storms of steel, the skylarks went up into a cerulean sky. (Sassoon called the weather 'heavenly'.) Even on the Somme, nature impressed itself on the experience. The correspondent for *The Times* informed readers that the skylarks could be heard singing during the battle 'whenever there was a lull in the almost incessant fire'.[31]

A month later, with the battle still raging, Sergeant Leslie Coulson, 1/12 London Regiment, in the line at Hébuterne, paid his admiring respects to the magnificent tenacity of the Somme's *Alauda arvensis* in poetry:

> From death that hurtles by
> I crouch in the trench day-long,
> But up to a cloudless sky
> From the ground where our dead men lie
> A brown lark soars in song.
> Through the tortured air,
> Rent by the shrapnel's flare,
> Over the troubleless dead he carols his fill,
> And I thank the gods that the birds are beautiful still.[32]

As a boy, Coulson had attended a Norfolk boarding school which, contrary to the commonplace view of Edwardian private schools as uniformly arid, soulless, snobbish institutions, actually fostered a love of nature and the principles of natural justice. He worked as a journalist for Reuters before signing up. He refused a commission.

Coulson was fatally wounded charging the German line at Le Transloy on the Somme in October 1916.

Second Lieutenant Otto Murray-Dixon, Seaforth Highlanders, was amazed during a German 'hate' or shelling that:

> The larks continue to sing right through the shelling and kestrels hover about, not at all concerned by all the noise; it is very cheering to see them.

Murray-Dixon had spent his childhood rambling and bird-nesting around his home, the Old Rectory at Swithland in Leicestershire, prior to attending Calderon's School of Animal Painting. Before joining up, he had been commissioned by J.G. Millais to provide drawings for his *British Diving Ducks*. One of the obituaries for Murray-Dixon, following his death in 1917, observed 'wild flowers filled his soul'.

The skylarks were there in Flanders too. Poppies might dominate the landscape of Lieutenant-Colonel John McCrae's iconic 'In Flanders Fields', but there's nonetheless a significant place for the skylark:

> In Flanders fields, the poppies blow
> Between the crosses, row on row
> That mark our place; and in the sky
> The larks still bravely singing, fly
> Scarce heard amid the guns below.

The song of the skylark was the soundtrack of the war on the Western Front wherever, and whenever. Lance Corporal Alfred Vivian, 4/Middlesex Regiment, fought in Britain's first land battle of the conflict, at dusty Mons, in August 1914:

> Church bells chimed sweetly in the towns and hamlets about us, and dimly, from the distance, we discerned faint strains of music being poured out at the service being held in the convent in our rear.

A lark hovering immediately above our hole in the roof trilled out a glorious burst of song, and we craned our necks the better to view it. A strange and indefinable sense of unreality stole over me and, for some extraordinary reason, I became attacked by a strong desire to cry. I endeavoured to impart my sensations to my colleague, and I said to him: 'There is something so extraordinary hanging in the air, that I feel the thing I would most enjoy would be to visit a church. I don't like this quietness and –'

'Smack!' the tile within two inches of our heads was shattered into a thousand fragments, and the two of us flopped simultaneously to the floor.[33]

At the other end of the war, the larks were still trilling. Private Wilfrid Edwards, 15th London Regiment (Civil Service Rifles), noted in 1918:

There was a front-line trench on the slopes above Albert, in standing corn over the chalk, which was memorable in a number of ways. A typical sequence of events on quiet days was as follows: at 'stand-to' an hour before dawn, the darkness of no-man's land would become musical with the songs of skylarks, which continued until sunrise.[34]

For Private Norman Edwards, 6/Gloucestershire Regiment and in the line at Plugstreet Wood in May 1915, the melody of the skylark was part of the pattern of the soldier's day:

One realised how close one was living to nature, closer perhaps than ever before, and the thought that possibly each dawn might be the last accentuated the delight.

The dawns at this time were particularly beautiful. Before any definite light appeared, the larks would soar up and a faint twittering in the wood grew to a buzz of noise as the birds stood-to with us.[35]

'The song of the Skylark at dawn over No-Man's-Land was as usual as the song of the sniper's bullet,' believed the *Daily News and Leader*.[36] The matins of the skylark was more than an alarm clock, it was confirmation that the black night was over. Lieutenant Harold Rayner of the Devonshires was eloquent in his expression of this post-nocturnal relief:

> The larks sing all day here but they are best at dawn. The larks of the morning 'stand-to', deserve a poem of their own, they are wonderful after a night of doubt and terror in the trenches, they are the returning light transformed to music; they are the renewed blue trembling into song, they sing of the permanence of the joy of life, of the sweets of light and warmth, and the war-indifferent exquisiteness of Nature. They have to be experienced in much-strafed trenches where the night is hideous, to be understood. Punctually as we stand-to about 3 a.m. hark! and their thin sweet voice intensening with the growing light 'droppeth as the gentle rain from Heaven upon the place beneath'.[37]

Rayner had just made acquaintance with George Meredith's 'The Lark Ascending' ('a priceless appreciation of that joymaker'), the poem which inspired Ralph Vaughan Williams' composition of the same name. In retrospect, Vaughan Williams' music seems a predictive requiem for the coming pale-faced battalions of the dead; more certainly, 'The Lark Ascending', written as Vaughan Williams ambled Margate's cliff top in the first week of the war, was an attempt to capture the spirit of Britain's pastoralism. Vaughan Williams enlisted as a private in the RAMC, before being commissioned in the Royal Garrison Artillery.[38]

The skylark played on chords deep within the psyche of the educated nation; it was the bird of the poets, of Meredith, Gerard Manley Hopkins, A.E. Housman, John Clare, Christina Rossetti and, above all, of Percy Byshe Shelley and his 'Ode to a Skylark'. Private Isaac Rosenberg implicitly acknowledged the debt to Shelley in 'Returning,

We Hear Larks', with its metaphorical description of the bird's song as light rain: 'Music showering our upturned list'ning faces'. (Shelley has 'As from thy presence showers a rain of melody'.) Rosenberg and his mates, coming back to camp after a night stint of trench maintenance, are, like Harold Rayner, delighted to hear larks in the sky rather than the expected whine of bombs. It's an interlude from death, a delight shared by all men, with the larks themselves forming an invisible shield:

> . . . Death could drop from the dark
> As easily as song –
> But song only dropped . . .[39]

Less than a year later, on 1 April 1918, Private Rosenberg was sniped at dawn after a night patrol. A bullet, not song, had dropped from the sky. The war was always rich in irony.

While Rosenberg was elliptical in his homage to Shelley, Sergeant John William Streets, 12th (Service) Battalion York and Lancaster Regiment ('Sheffield Pals'), was explicit in acknowledging the debt. In 'Shelley in the Trenches' Streets, like his Romantic inspiration, is transported by the song of the skylark into transcendent euphoria:

> A lark trill'd in the blue: and suddenly
> Upon the wings of his immortal ode
> My soul rushed singing to the ether sky
> And found in visions, dreams, its real abode –
> I fled with Shelley, with the lark afar,
> Unto the realms where the eternal are.[40]

Eldest of twelve children, unable to take up a place at grammar school due to poverty, Streets had worked on the coal face at the Whitwell mine, Derbyshire, but filled his spare time studying French and the Classics. The pit and the trench were both troglodyte worlds.

Streets was killed on the first day of slaughter on the Somme, when the 'Sheffield Pals' went over the top at Zero Hour – 0730 hours – near Serre, to be met, in the words of the battalion's war diary 'with very heavy machine gun and rifle fire and artillery barrage'. The German barbed wire did its job; 'the few men who reached the wire were unable to get through'. Wounded himself, Streets was last seen going to help another man. By the time his battalion was taken out of the line on the evening of 3 July, 513 officers and men had been killed, wounded or were missing; a further 75 were slightly wounded. The Somme was the graveyard of the Pals, those men who had answered Lord Kitchener's call in 1914, the selfless and the public spirited.

Streets was aged thirty-one when he died. In May 1917 a collection of his war poems was published posthumously as *The Undying Splendour*, which was reasonable titling, both for the quality of the poetry and the manner in which Streets and his Pals met their deaths.

Appreciation of the skylark, however, was not dependent on being groomed, or even self-educated, in culture. The musical song of the bird was intrinsically beautiful, and lifted spirits. Private Ivor Gurney, doing his rifle training, lying on his belly, reloading 'with the quickness of those who get extra pay for it', saw a skylark fly up. Stretched out next to him was Tim Godding, 'a Shakespearean character':

Now Tim Godding has little bits of jargon, some of which I strongly suspect to be Hindustani. One of these is 'ipsti pris' a sign of high spirits, of salutation to a passing battalion or the crown of a joke: anything joyful. So Tim Godding half turned over, looked up to the first blue of spring – 'Ipsti pris, skylark, ispti pris'![41]

Skylarks turned the eyes upwards from present problems. When Siegfried Sassoon wrote in his diary on 3 June 1916 from near Sailly-Laurette that 'A lark goes up, and takes my heart with him',[42] it was nature pure providing the uplift rather than literary association.

There were negatives in the singing of the 'blithe spirit'. For

Sergeant-Major F.H. Keeling the skylark's trilling caused aching homesickness:

> Every morning when I was in the frontline trenches I used to hear the larks singing soon after we stood-to about dawn. But those wretched larks made me more sad than anything else out there ... Their songs are so closely associated in my mind with peaceful summer days in gardens or pleasant landscapes in Blighty.[43]

Another sergeant, Ernest Boughton from Nottingham, aged forty, also understood the melancholy the skylark's song could engender. In a letter home in 1917 he wrote that the 'ecstasy of the lark' was 'inseparably connected with "stand to" in trenches'. In the mind of Second Lieutenant Ford Madox Hueffer, there developed a worse association still: larks and German shells. Birdsong became the harbinger of death itself:

> Now that the shells were coming back from a mile or so off, the sky was thick with larks ... You might almost say that it was a sign that the Germans were going to shell you again. Wonderful 'Hinstinct' set by the Almighty in their little bosoms. It was perhaps also accurate. No doubt the shells as they approached more and more shook the earth and disturbed the little bosoms on their nests. So they got up and shouted; perhaps warning each other; perhaps mere defiance of the artillery.[44]

Hueffer, instead of finding concord in the song of the skylark, heard only discord. He likened the bird's trilling to 'a heartless noise like that produced by the rubbing of two corks one on the other'. Hueffer's literary alter ego, Christopher Tietjens in *Parade's End*, receives the 'fright of my life!' when, in looking over the trench top, a skylark almost lands in his mouth, he thinking it a German shell. Some nervous men visually misidentified skylarks at the apex of their ascension; Captain Patrick Chubb wrote: 'Skylarks are continuously up in the air, and are continuously being mistaken at first sight for aeroplanes.'[45]

Under the weight of war, there were men for whom the skylark flew away from being the bird of sunlit British meadows or the blithe raiser of spirits. It became the war bird.

The *Daily Mail* reported in August 1915 from a battlefield suffering 'scores of our dead and wounded', that a skylark darted into the sky pouring forth his song: '"What the 'ell is 'e singing about?" irritably asked a prostrate Tommy.'[46]

What indeed.

*

'Ye fearless birds that live and fly where men
Can venture not and live, that even build
Your nests where oft the searching shrapnel shrilled . . .'

*From* 'Birds in the Trenches', *Lieutenant Willoughby Weaving, Royal Irish Rifles*

The skylark was not the only avian species which refused to retreat in the face of war. Far from it. Although it was expected that birds would entirely desert the war zone – except for those grim camp-followers of Mars, the hooded crow, the magpie, the raven – the apparent obduracy of birds, those 'Sweet disregarders of man's miseries' as Lieutenant Weaving termed them, was a constant wonder for soldiers, and was reported extensively in the British home newspapers ('a seemingly inexhaustible topic', opined *The Times*).

Writing to his young niece Nancy, Captain James Bell Foulis, 5/Cameron Highlanders, told her:

We are living in a lovely big green wood and you'd be surprised at the number of birds and things there are in it. They don't seem to care a button for all the shells that are flying about and keep on singing merrily all the time. There are cuckoos, and turtle doves, blackbirds, thrushes, robins, linnets, and all sorts of other, and even one or two pheasants.[47]

Aside from the evidence of the persistence of bird life, there is another remarkable feature in Foulis's letter: the assumption that a young child would automatically be interested in birds, and know the species mentioned.

Were some birds less affected by shell and shot than others? Lieutenant Douglas Gillespie thought magpies 'much more frightened by sounds than the smaller birds – we have a good many chaffinches and wagtails here, as well as blackbirds and thrushes'.[48] This was in Flanders. He found a sparrow's nest in a pollard willow on the front line, 'but there were three bullet holes scored on the bark within a foot of it, so that I did not care to climb up and look inside'.[49] Wood pigeons nested in the fork of a tree behind the trench: 'I hope a stray bullet will not put an end to their nursery.'[50]

Captain Patrick Chubb, RE, a soldier correspondent for *British Birds*, wrote at length on birds unaffected by fighting: 'These include House-Sparrow, Swallow, House Martin, Chaffinch, Yellow hammer, Sky-Lark, Willow-Wren, Magpie, Kestrel and Wood-Pigeon. All of these I have seen flying about in front of our own and the French artillery during an artillery duel.'

Some observers were convinced that birds chorused louder on the front line, as if to compete with the guns. The journalist H. Perry Robinson, war correspondent for the *Daily News*, reported on the June 1917 artillery prelude to Third Ypres, the 'Big Push' battle of 1917 – 'a truly terrible dawn'.

The sun as it rose was invisible behind the bank of smoke, but it flushed the sky above with red. It was a truly terrible dawn, most beautiful in its terror, and, if ever dawn did indeed come up like thunder, it was this. Then came the greatest miracle of all, for with the rose-flush in the sky the whole bird-chorus of morning came to life. Never, surely, did birds sing so – Blackbird and Thrush,

Lark and Black-cap and Willow Warbler. Most of the time their voices, of course, were inaudible, but now and again in the intervals of the shattering noise of the guns their notes pealed up, as if each bird were struck with frenzy and were striving to shout down the guns.[51]

This was not fancy. Male birds do increase the volume and pitch of their songs so they can be heard above background noise.[52]

The nightingale's mellifluous trillings between artillery crescendos were marked by many. Little, it seemed, could deter a male nightingale from singing his heart out. According to *The Times*, a nightingale began to sing at 3 a.m. on 23 May 1915 in the garden of a chateau; half an hour later German shells were rained upon the garden for the remainder of the day. The nightingale sang throughout the shell-storm until midday. The next morning it tuned up again as enthusiastically as ever.[53] Since it sang from high in bushes, the nightingale was little affected by poison gas, which lurked low.

The black rook was no songster, yet Sergeant H.H. Munro was much taken with its stoicism under fire. On British farmland the rook was shot as pest and as food, making it so 'gun-shy' that the bang of a barn door could set a rookery in commotion. Whereas, in France, the rook 'might have been in some peaceful English meadow on a sleepy Sunday afternoon' for all the notice he took of shot and shell.[54]

In the brave new world of the Colony, the Man–Bird relationship could be topsy-turvy. As Munro drolly observed, the birds 'must be rather intrigued at the change' that has come over the erstwhile fearsome human, who stalked everywhere over the earth as its possessor; now it is man who 'creeps about in screened and sheltered ways, as chary of showing himself in the open as the shyest of wild creatures'.[55]

Lance Sergeant Hector Munro, 22/Royal Fusiliers, was killed by a German sniper near Beaumont Hamel on 14 November 1916 during the battle of Ancre, as he sheltered in a shell hole. Reputedly, he had been admonishing a soldier for insufficient shyness. 'Put that damned cigarette out!' were his last words. He was forty-five.

The examples of birds 'sticking out' battles were legion. For years swans nested in the moat below Ypres' shell-ruined ramparts, successfully hatching cygnets in 1918 (at least), and were so deeply admired that when one Tommy tried to steal their eggs he found the sentries shooting at him in earnest – 'they would have shot him as calmly as a rat' wrote a witness of the incident; a blackbird laid her eggs in a siege-gun daily in action, leading one of the gunners to observe that she was 'as saucy as she was confident of our protection'; Corporal R.H. Tawney, serving with the 22/Manchester Regiment and already famous as an economic historian, saw 'kestrels hover for rats and mice when shells must have been passing within 50 yds of them'[56]; the swallows and martins on Ypres cathedral, a favourite target for German artillery, used mud from shell holes for their nests; waiting to 'go over the bags' at Fleurs on 25 September 1916 in the middle of an artillery storm, Second Lieutenant Alexander Aitken, 1/Otago Battalion (New Zealand Expeditionary Force), watched a partridge and a hare run along no man's land, then:

> Some man grins and jerks his bayonet upward towards a tree ... hardly any time to glance up, but – an owl! How in the name of all that shrapnel?

The Germans, seeing the unbroken line 'coming at speed with fixed bayonets,' fled 'like the partridge and the hare'.

It was the partridge that caused Corporal Garnet W. Durham of the Canadian Corps Cyclists' Battalion to witness a sight many Tommies thought impossible, a Frenchman being kind to birds. Durham was on his way through Death Valley, Pozières, when he passed a French gun battery:

> They stood back and the gunners stood with the trigger lines taut waiting for the word to fire – when suddenly a covey of partridges

flew out over the ridge and settled twenty yards in front of the gun muzzles. The colonel held up his hand. 'Attendez, mes enfants,' he said, and sent a sergeant to chase those 'oiseaux' to one side. When the birds had been driven out of the line of fire, and not till then, Fritz got his iron rations. The birds would not have been killed, but would have been deafened, for, of all the bitter barks, a French 60 pr has the wickedest: but the French officer was too kind to hurt them. (There are partridges all through the trench area.)[57]

In the resilience of birds the soldier hoped to see something of himself. If the birds stayed put, so could he. Birds were encouraging mirrors. They had the necessary qualities of the good soldier: courage, self-sacrifice, strength.

One form of avian obduracy was seen as a blessing upon men. Due to the absence of traditional nesting places in the battle area, birds deigned to share the rudimentary living and working quarters of soldiers. While the birds doubtless merely tolerated humans, the attitude of their soldier cohabitees leaned towards reverential gratitude. The swallow family led the cohabitation effort, and as every student of Shakespeare's *Macbeth* knew, there was benediction in having a 'martlet' nesting in one's lodgings. (It is the martlet who by 'his loved mansionry' on Duncan's castle indicates that goodness resides within.) Major W. Maitland Congreve noted that swallows 'often used the circular Nissen huts put up for troops and were extremely tame and confiding'. One pair, meanwhile, made:

valiant efforts to build their nest under the hood of one of the Battery lorries. The lorry went out regularly but the old birds carried on building operations on its return and only gave up after two or three days.[58]

As Captain Arnold Boyd confirmed, the war swallows of the Somme could be 'astonishingly tame', with a pair successfully raising a brood in the officers' mess at Bertincourt, despite 'the noise, tobacco smoke and candle-light at night'. In his den-ish observation post at Plugstreet, Richard Talbot Kelly had swallows nesting alongside his head, a sight he lovingly reproduced in black-and-white in his artist's sketchbook (the savvy and the experienced always carried a time-killer about their person, whether drawing pad, book to read or pack of cards). Talbot Kelly's interest in drawing birds never left him, and post-war he provided illustrations for bird guides, including his own *The Way of Birds* and R.M. Lockley's classic *Birds of the Sea*. At Wanquentin in May 1918 the ever reliable diarist, Second Lieutenant Arnold Monk-Jones, recorded:

> This evening, while undressing for a bath (at the bath house near the church) I was interested to watch a Swallow building, on a beam just above me. She was a little nervous of entering, but overcame her fears two or three times: on each occasion she brought a piece of straw (about 1 inch long) or some mud, which she laid on the edge of the nest, and proceeded to spit on it, this cementing it on.[59]

In the April 1917 fighting at Vimy Ridge, an escarpment northeast of Arras, Captain Charles Raven's battalion had been 'cut to pieces' (down to 150 from 800 men) and was in 'venomous mood'. But when the battalion went into reserve at La Comté a 'minor miracle' occurred. A pair of swallows built their nest in the entrance to company HQ:

> These birds were angels in disguise. It is a truism that one touch of nature makes the whole world kin: those blessed birds brought instant relief to the nerves and tempers of the men. We all regarded the pair with devoted affection.[60]

The whole battalion, officers and men alike, became obsessed with the swallows' fortunes, placing bets on when the first egg would appear. A daily inspection was held – via a trench periscope, one of the instrument's more novel applications. When the battalion was relieved strict instructions were given on the care and protection of the birds from harm, especially from a German bombardment, 'our chief anxiety'.

The migratory swallow was a bird of spring. For soldiers on the front it was a calendar bird, a marker of the change of season. On seeing the first swallow of the year on Saturday 14 April 1917 at Candas, Captain Collingwood Ingram, RFC, exclaimed in his journal, with a delight still audible to this day:

> The first swallow! What a welcome sight it was to see the steely glint of sunlight upon its back as it sped with sharply pointed wings across a field that, only 48 hours ago, was a white sheet of snow.[61]

Captain T.P.C. Wilson, writing home on 26 April 1916 'from a trench not very far from the Germans', wanted to tell his mother *the* news: he had just heard the first cuckoo.

In trench-land, the flapping of bird's wings turned the seasons.[62] The call of birds, the lark in the morning, the nightingale at night, were the soldiers' clock.

\*

There was spiritual uplift too from the birds of the battlefield, as Robert Sterling of the Royal Scots Fusiliers explained in a letter home:

> I've been longing for some link with the normal universe detached from the storm . . . I did find such a link about three weeks ago. The enemy had just been shelling our reverse trenches, and a Belgian patrol behind us had been replying, when there fell a few minutes silence; and I still crouching expectantly in the trench, suddenly saw a pair of thrushes building a nest in a 'bare ruin'd choir' of a tree, only about five yards behind our line. At the same time a lark began to sing in the sky above the German trenches. It seemed almost incredible at the time, but now, whenever I think of these

nest-builders and that all but 'sightless song', they seem to repeat in some degree the very essence of the Normal and Unchangeable Universe carrying on unhindered and careless amid the corpses and bullets and the madness.[63]

Although birds lived in their own world, they were also the 'link' to God.[64] More than other fauna, birds possessed the ability to carry the watcher 'heavenwards'. One sapper told Captain Thomas Tiplady, the Methodist chaplain of the Queen's Westminster Rifles how, after shelling, he was enjoying the calm and a lark commenced singing:

Then some impulse seized me and, hardly knowing what I did, I cried aloud, 'Why bless, me, it must be Sunday,' and so it was, although I had forgotten.

Then we jumped up for we saw that the dawn was breaking and, lifting the sergeant out of the trench, we rushed across the open ground in the direction of the dressing station. Talk about 'feeling protected!' Why, I felt that God was all around us – that no harm could touch us. A great calm stole over me, and I felt utterly devoid of fear. We had, as you know, to bring the sergeant some two miles to the dressing station, just down the road there, but we got him safely in, and I think he will get better.[65]

Having arrived at Cambridge as 'a pure pagan' Captain Charles Raven had discovered faith in 1906, switching from Classics to Divinity, a conversion which enriched his passion for nature. Thereafter he was able to see:

something of what Wordsworth and the mystics have made familiar – the sense for a moment time had stopped, that suddenly the visible world had become transparent, that the eternal reality, beyond and behind things of sense had been unveiled and in an instant of rapture had enfolded me into union with itself.[66]

He went to the Western Front as a chaplain. If the nesting swallows restored his morale after Vimy, being then billeted 'to my joy on the edge of a wood where golden orioles were nesting' resulted in an almost permanent flotation aid. This was at La Comté. The encounter with orioles was one of the small incidents 'which brought back my love of birds with a rush'.[67] Post-war, Raven wrote three books connected with birdwatching and ornithology – *In Praise of Birds* (1925), *The Ramblings of a Bird Lover* (1927) and *Bird Haunts and Bird Behaviour* (1929) – as well as becoming canon of Liverpool Cathedral, then Regius Professor of Divinity at Cambridge. As a theologian his concern was to maintain nature and the natural world in the Christian faith.

Birds performed other transports. They could carry men across geography and time. Birds had a Proustian capacity for making nostalgia, especially remembrance of home. Private Ivor Gurney wrote to Catherine Abercrombie, wife of the Dymock-based poet Lascelles Abercrombie, that in June 1916:

Once we were standing outside our dugout cleaning mess tins, when a cuckoo sounded its call from the shattered wood at the back. What could I think of but Framilode, Minsterworth, Cranham, and the old haunts of home.[68]

In his billets in Albert, Second Lieutenant Ford Madox Hueffer, 9/Welch Regiment, put pen to paper on 22 July 1916 to write 'The Iron Music':

The French guns roll continuously
And our guns, heavy, slow:
Along the Ancre, sinuously.
The transport wagons go,
And the dust is on the thistles
And the larks sing up on high . . .
But I see the Golden Valley
Down by Tintern on the Wye . . .[69]

*

It was only in 1903 that the Wright Brothers had made the first powered flight at windswept Kitty Hawk, and only in 1909 that Louis Blériot had crossed the Channel wastes. Blériot's flight, which had taken a mere forty minutes, meant that Britain was no longer an untouchable island off the coast of the Continent but an eminently reachable destination for an enemy. The heads of the War Office, army and navy, often portrayed as antediluvians uninterested in technology, were as alive as anyone to the need to command the skies. The great men's minds were also concentrated by aeronautical developments in southern Europe. Purportedly the most unmilitary of nations, Italy, in a revolt into modernism hymned by the poet Filippo Marinetti in his 1908 *Futurist Manifesto*, had employed the new-fangled aircraft for war work as early as 1911.[70] No nation could afford to be without an air force. While Britain may not have pioneered aircraft design, it had the technical know-how to improve flying machines and the factories to put them into production. Our image of Edwardian Britain hovers between the pastoral and the industrial, the green country and the Black Country, the birdsong and the pandemonium. Less easily brought to focus is Edwardian Britain as the world centre of technology, the Silicon Valley of its time.

Aeroplanes captured the public imagination like nothing on earth. Humans had dreamed of flying like birds if not forever for centuries at least (witness Leonardo da Vinci's 1485 design for an 'ornithopter'), while, as the Futurists had known from the outset, aircraft had the shocking glamour of the new. Hendon 'aerodrome', a field by any other description, regularly attracted crowds of twenty thousand to see flying machines and the magnificent men who flew them. Young daredevils tried to outdo each other in stunts, though the wittiest prank belonged to J.T.C. Moore-Brabazon, who took up a porker in his Short biplane in 1909, so that 'pigs might fly'. The party piece of aviator Gustav Hamel, a Briton despite his Teutonic-sounding surname, was to loop the loop. Winston Churchill, then First Lord of the Admiralty, thought the glamorous Hamel 'three parts a bird and the rest genius'.[71]

At the beginning of the Great War the aviation forces of Britain, the Royal Flying Corps and the Royal Naval Air Service, numbered 250 aircraft. (Germany had 246.) By 1919 the British had around 4000 combat aircraft. The growing flock of warbirds gave ornithologists in uniform the opportunity to answer a question which had long rumbled around the collective ornithologists' brain: At what height do birds fly? In the words of one wartime ornithologist:

The height at which birds migrate is one of the branches of orni-thology upon which we are still profoundly ignorant.[72]

As well as the specialist birding magazines, *British Birds* and *Ibis* and the like, the national press regularly pondered the matter. *The Times* felt sufficiently moved to publish a request from the explorer-soldier-ornithologist Colonel Richard Meinertzhagen DSO (to whom the noun 'legend' is so easily attached along with 'fraudster', since many of his coups as an intelligence officer and birdwatcher have since proven false), asking for RFC pilots to inform him of their aerial encounters with birds.

Any pilot, if not himself interested in things feathered, was likely to be pestered by those who were. Birdmen pursued by birdmen. Proba-bly the most persistent inquisitor was Captain Collingwood Ingram. During two years of service on the Western Front with the RFC and RAF he, in his own words, 'interrogated a very large number of pilots and observers – possibly as many as seven to eight hundred' on the great subject of the height at which birds fly.

Collingwood Ingram, one feels, was born to birdwatch. He was the son of Sir William Ingram, owner of the *Illustrated London News*, and his wife Mary. They were both animal mad. Sir William had a small private zoo at their seaside home at Westgate-on-Sea, and bought an island, Little Tobago, to make a reserve for the Greater Bird of Para-dise. Mary allowed wild birds the run of the house; sparrows slept in her nightgown and she provided them with locks of her hair and fur from her sable cape for their nests. Collingwood Ingram, who had no need for work, courtesy of the family fortune, devoted his early life to birds and blood sports. The fixed points of his year as boy and young man were birdwatching in spring, grouse shooting in August, deer stalking in November and fox-hunting in December. (In those days few saw any troubling moral divide between the sporting and birding life; a naturalist could be a sportsman and vice versa.)

By the outbreak of war in 1914 Collingwood Ingram, aged thirty-four, had published many ornithological papers. Initially commissioned in the Kent Cyclist Battalion, Ingram transferred in 1916 to the Royal Flying Corps as an adjuster of compasses, which were the service's principal navigational aid. The work was emotionally wearing, because the pilots whose compasses Ingram tuned invariably died. Life expectancy was measured in days. During 'Bloody April' 1917 the RFC lost a third of its force in France to German Albatros D.I and D.II fighters of Die Fliegertruppen des deutschen Kaiserreiches ('Imperial German Flying Corps'). New RFC pilots lasted, on average, seventeen days before becoming a casualty.[73] Revisiting one aerodrome in France, Ingram recorded in his diary:

> The place awakens sad memories for how many of the old crowd are still alive? Lubbock, Branby Williams, Truscott, Griffiths and a dozen others have been killed . . . in fact I should say that no more than four or five are still alive. And what good fellows they were too![74]

Eric Lubbock, killed in an aerial flight on 1 March 1917 was godfather to Ingram's daughter, Certhia. (If evidence of Ingram's love for birds is needed this is it: *Certhia* is the genus containing the treecreeper.)

Amid the deaths of friends and colleagues, there was some solace for Ingram in birding and the quest for knowledge of high flying birds. As he discovered, RFC types made good, if accidental birders. Ingram wrote:

While on a patrol over the enemy's lines, vigilance was always of such vital importance that a pilot was extremely unlikely to overlook the passing of a flight of birds, and, moreover, an encounter of this kind was always regarded as an interesting event and one sufficiently unusual to warrant comment on return to the squadron, and generally an entry in the observer's diary.

For these reasons I think the data obtained can be regarded as tolerably reliable with regard to heights, dates, etc.

Ingram questioned what was, in retrospect, a Who's Who of Royal Flying Corps heroes. At Filescamp he chatted to 'ace' James McCudden VC:

In reply to my enquiries as to whether any of the pilots in this squadron [26 Squadron] had ever met birds at considerable elevations, McCudden declared he had seen some once, apparently geese, at 9000 ft. This was near Albeaute.

At Camblain l'Abbé:

Major C.F. Portal OC of this Squadron, No. 160 happens to be the author of two interesting communications that appeared in The Field about a year and 18 months ago, describing birds migrating at considerable heights. I subjected him to a rather severe cross-examination, as he is one of the few pilots I have met who possesses more than a layman's knowledge of ornithology.

Portal appears to have encountered birds at over 5,000ft on at least five occasions during the 800 hours he has flown.[75]

Unlike McCudden, Portal was among the few long-serving pilots to survive the war. He was Chief of the Air Staff in the Second World War.

Being a good scientist, Ingram eventually published his research, his 'Notes on the Height at which Birds Migrate' appearing in *Ibis* No. 2, 1919. According to Ingram:

> The birds most frequently observed appear to have been Green Plover or Lapwings (Vanellus vanellus), and I have fourteen records of this species between 2000 ft. and 8500 ft., the majority being about 5000 ft. or 6000 ft. They were met with in flocks during the spring and autumn passage, the earliest dates being 1 February, 1918, and 15 July, 1917. On 26 February, 1917, Col. C. F. Portal, D.S.O., M.C., of No. 16 Squadron, encountered a flock of Green Plover at 6000 ft. over Candas.

While:

> The greatest height of which I have a record is 15,000 ft. Lieut. J.S. Rissen, of 57 Squadron, met with 'two large birds' at this elevation when flying a D.H. 4, in August 1917, over the country lying between St. Omer and the coast. Rissen informed me that he was certain of the height, and, from his description, I should say the birds were most probably Cranes.[76]

A flock of five hundred ducks, or geese, was observed on 26 November 1915, at about 11,500 feet. Birds resembling linnets were seen over Béthune on 22 August 1917, at a height of 10,000 feet; about fifty rooks, jackdaws or crows were noted over Lens on 1 March 1917, at 6000 feet, and 'six birds about the size of Rooks' over Arras, at 3000 feet, on 10 July 1918; starlings and field-fares (or redwings) were observed at 3000 feet in March 1917; some species of sandpiper was met with over Arras, towards the end of March 1917, at an elevation of 12,000 feet, and other limicoline birds at 9500 and 10,000 feet; whimbrel were observed at 4000 feet, and herons at between 2500 and 3000 feet.

Wherever men were sent for service they birdwatched. In an age when foreign travel was the prerogative of the very few, soldiering in the Great War offered many an ornithologist a new horizon. A Royal Navy surgeon aboard HMS *M28*, J.M. Harrison declared the Aegean 'a veritable Paradise to the ornithologist', and wrote up his notes for *British Birds* in the hope they 'may be of interest to others about to embark O.H.M.S. [On His Majesty's Service] for that quarter, and help to send them on their way one degree cheerier, and hold out some consolation for Foreign Service in war-time'. And this despite the fact that HMS *M28* had been sunk on 20 January 1918, during an action off the coast of Imbros in the Aegean.

Denis Buxton, one of the descendants of Thomas 'Liberator' Buxton, the emancipator of the slaves, ended up on the peninsula of Gallipoli in 1915 as a private with 889th Field Ambulance. He was very young; in July of the previous year he had still been a schoolboy, writing home to his mother from Rugby, 'I have not got mumps yet'. His elder brother also served with the RAMC. Like many a young gentleman going Gallipoli way, Buxton took a copy of Homer's *Iliad* with him, recounting as it did an earlier war thereabouts. 'I enjoy it much. It is by far the best book for this part of the world,' he wrote to his parents. His father provided him with a small black leather notebook, complete with marbled fly pages and inlaid with 'Private Buxton 2055 889th The Field Ambulance' in gold lettering, to use as a nature diary. The boy did not disappoint, writing his first entry even as he departed Britain; 'I saw some gannets off the Bristol channel'. Arriving off Gallipoli on 25 April 1915 – amid the bombardment of the shore defences by the fleet of ships – he took time to write: 'There are a good many birds flying hither and thither in parties of 12–20, large and dark, but I cannot say what species at all.[27] One Cormorant.'

His diary continued to weave war and the peaceful pursuit of ornithology:

Tuesday 18 May 1915. Woken by shrapnel quite near us. Went up road about two [?] and a quarter miles to the ruined white house, whence we usually fetched wounded. But there were none. A very enjoyable walk. Found a rose bush in flower in the garden here, a 6 inch shrapnel shell (British) with the nose off, otherwise unexploded. Magpies, Bee Eaters, Turtle Doves (they seem darker than in England). A pair of Wheatears had a nest in a ruined house on the road. The Cock (?) was grey above, white below: black wings and tail and a black patch round the eye. Saw V. Atalanta and cardui, C. pamphilus, Th. rubi. A (greater spotted?) Woodpecker where I saw the last: scarlet under t[ail]. covers: black back and tail: white on wings. We came home down the middle of the peninsula. I saw another woodpecker in some tall elms: head seemed white on top, with black patch behind eye and black eye stripe.[78]

By the time of the evacuation from the peninsula, Buxton had totted up quite a list of birds observed: Barbary partridge, wheatears, swallows, jackdaws, 'a large dumpy lark with short tail and black on throat', shearwaters, sandmartins, woodpecker, magpies ('whiter than ours I think'), jay ('heard, not seen'), hooded crows, lesser kestrels, great tits, several kinds of warblers ('which I am afraid cannot be identified'), goldfinch, sparrows, vultures, spotted flycatcher, turtle doves, vultures ('Or were they pelicans?'), linnets, house martins, cuckoo, rollers ('fairly common. Their note is a harsh caw'), red-backed shrike, swifts, herring gull, hobby, yellow wagtail, robin ('very shy compared with our'), huge flocks of cranes in August, blue tits, mistle thrushes, bee eaters, little owl, and once he thought he saw a hoopoe.

The Buxtons were naturalists down the generations, so Denis, who was nineteen when he landed on the peninsula, unsurprisingly discussed with his father, via letter, the birds he had seen. Sometimes, as with an unidentified black-and-white bird, Denis asked for advice. (His father, probably correctly, suggested a stork.) More than empirical information was being exchanged in the birding letters between Buxton *fils* and *père*. Birds were a pretext for communication between the boy and the father.

There were places to serve and to birdwatch more exotic still than the Mediterranean. And as dangerous. Captain Claud B. Ticehurst RAMC, the lead writer of the paper 'The Birds of Mesopotamia', published in the *Journal of the Bombay Natural History Society*, apologised that:

The working up of the notes of various observers has been no simple task; many notes were made in the trenches, or at least under active service conditions where baggage was reduced to a minimum, and were therefore not presented in a manner which lent themselves to easy abstraction.[79]

The paper was a great co-operative effort. Ticehurst, a Member of the British Ornithologists' Union (MBOU), was assisted by Captain P.A. Buxton, RAMC (MBOU), Major R.E. Cheesman, 5th Buffs (MBOU), and thirty-four other military and political officers, among them Major-General Sir F. Brooking, Major-General Sir Percy Cox and the Arabist and explorer Harry St John Philby, then serving as political officer with the Mesopotamia Expeditionary Force. Philby, in his wartime and post-war explorations of Arabia took a keen interest in wildlife and gave the scientific name to the Arabian woodpecker (*Desertipicus dorae*; Dora being his wife), while he is remembered in ornithology by the name of Philby's partridge (*Alectoris philbyi*). History has been less kind, since 'Philby' is indissolubly associated with his traitor son, the Soviet spy Kim.

The same journal that published 'The Birds of Mesopotamia' by Ticehurst et al., also saw Major A.G.L. Sladen's 'Notes on Birds Observed in Palestine'.[80]

Sladen won the Military Cross for bravery, suggesting that birdwatching supplemented rather than distracted from devotion to duty. (A proposition supported by Arnold Boyd's Military Cross (MC) at Gallipoli; Maitland Congreve and Sassoon were also awarded the purple and white ribbon for bravery.) Africa did not pass unobserved; *Ibis* printed Captain H. Lynes and Major Cuthbert Christy's paper 'A List of the Birds of the Anglo-Egyptian Sudan', not to mention a letter from the appositely named Lieutenant C.G. Finch-Davies on South African hawk eagles.

Birds were everywhere, even in the desert. Swallows, both European and Egyptian, invariably accompanied mounted troops to catch the insects disturbed by their horses' feet.[81] General Edmund 'Bull' Allenby made good misuse of one of his sergeants, stationing him next to a water hole in Palestine, purely so Allenby could receive news of the birds that attended it.

In the Great War, birds also appeared in the soldier's life as instrument and as target. Such are the inconsistencies of humans in uniform that the same group of endothermic vertebrates which were believed a blessing, an aid to nostalgia, a sign of God's grace, could also be shot for food (see pp. 281–8) and employed as tools. While some soldiers risked their lives to carry partridges to safety on the Somme, others hunted them down.

War can brutalise. As vandalistic recreation, Captain Charlie May went with his friend Don Murray out into the French country and:

> forgot building operations and rest billets and every other such objectionable thing in trying to shoot crows with our revolvers. Needless to say we did not succeed. But it took us completely out of ourselves and was therefore quite a success.[82]

In the Struma Valley in Salonika, Lieutenant H. Birkett Barker, 134th Siege Battery, RGA, encountered a similar cathartic shooting of birds, but in high tech form. An RFC officer, frustrated after many non-appearances of 'the Hun' in the sky:

> as outlet for his feelings ascends in pursuit of a large flight of geese overhead and tackles them with his machine gun, making several dives and skilful turns after them as they wheel about obviously a little bewildered by this novel form of disturbance. Doubtless

this sort of thing will soon oust fox-hunting from its honoured position in the hearts of British sportsmen.[83]

There was official employment for birds too. In what was simultaneously charming and cruel, ambulance trains were fitted with canary cages, so the birds could sing to wounded troops in transit to hospital. As everyone Edwardian knew, birdsong was a guaranteed cheerer-upper. Caged songbirds were still a common fixture in the back street homes of Britain.

Even the underground war fought by the sappers saw the utilisation of birds. Caged canaries were gauges for ascertaining the presence of toxic gas and poisonous fumes in tunnels dug by the Royal Engineers below enemy positions, just as they were in the coal pits of Britain. The little yellow canary was also used as a gas-detector in other enclosed spaces, such as dugouts, where fumes of chlorine, phosgene or sulphur mustard might linger after a German chemical weapons attack. Canaries are about fifteen times more sensitive to gas than humans. Although it is mawkish doggerel, there is genuine gratitude to the detector bird in the soldier's poem 'To a Canary in a Trench':

*Bon suis*, merry bird!
In war you've played your part –
Nor knew that death
Was in the breath
That stilled your little heart.
Your perch swings idly in your cage –
Unscathed we march along
So we may learn
To greet death 'with a song.'[84]

British soldiers in the trenches were said to have been warned of nighttime gas attacks by wild birds shrieking and calling. 'Owls are greatly excited. Behind the front fowls and ducks are said to become restless a quarter of an hour before the gas clouds approached,' recorded Major-General C.H. Foulkes CB CMG DSO in his *Gas!: The Story of the Special Brigade (RE)*. Whether by highly sensitive hearing or by a sophisticated ability to detect vibrations, birds were also believed to be able to give warning of enemy air raids by up to half an hour.[85] Pheasants, in particular, were said to possess the gift, abroad and at home. During the first Zeppelin raid in January 1915, pheasants at Thetford and Bury St Edmunds, thirty-five to forty miles from the area over which the Zeppelins sallied, crowed themselves hoarse.[86]

Carrier pigeons already had a long and distinguished career in warfare as conveyors of messages. (Solomon is, wisely, alleged to have used them; after Caesar's conquest of Gaul relays of carrier pigeons took the news to Rome.) With wireless in its infancy, with field telephones prone to break down, with human runners slow, the carrier pigeon and the dog (see p. 263) were the pre-eminent battle-field messengers in the Great War. The pigeons flew when the wires were down, where there were clouds of gas, storms of shot and shell.

An official carrier pigeon unit, the Carrier Pigeon Service (CPS), commanded by Captain A.H. Osman, sent its first batch of birds to the Western Front in March 1916; they were taken to the front line in wicker baskets attached to motorcycles. The messages themselves were placed in small cylindrical aluminium tubes clipped to the bird's leg, and the bird was then released to fly to its 'home' – a mobile loft, either a hut on wheels, or a converted lorry. As many as 1000 birds were deployed in a single engagement. In this happy instance where the overburdened army put square pegs into square holes, the men in charge of pigeons tended to be pigeon fanciers; the vast majority of British war pigeons themselves were supplied by the racing pigeon clubs of the Midlands and the North.

On the Western Front the speed of the carrier pigeon – about sixty miles an hour – meant it could gain height quickly and thus rise supreme above some of the dangers posed by shot and shell and gas. Of the 100,000 pigeons put into service by the British on the Western Front, 95 per cent got through with their messages. Some birds achieved marvels. In the action on Menin Road on 3 October 1917 pigeon No. 2709 was dispatched with a message from the front line to divisional HQ at 1.30 p.m. During its passage it was struck by a German bullet which broke one of its legs and drove the metal cylinder containing the message into the bird's body; the bullet passed out of the bird's back. Although wounded and sodden from rain, the bird struggled home to its loft, a distance of nine miles, and delivered its message at 10.53 a.m. the following day, 4 October, dying shortly after its arrival.[87] After receiving the attention of a taxidermist, the bird was added to the museum of the Royal United Services Institute. The glass case was labelled 'Died of wounds received in action'.

There were occasions when the birds saved the day, as in the famous case of the American 'Lost Battalion' during the 1918 Argonne Offensive, when Major Charles Whittlesey and more than 500 men were trapped in a small depression receiving both friendly and enemy fire. Two pigeons were shot down, then a third homing pigeon, Cher Ami, given to the US Signal Corps by British pigeon fanciers, was dispatched. The note in the canister on the bird's leg read: 'We are along the road parallel to 276.4. Our own artillery is dropping a barrage directly on us. For heaven's sake, stop it.'

When the Germans saw the pigeon lifting off they opened fire. The pigeon was shot down but managed to take flight again, arriving back at its loft at division HQ 25 miles to the rear in 24 minutes, so helping save the lives of 194 men. Cher Ami delivered its message despite having been blasted through the breast, blinded in one eye and with one leg hanging on by a tendon. The medics of the 77th Infantry Division managed to save its life, and Cher Ami was sent off to a hero's welcome in the USA. The French awarded the pigeon the Croix de Guerre with palm Oak Leaf Cluster.

Pigeons served at sea, as well as on land. One RAF seaplane forced down in heavy seas released a pigeon with an SOS message; in twenty-two minutes the bird reached its loft twenty-two miles distant. Help was sent at once and the airmen were found clinging to the wreckage of their machine while it was breaking up.[88] By the end of 1918 pigeons had brought in no fewer than 717 messages of distress from naval aircraft.

Late in the war, aerial photographs were taken by cameras attached to specially trained pigeons. More fantastic still, *The Times* reported that large numbers of pigeons in baskets were dropped behind enemy lines in Northern France and Belgium. Like the Midlands and North of England, these were centres of pigeon-fancying, so the War Office surmised that the populace would know what to do with the feathered gifts. In due course, quite a large percentage arrived at British lofts bearing secret messages about enemy dispositions and troop movements.

So concerned became the British government about the disruption to the war effort that might come from the loss of carrier pigeons to hungry or sporting shooters that it imposed dire penal measures for those found interfering with the birds. Defence of the Realm Regulation 21A ('Shooting Homing Pigeons') warned:

Killing, wounding or molesting homing pigeons is punishable under the Defence of the Realm Regulations by Six Months Imprisonment or £100 Fine.

The public are reminded that homing pigeons are doing valuable work for the government, and are requested to assist in the suppression of the shooting of these birds.

£5 Reward will be paid by the National Homing Union for information leading to the conviction of any person SHOOTING HOMING PIGEONS the property of its members.

Woe betide too the British soldier who, intentionally or accidentally, shot an Allied carrier pigeon. Or indeed, cooked one. In an incident that is pure *Blackadder Goes Forth*, a faithful Baldrick-like batman, unable to find dinner for his officer, somehow served up a 'brace of birds'. A subsequent enquiry from HQ about the loss of two valuable homing pigeons led to an investigation. The well-dined officer, when the origin of his slap-up feast was revealed to him by his servant, asked if there was any evidence, since, if caught, it would mean a court martial. The batman replied: 'Couldn't cook 'em without making a fire, Sir.' He'd used the wicker basket for carrying the pigeons as fuel, thus destroying all evidence of the crime.

On the front line, of course, shooting enemy pigeons was applauded and units were issued with shotguns for the purpose. (It helped to know one's birds: Captain Boyd recalled that wood pigeons were repeatedly reported to Brigade Intelligence as 'enemy carrier pigeons' by 'gullible and enthusiastic subalterns'.[89]) Another minor method of stopping German pigeons was flying birds of prey; the gauntlet-wearing falconers brought a distinctly medieval tone to the trenches.

With war's end, demobbed birds were sold and the proceeds divided among charitable institutions in accordance with the wishes of the breeders who gave the birds to the country for war. In the pageant of the Lord Mayor's Show in London, 1918, a travelling pigeon loft took part in the procession to remind the public of the achievements of the Carrier Pigeon Service, dubbed by wags the 'First Flying Corps'.

In one way or another, the birds did their bit.

# *Interstice 2*

## *Poems about Birds*
## *Written by Serving Soldiers*

### A lark above the trenches

Hushed is the shriek of hurtling shells: and hark!
Somewhere within that bit of soft blue sky –
Grand in his loneliness, his ecstasy,
His lyric wild and free – carols a lark:

I in the trench, he lost in heaven afar,
I dream of Love, its ecstasy he sings;
Doth lure my soul to love till like a star
It flashes into Life: O tireless wings

That beat love's message into melody –
A song that touches in this place remote
Gladness supreme in its undying note
And stirs to life the soul of memory –

'Tis strange that while you're beating into life
Men here below are plunged in sanguine strife!

*Sgt John William Streets, 12/York and*
*Lancaster Regiment, France, 1916*

## Hark, hark the lark

Hark, hark, the lark to heaven's gate uprisen,
Pours out his joy . . .
I think of you, shut in some distant prison,
O Boy, poor Boy;

Your heart grown sick with hope deferred and shadows
Of prison ways;
Not daring to snatch a thought of Severn meadows,
Or old blue-days.

*Pte Ivor Gurney,*
*5/Gloucestershire Regiment*

## To a skylark behind our trenches

Thou little voice! Thou happy sprite,
How didst thou gain the air and light –
That sing'st so merrily?
How could such little wings
Give thee thy freedom from these dense
And fetid tombs – these burrows whence
We peer like frightened things?
In the free sky
Thou sail'st while here we crawl and creep

And fight and sleep
And die.

How canst thou sing while Nature lies
Bleeding and torn beneath thine eyes,
And the foul breath
Of rank decay hangs like a shroud
Over the fields the shell hath ploughed?
How canst thou sing, so gay and glad,
Whilst all the heavens are filled with death
And all the world is mad?

Yet sing! For at thy song
The tall trees stand up straight and strong
And stretch their twisted arms.
And smoke ascends from pleasant farms
And the shy flowers their odours give.
Once more the riven pastures smile,
And for a while
We Live.

*Captain Edward de Stein, Machine Gun Corps*
*and King's Royal Rifle Corps*

### Returning we hear the larks

Sombre the night is:
And, though we have our lives, we know
What sinister threat lurks there.

Dragging these anguished limbs, we only know
This poison-blasted track opens on our camp –
On a little safe sleep.

But hark! Joy – joy – strange joy.
Lo! Heights of night ringing with unseen larks:
Music showering on our upturned listening faces.

Death could drop from the dark
As easily as song –
But song only dropped,
Like a blind man's dreams on the sand
By dangerous tides;
Like a girl's dark hair, for she dreams no ruin lies there,
Or her kisses where a serpent hides.

*Pte Isaac Rosenberg, 12/Suffolk Regiment,*
*later 11/King's Own Royal Lancaster Regiment*

## Birds in the trenches

Ye fearless birds that live and fly where men
Can venture not and live, that even build
Your nests where oft the searching shrapnel shrilled
And conflict rattled like a serpent, when
The hot guns thundered further, and from his den
The little machine-gun spat, and men fell piled
In long-swept lines, as when a scythe has thrilled,
And tall corn tumbled ne'er to rise again.
Ye slight ambassadors twixt foe and foe,
Small parleyers of peace where no peace is,
Sweet disregarders of man's miseries
And his most murderous methods, winging slow
About your perilous nests – we thank you, so
Unconscious of sweet domesticities.

*Lt Willougby Weaving, Royal Irish Rifles*

## The rainbow

I watch the white dawn gleam,
To the thunder of hidden guns.
I hear the hot shells scream
Through skies as sweet as a dream
Where the silver dawn-break runs.
And stabbing of light
Scorches the virginal white.
But I feel in my being the old, high, sanctified thrill,
And I thank the gods that the dawn is beautiful still.

From death that hurtles by
I crouch in the trench day-long,
But up to a cloudless sky
From the ground where our dead men lie
A brown lark soars in song.
Through the tortured air,
Rent by the shrapnel's flare,
Over the troubleless dead he carols his fill,
And I thank the gods that the birds are beautiful still.

Where the parapet is low
And level with the eye
Poppies and cornflowers glow
And the corn sways to and fro
In a pattern against the sky.
The gold stalks hide
Bodies of men who died
Charging at dawn through the dew to be killed or to kill.
I thank the gods that the flowers are beautiful still.

When night falls dark we creep
In silence to our dead.
We dig a few feet deep
And leave them there to sleep –
But blood at night is red,
Yea, even at night,
And a dead man's face is white.
And I dry my hands, that are also trained to kill,
And I look at the stars – for the stars are beautiful still.

*Sgt Leslie Coulson, 1/12 London Regiment*


## Shelley in the trenches

Impressions are like winds; you feel their cool
Swift kiss upon the brow, yet know not where
They sprang to birth: so like a pool
Rippled by winds from out their forest lair
My soul was stir'd to life; its twilight fled;
There passed across its solitude a dream
That wing'd with supreme ecstasy did seem;
That gave the kiss of life to long-lost dead.

A lark trill'd in the blue: and suddenly
Upon the wings of his immortal ode
My soul rushed singing to the ether sky
And found in visions, dreams, its real abode –
I fled with Shelley, with the lark afar,
Unto the realms where the eternal are.

*Sgt John William Streets, 12/York and Lancaster Regiment*

## Magpies in Picardy

The magpies in Picardy
Are more than I can tell.
They flicker down the dusty roads
And cast a magic spell
On the men who march through Picardy,
Through Picardy to hell.

(The blackbird flies with panic,
The swallow goes like light,
The finches move like ladies,
The owl floats by at night;
But the great and flashing magpie
He flies as artists might.)

A magpie in Picardy
Told me secret things –
Of the music in white feathers,
And the sunlight that sings
And dances in deep shadows –
He told me with his wings.

(The hawk is cruel and rigid,
He watches from a height;
The rook is slow and sombre,
The robin loves to fight;
But the great and flashing magpie
He flies as lovers might.)

He told me that in Picardy,
An age ago or more,
While all his fathers still were eggs,
These dusty highways bore

Brown singing soldiers marching out
Through Picardy to war.

*Lt T.P. Cameron Wilson, Sherwood Foresters*

## To a sparrow

Because you have no fear to mingle
Wings with those of greater part,
So like me, with song I single
Your sweet impudence of heart.

And when prouder feathers go where
Summer holds her leafy show,
You still come to us from nowhere
Like grey leaves across the snow.

In back ways where odd and end go
To your meals you drop down sure,
Knowing every broken window
Of the hospitable poor.

There is no bird half so harmless,
None so sweetly rude as you,
None so common and so charmless,
None of virtues nude as you.

But for all your faults I love you,
For you linger with us still,
Though the wintry winds reprove you
And the snow is on the hill.

*Lance Corporal Francis Ledwidge, 5/Royal Inniskilling Fusiliers*

# CHAPTER III

# All the Lovely Horses

*Equus as Beast of Burden, War Horse, Comrade*

'Concerning the war I say nothing – the only thing that wrings
my heart & soul is the thought of the horses – Oh! My beloved
animals – the men – and women can go to hell – but my horses; –
I walk round & round this room cursing God for allowing
dumb brutes to be tortured – let Him kill his human beings
but – how CAN HE? Oh, my horses.'

*Sir Edward Elgar, Hampstead Volunteer Reserve, 1916*

The horses were there at the beginning, the horses were there at the
end.

When war commenced on 4 August 1914, the British army had
25,000 horses and mules. Within twelve days, military 'impressment'
units from the Army Service Corps Remount Scheme had rounded
up 160,000 horses from farms and stables for the colours, much as
Nelson's press gangs had once seized men. Requisitioned horses were
bought at a 'fair price' – £60 for an officer's charger (around £5800

at today's prices) for instance. The war horse was generally 'a Light Draught' used for transportation; many an 'Officer's Charger' was really a pony.

The countryside was emptied of draught horses, hunters and riding ponies, a heartbreaking happenstance for farming families who saw their finest and most loved horses go off to war. 'I had seen the last of my faithful friend Cockbird,' wrote Siegfried Sassoon on having to hand over his hunter on enlistment. He found it 'a step nearer to the bleak realization of what I was in for'.[1] And what he was in for, was war. One young schoolgirl, Elizabeth Owen, seven when war burst out of the clear summer sky of 1914, remembered how 'the khaki men' put the village horses on a long rope, 'all the horses we used to know and love and feed. Then they started trotting them out of the village and as they went out of sight we were all terribly sad.'[2]

The horse was the soul of the village, because it delivered mail, collected milk, pulled hay wagons, brought ale for the pub, carried the dead to church, transported the doctor on his rounds, provided a petting attraction for young mothers with tantrummy toddlers.

Lieutenant Will Harvey, incarcerated in German PoW camps from 1916 onwards, frequently let his mind drift back to his native Gloucestershire. There were memories which hurt, such as the day in 1914 that the horses were taken from his father's farm in Minsterworth:

My father bred great horses,
Chestnut, grey and brown.
They grazed about the meadows,
And trampled into town.

They left the homely meadows
And trampled far away,
The great shining horses,
Chestnut, and brown, and grey

Gone are the horses
That my father bred.
And who knows whither? . . .
Gone are the horses,
And my father's dead.[3]

To be one of the 'khaki men' on requisitioning duty was joyless too. Sergeant George Thompson, a Territorial with the 1/7th Durham Light Infantry wrote in his memoir based on his wartime diary:

I was stationed in the drill hall for a while whilst the government was buying up horses. I can still remember the old drivers saying, 'Take care of him, he is quiet and a good worker and will go anywhere'.[4]

Three children from Wigan managed to save their pony, Betty, by the expedient of writing to Lord Kitchener, Secretary of State for War, asking that Betty be spared because she was pregnant:

Dear Lord Kitchener
    We are writing for our pony, which we are very afraid may be taken for the army. Please spare her. Daddy says she is going to be a mother early next year, and is 17 years old. It would break our hearts to let her go. We have given 2 others and 3 of our family are fighting for you in the Navy. Mother and all will do anything for you but do please let us keep old Betty, and send official word quickly before anyone comes.

The children signed the letter as 'Your troubled little Britishers'.[5]
    Lord Kitchener was suitably moved, and instructed that 'no horses under 15 hands shall be requisitioned belonging to the British family: P., L. and Freda Hewlett'. When the mare of novelist, playwright and animal campaigner John Galsworthy was rejected as unfit he wept with unashamed relief.[6]

Some horses went to war because their owners did. The horse riding class of Britain was ardent for duty. The Sinnington hunt in Yorkshire saw fifty farmers, their sons and other huntsmen join the colours, each providing his own horse. Hunting men were prominent in the Cavalry, the Yeomanry (the mounted Territorials), the Veterinary Corps and the Army Remount Service, which existed to horse newly created units, to make good wastage and to distribute animals from the veterinary hospitals.

In Britain, to make up for the exodus of the horse, tractors were imported to take their stead. To avoid putting British patriotic noses out of joint, US tractors were often rebranded for the British market; the Parrett tractor became the Clydesdale – and there was irony, since the Clydesdale along with the Shire and the Suffolk Punch, horses which had strode so magnificently over the farming landscape of Britain for hundreds of years, would be driven to the edge of extinction by tractors. In 1917 the government bought 400 British Saunderson tractors and a further $3.2 million was invested in US models such as the Fordson. By 1918, 6000 tractors were in operation in Britain.

Though few guessed it, the August 1914 round-up of 160,000 would come nowhere near sating the demand for horses. Three years on, 869,931 equines would be in British harness. Over the course of those four long years of total war more than two million horses, mules and donkeys would serve His Majesty.

Since there were not enough horses in Britain to go round, the Remount Service cast the rope further afield for new 'recruits' and replacements for those that had been lost, or were no longer fit for duty – what was officially called 'wastage'. North America, the cowboy country, was the obvious place to look, and Purchasing Commissions were sent to Canada and the USA. With their vast plains and intensive farming, the North Americans had produced a light draught horse that was a breed apart from its European ancestors and, importantly, there were plenty of them. At first sight, the 'Yankees' were in a rough and ready shape – they were shoeless, long-haired, tousle-maned. And they were tough; generations of their kind had become completely at home with roaming out in the open and in all kinds of weather.

The purchasers of the Remount Commission consisted 'largely of country gentlemen, large landowners, and competent masters of hounds'[7]; equine experience was necessary so purchasers were not conned into buying 'duds'. The Commission travelled throughout the American West and Midwest buying between ten thousand and twenty-five thousand horses a month, the first batches arriving in Britain in October 1915. By the end of 1916 there were purchasing depots at Lachine and Calumet (Michigan), Chicago and Grand Trunk (Illinois), Rosemount and St Paul (Minnesota), Le Pester Miller Stock Farm (Ohio), Green Island, Jersey City and Goshen (New York State), St Louis (Missouri), Cedar Rapids and Sioux City (Iowa), Lathrop (California), Portland (Oregon), Newport News (Virginia), Ogden (Utah), Halifax (Nova Scotia) and Toronto. After being bought, the American horse or mule was branded with the British army's broad arrow symbol, and then taken to the nearest railhead for immediate transportation. On 11 November 1918, when the war ceased, the Canadian Commission had shipped from North America 428,608 horses and 275,097 mules.[8]

Purchasing Commissions were also sent out to Spain, but only 3000 equines were obtained. Seven hundred mules were bought in Portugal. The Indian government was asked to undertake horse purchasing on Britain's as well as its own behalf in Australia, and 1600 mules were sent from there to East Africa. South America was drawn on for 6819 horses and cobs. Captain Robert Bontine Cunninghame Graham, whose ornate name, army service and Harrow education disguised a die-hard socialist (he was the co-founder with Keir Hardie of the Scottish Labour Party), was the natural choice to lead the Uruguay Remount Commission, as he had spent a stint as a rancher down Argentina way. 'Don Roberto', along with five officers and three vets, established his collection point at Fray Bentos; in 1915 he sent about 2300 horses by train to Montevideo or

Buenos Aires, from where they were shipped to Liverpool or Avonmouth. The horses were ill bred, with little care given to selection – the country was given to instability – though, the official report observed, the horses 'possessed of good powers of staying, and meeting the requirements of the people of the country as general utility animals'.

Whether British or foreign, there was hardship for horses from the outset. The North American horses turned out en masse into coverless winter paddocks often died of exposure; in one seven month period no less than 80,000 of the North American remounts were too ill to be shipped to Britain; and 15 per cent died or were destroyed. Crammed twenty per wagon in trains for the USA's Eastern ports, a journey of 1300 miles or more, many died of 'shipping fever' (that is, pneumonia).[9] Pink-eye influenza killed thousands, as did paraplegia, while thousands more suffered from acute tendonitis. After 1915, careful shipping reduced the mortality rate. Even so, one vet recorded that of the 1800 horses which landed at Rouen (via Britain) between 1 February and 7 March 1915, 1040 went straight to veterinary hospitals with colds or pneumonia.

Captain Eliot Crawshay-Williams, formerly Liberal MP for Leicester, who had resigned following a divorce case brought by a friend and fellow MP, sailed with the Royal Horse Artillery to Egypt. In his diary for 17 February 1916 he wrote:

This horse business is becoming very serious. It is septic pneumonia, and there is no disease more deadly or more contagious. Already we have thrown three overboard, and there are quite a number of cases sickening. Poor Billy, my first charger, is in the clutches of the thing; his temperature was 106 this morning. It is very distressing even to witness: the horse becomes dull and sluggish, droops his head till it rests on the bar of his stall; then develops fever and refuses food; lastly breathes with more and more difficulty, till at last he collapses and dies. It is swift, too, this stroke; for from first to last it may be only a day and a half from a well horse to a carcass floating astern. Alas! I am afraid we have the worst to come. They will not assure me, too, that septic pneumonia in horses is not contagious to human beings. But, thank goodness! there are no signs that it is as yet.

The horses die with persistent regularity. We have lost eight, but I think the worst is over. Billy, my charger, is much better, I'm glad to say, but the Adjutant has lost one of his chargers.[10]

Even without disease, there were problems with transportation. The value of horses was known to all. German agents in America attempted to poison the horses on the docks.

Loading horses, whether in America, Britain or elsewhere was always a tribulation. Second Lieutenant Arnold Gyde, 2/South Staffordshire Regiment, recalled the embarkation of his unit's equines:

There was plenty of excitement on deck while the horses of the regimental transport were being shipped into the hold. To induce 'Light Draught', 'Heavy Draught' horses and 'Officers' Chargers' – in all some sixty animals – to trust themselves to be lowered into a dark and evil-smelling cavern, was no easy matter. Some shied from the gangway, neighing; others walked peaceably onto it, and with a 'thus far and no farther' expression in every line of their bodies, took up a firm stand, and had to be pushed into the hold with the combined weight of many men. Several of the transport section narrowly escaped death and mutilation . . .[11]

'Impossible' horses which refused to board were slung in hammocks and winched in. Once aboard grooms, drivers and other horse men took turns down in the hold caring for their charges, one hour on and four hours off. Driver Rowland Luther, Royal Field Artillery, remembered that 'one hour down that hold, with the heat and the smell and sweat was gruelling', and he was only traversing the Channel to Le Havre. Major Patrick Butler, 2/Royal Irish Regiment, crossed the English Channel on the *Armenian* in 1914 for service as a 'galloper' – an aide-de-camp – in the Ypres Salient. (The Butlers were Irish gentry, and consequently horsey to the core; his mother, Lady Butler, had painted portraits of his chargers 'Sportsman', 'Dawn' and 'Brightness' before his posting.) As Butler wrote in *A Galloper at Ypres*, his memoir of service, on going across the Channel:

I went below to look for my belongings. The dim and stuffy vistas swarmed with men, and down both sides the horses were jammed in long, uneasy rows. This was the lowest deck of all.

Just above it there were more men, and a sort of loose boxes in which were tied the huge, heavy draught horses allotted to our transport. One of these poor animals was behaving like a mad thing, and threatened to smash his way out of his pen, secured by the head as he was, by sheer weight and violence. Every now and then he would rear aloft, and get a leg over the side of the box in a sort of paroxysm of fear and rage.

Poor brute! There was a crowd of men round him, and at first I could not see what was taking place; but soon I heard the drip, drip of blood, and a trickle began to make its way through the planks on to the deck below, close to the companion at the foot of which I was standing. The sight was not pleasant. After an interminable delay the cooks, groom and servant all reported to me, and I located my three chargers. As I escaped up to the light and air I had to pass again near the monster draught-horse. I could see his huge bulk filling the stall, but he seemed strangely quiet now. I noticed that the men still crowded round, but they were more intent and reassured, and with a sort of curiosity in their faces. There were horror and pity in their looks, not cruelty. The drip, drip was now a steady outpouring of blood. It flooded the deck. They were bleeding him to death, a man told me. He had already staggered once, and would fall now at any moment.

As I gained the deck I fancied I heard the thud.

The 'merciful bullet' was impracticable here, on account of the congested state of the decks.

Poor beast, his troubles were over early.[12]

On unloading, horses were often frantic for water. Arriving at the entrepôt of Le Havre, Driver Luther, an ex-South Wales miner, first tried out his French on the watching civilians on the quayside: 'Bonjour, Monsieur, Bonjour Madame'. Then came the unloading of the RFA brigade's horses. The horses scented water in the troughs on the quayside and despite shouted instructions, men holding onto their reins, they lurched forward; 'nothing would stop this mad rush'. Luther was dragged along. Finally, the horses were yoked to their wagons and limbers, and paraded on the dockside, but then 'all hell let loose again'. The horses slipped on the cobble stones and tram tracks, 'sparks flying from their hooves, and they crashed to the ground'.[13] Luther, who had volunteered in September 1914 aged nineteen, 'eventually came to like horses and I became a good rider'.

As with novice horseman Driver Luther and the unloading of the Royal Field Artillery's horses at Le Havre, the lack of horse sense among handlers (experienced hands would have taken buckets of water to the horses while they were still on board) compounded equine welfare problems. Even the Remount Service, the specialist equine branch of the army, endured poor horsemanship. Originally, in the words of Lionel Edwards, sporting artist turned Remount officer:

The Army Remount Service consisted of . . . old crusted cavalry officers and NCOs, with Masters of Foxhounds, racehorse trainers, horse dealers etc as their opposite numbers – jockeys, huntsmen and grooms filling 'other ranks'.[14]

Owing to the need to release all fit men from Remount squadrons for active service, together with the expansion of the service (on 1 August 1914 it comprised 351 officers, non-commissioned officers

(NCOs) and other ranks; on 30 November 1918 it consisted of 8766 officers and men), more and more Remount personnel had no previous knowledge of horses. Captain Sidney Galtrey thought men in the remount depots mostly 'piano tuners, paper-hangers or fried-fish merchants before King and Country called – or fetched – them'. The churn of men during the last two years of the war was approximately 40 per cent per annum.

Cecil Aldin, like Lionel Edwards a sporting artist turned Remount officer, came up with the novel idea of employing women at his remount depots in Berkshire. Aldin wrote about his stable girls:

> At first they had only quiet R2s (small riding horses) under their charge, but as time went on and their horses were often better 'done'; and more quickly made fit for issue, more and more of my depots were placed entirely under woman control.[15]

Some other remount establishments followed feminine suit.[16] But turnover among Remount staff meant that the equine supply system was always susceptible to inefficiency, if not danger to horse and man alike.

All this and horses had not yet entered the war zone.

In the Colony across the Channel lorries and cars were rarities, while the French-run railway system was so decrepitly slow that passengers would routinely step down from carriages, walk alongside, then climb back aboard.

In the Colony the horse therefore reigned supreme as transport.

All horses and most of their feed and tack entered France via Le Havre, where the depots included Hangar au Coton, a nine acre shed, the contents of which included tens of thousands of horseshoes – thirty-four sorts in seventeen different sizes. Horses were dispersed from the remount depot or, more accurately, the remount depots, since by the end of the war there were five such establishments on the north coast of France.

The sheer scale of the logistical operations required to equip and fodder the warhorses of Britain during the Great War beggars belief: the British army provided 2,978,301 tons of oats and 2,460,301 tons of pressed hay for its equines between 1914 and 1918. The average ration for the light draught horse during a 'normal' spell in France was 12lbs of oats, 10lbs of hay as well as bran for a mash at least once a week.

Without horses, the British army would have failed. Horses in the British Expeditionary Force (BEF) fell into three general types. Firstly, there were the 'Light Draught' animals (from a height of 15 hands 2ins to 16 hands and a weight of up to 1200lb) for field artillery limbers, general transportation of supplies and munitions, ambulances, either singularly or in teams. To draw a large field artillery gun, such as the standard British 18-pounder, weighing 2900lb, across broken country required six draught horses harnessed in pairs. The light draughts were the mainstay of the army's logistical support. They were cheap, easy to maintain and they could traverse broken ground impassable to four wheels powered by internal combustion. Four motorised wheels were good but four horse legs were better. Major-General Jack Seely, Canadian Cavalry Brigade, proffered the following affidavit for the horse in the winters of the war, which were some of the worst of the twentieth century:

> . . . we learnt that the horse is the only certain means of transport. The horse is vital to man in modern war. All the mechanical contrivances fail when the mud gets deep; the horse suffers, but some survive to pull up the batteries, to bring up food and ammunition, to drag back the melancholy lines of ambulances.[17]

The light draughts served at the front, in the rear and in the support lines. They stumbled through the tangle-wire Hell of no man's land, closely following every British and Commonwealth push. Taken from the fields, cities, factories and coal pits of Britain and from the rolling plains of America and Canada, the light draught horses worked in

a world as unfamiliar to them as it was for their human counter-
parts. In the mud, rain and terror of the trenches they supplied their
human comrades with food, water and ammunition, even though
they themselves were hungry, sodden and spent. Their numbers
with the BEF in France alone rose to over 475,000 by the autumn
of 1918.

Secondly, there were 'Heavy Draught' horses, which were of a
bigger and sturdier type, such as the Shire and the Clydesdale.
They were teamed together to pull the larger artillery pieces, which
could weigh up to 5000lbs. Despite their formidable size, Shires and
Clydesdales were of a delicate constitution and tended to contract
pneumonia, while their hairy feet made them prone to necrotic and
eczematous foot conditions. As time went by, the heavy draughts
were replaced – the largest guns of war had become ever bigger and
needed tractors and even locomotives to pull them.

Thirdly, there were the riding horses, the cavalry trooper's mount
and the officer's charger. For anyone from a non-country background, army lessons in riding were one of the tribulations of service.
The Royal Welch Fusiliers made all subalterns unable to ride attend
riding school every afternoon when in billets. 'At Laventie,' recalled
Lieutenant Robert Graves, 'I used to look forward to our spells in
the trenches. Billet life spelt battalion mess, also riding school, which
turned out to be rather worse than the Surrey-man had described.'[18]
To the dismay of the equally green Second Lieutenant Edmund Blunden his colonel decided on an impromptu riding school behind the
line. The rain dripped dismally off the poplars, and:

A body of spectators was soon on the scene. Sergeant Ashford
would say to me afterwards, with the smile of Ah Sin, 'Yes the
first time they went round you were there. The second time you
weren't. It was very puzzling'.[19]

Blunden, at least, fared better than Captain A.E. Bundy in Salonika:

Attended riding course for officers. Second day horse bitten by horse fly and careered for about 3 miles in frantic gallop and finally fell and threw me, but I was uninjured.[20]

Officers were expected to be able to ride. An officer was by definition a gentleman, and gentlemen rode. Neither was the army oblivious to the natural authority a man on horseback has by virtue of height and the resonances of history. Knights rode, pikemen did not. More prosaically, the horse was a mode of transport, the car of its day, and officers required transport for the endless round of duties that were their lot, from briefings with the colonel to collecting the wages of the men.

In the rush to build a mass citizen army, the requirement that an officer rode was sometimes dispensed with, though the smarter the regiment – and Graves' Royal Welch Fusiliers were pukka – the more likely was an officer to find himself on the deck of a 'charger'. NCOs and men working in transport or with artillery also had riding lessons, invariably of the intensive type, condensed into a week, as Sergeant George Thompson recalled:

All the drivers were taken to 50th Division RFA and went through a week's training to learn both to ride and to drive. They gave us some stick, I can tell you. First came riding bareback and then with saddles on; we were sore for days.[21]

There was a fate worse than riding lessons. Edwin Campion Vaughan's quiet satisfaction at having escaped battalion riding lessons in Britain turned to horror in France when he was informed that his mess was to ride over en bloc to watch a football match. Second Lieutenant Vaughan had never been on a horse before. For half an hour of embarrassment and agony he 'bumped up and down at an alarming rate'. He would have sympathised with Captain Stormont Gibbs, 4/Suffolks who, on his elevation to adjutant inherited 'Kitty', the horse of wilful character which came with the office; the luckless

Gibbs was required to ride Kitty at battalion parade. Having no interest in ceremony, Kitty decided to bolt, leaving Gibbs hanging on to her mane, his tin hat off the back of his head, and both feet out of the stirrups. After finally reining her in, 'I rode sheepishly back on parade and everyone spent a difficult few minutes trying not to catch anyone else's eye with the "Old Man" glaring around waiting for anyone to flicker an eyelid.'[22]

This mortifying parade ground mishap did not prevent Stormont Gibbs from coming to love his regiment 'more than any other corporate institution of which I have ever been a member'.[23]

There were so many ways for a horse to die on the Western Front and the other battle zones of the war.

On average the British army lost 15 per cent of its horses every year, 484,000 in total. Horses were shot by bullets, shattered by shells, overcome by poison gas, consumed by disease. Tens of thousands wasted away due to debilitation, despite the gargantuan supply of fodder.

The slaughter of the horses began with the chaotic retreat of the British Expeditionary Force from Mons in August 1914. According to Gunner J.W. Palmer, RFA:

> We had strong feelings towards our horses. We went into the fields and beat the corn and oats out of the ears and brought them back, but that didn't save them . . . the cry was frequently heard down the line, 'Saddler – a plate and a punch!' This meant that the saddler had to come along and punch some more holes in the horse's leather girth to keep the saddle on.[24]

On the retreat from Mons one of the 4th Dragoon's horses was so hungry that, overexcited, it 'shot forward and in one movement bit my stomach' remembered Trooper Ben Clouting. In excruciating pain, Clouting lifted his shirt: 'My stomach oozed blood from a wound.'

Horses unable to complete the retreat were shot by the wayside to put them out of their misery.

Equus had been introduced into warfare in the first century BC, when the Hyksos invented a chariot pulled by horses. Thereafter, whether it had been Alexander on Bucephalus, Genghis Khan's Mongol hordes, Cromwell at Marston Moor or Maréchal Murat at Eylau, the horse warriors had reigned supreme. But the development of artillery turned the horse from unalloyed asset to soft target for shrapnel. Since it was almost impossible to shelter horses during shelling, the casualty rate for horses on the Western Front could be catastrophic, particularly when gun teams were caught manoeuvring over open ground. A familiar battlefield tableau of the Great War was of horses with broken backs hauling their useless hindquarters along, while others galloped pointlessly, foam-flecked and wild-eyed, amid the strewn corpses of their species. Second Lieutenant Arnold Gyde came upon a post-battle scene where horses had been 'slaughtered by the score':

> They looked like toy horses, nursery things made of wood. Their faces were so unreal, their expressions so glassy. They lay in such odd postures, with their hoofs sticking so stiffly in the air. It seemed as if they were toys, and were lying just as children had upset them. Even their dimensions seemed absurd. Their bodies had swollen to tremendous sizes.[25]

In order to lessen the loss of horses, the army put horse transports to work at night, or behind screens, so the enemy could not see them. Even so, the horse continued to make an easy flesh-and-blood victim. Second Lieutenant George Atkinson, RE, recorded in his diary, 29 July 1918:

> A very favourite trick [of the Germans] is to shell some point on the road and thus compel traffic to wait. In five minutes they know that there will be a solid column of wagons on the far side of the

block, and then they lengthen range – preferably with shrapnel.

Then it is like all hell let loose. Half a dozen shells among those crowded limbers can do the most terrific damage, and men and horses go down together in a welter of blood and flying red-hot steel. Mules and horses go mad, and scream and kick, the harness breaks, they climb into the limbers, ammunition explodes, and in a few seconds there is nothing but a mass of wreckage in the ditch and the cries of wounded men and dying horses.[26]

A heart-wrenching account of a draught animal's plight post-shelling was given by Lieutenant R.G. Dixon, 14th Battery, Royal Garrison Artillery:

Heaving about in the filthy mud of the road was an unfortunate mule with both of his forelegs shot away. The poor brute, suffering God only knows what untold agonies and terrors, was trying desperately to get to its feet which weren't there. Writhing and heaving, tossing its head about in its wild attempts, not knowing that it no longer had any front legs.

I had my revolver with me, but couldn't get near the animal, which lashed out at us with its hind legs and tossed its head unceasingly. Jerry's shells were arriving pretty fast – we made some desperate attempts to get to the mule so that I could put a bullet behind its ear into the brain, but to no avail.

By lingering there, trying to put the creature out of its pain I was risking not only my life but also my companions'. The shelling got more intense – perhaps one would hit the poor thing and put it out of its misery.[27]

The armoury of German anti-horse weapons was not limited to shells and bullets. German aircraft dropped metal darts on to horses to kill them, or laid down caltrops (spikes) to lame them. Perversely, more horses were likely lamed by the Allied nails which littered the roads. 'These nails were mostly attributed to the firewood used in regimental cookers,' wrote Captain Francis Hitchcock of the Leinsters in his diary. 'On numerous trees along the Ypres-Poperinge road were nailed small boxes for the collection of picked-up nails.'[28]

An unfortunate 210 or so British horses on the Western Front died from the effects of poison gas. Sergeant E. Miles was waiting for a train at Barlin when a group of gassed horses was brought in. They made a pitiful, upsetting sight: 'Their eyes were being slowly burned away while their nostrils were covered with a sickly yellow fluid.' Initially, protection against gas for equines was crude, being gauze forced up the nostrils and held in place with safety pins through the nose. A development came with a gas helmet for horses. Driver James Reynolds of the Royal Engineers, though, was scathing about its efficacy:

On the night of the 30th I was on rations to our sappers at Fregicourt and had just got into Combles when I smelt gas and heard the 'Whew-w-w-flop' of some more shells coming over. I halted and adjusted my own helmet and proceeded to try to put on my horses'. One of my pair was a restive bay mare, and she evidently took a violent dislike to the thing I was trying to put over her nostrils. She swung her head about and managed to hit me in the face with it and tore my mask. I realised at once that I was for it as I smelt the gas coming in so I hopped up on their backs and flapped for our headquarters. The horses were none the worse for not having those wretched helmets on, but I got a decent little dose which left me with catarrh and face itching for several years afterwards. Those horse respirators were eventually scrapped thank goodness.[29]

Often the horses ate the gas masks intended to save them.

By far the biggest killer of equus, though, was 'debilitation' – cold, malnutrition, disease, harshness, especially in winter. Out of the 256,000 horses lost by the British on the Western Front 148,000 perished from debilitation. Stabling was invariably a rudimentary, or non-existent, affair at the front. In many cases a picket line – a strung rope – sufficed, which in winter was potentially lethal. Picketed horses suffered exposure. Gunner Sylvester remembered:

> The horses were up to their bellies in mud. We'd put them on a picket line between the wagon wheels at night and they'd be sunk in over their fetlocks the next day. We had to shoot quite a number.[30]

Sergeant George Thompson thought winter

> awful both for horses and men. I have many a time wondered how those poor horses stood it so long. I have seen them standing up to their knees in mud and for days.[31]

The forlorn horses on the picket lines were starved as well as soaked. Driver Rowland Luther wrote:

> In this cold and hunger, the horse now developed a new habit – they all started chewing – ropes, leather, or even our tunics ... So we reverted to chains, a big steel chain for pinioning down, another from the horses' nose-band, just like a heavy dog chain ... The horses then turned to chewing at one another, and they soon became hairless, and a pitiful sight.[32]

Luther then found a useful and plentiful supply of rubble to make a hardstanding for his horses: from the shelled and ruined village next door.

Alas, the army exacerbated the problem of picket line exposure by its stance on the clipping of equus's shaggy winter coat, which protects it from the elements, but which can also disguise various skin disorders and parasitical activity.

Army vets and those caring for the animals were told to 'clip out' the coats, a measure that would have been fine in peacetime when horses and mules could be stabled or placed in paddocks with rugs over them. The decision to clip meant that many animals were lost to exposure because of an order from on high which took no account of circumstances on the winter ground. Some horsey officers, among them Captain R.G.A. Hamilton, convinced in the wisdom that comes from experience, refused to clip; his black artillery horses instead enjoyed their natural cold season 'woolly-bear coats'. Next summer they looked 'magnificent' and 'more important, are all in hard condition'.[33] As the war years passed, men in charge of horses and mules increasingly left most of the winter coat unshorn. By 1918, the clipping of only the legs and bellies had become standard army practice.

It was always easier for an officer to ignore an order than it was for a ranker or an NCO. When Sergeant Thompson, stationed on the Somme, judged officialdom in the wrong he resorted to sly avoidance rather than up-front disobedience:

Animals like men are prone to disease. I remember when we were stationed in Fricourt there was a skin disease came out among our horses and an officer in the AVC came up one morning and ordered about fifteen horses to go down the line and one of them was one I had brought out from England and he had to go as well. So instead of sending him away, we sent another in his place and we built a stable for him away from all the other horses and looked after him ourselves and in a month we had him working again. The horses they took away from us we never saw again.[34]

The worst year for the 'wastage' of horses was 1917. In that year all of the above factors would concinnate, making this year, regardless of care received, the most lethal for the horse and the mule. Losses among horses were 14 per cent in 1916; the figure jumped to 28.5 per cent in 1917. The suffering was greatest during the fighting at Arras, when unseasonably cold weather ('weeks on end of rain, then weeks of rigorous cold and icy winds, and then rain again', remembered

Captain Sidney Galtrey) continued into April. There was also an oats shortage. In that month 20,319 animals were evacuated to veterinary hospitals behind the line in the Colony due to 'debility'.[35]

With so many horses and mules out of action, there came a transport crisis. By the end of the great Arras offensives in April 1917, the gunners were short of 3500 draught horses. The horses that remained were required to work day and night, night and day. The Royal Regiment of Artillery's 167th Brigade noted in its diary that: 'many horses died of sheer fatigue'.

And the mud-and-bloodbath of Passchendaele was still to come.

Mud, the sucking mud, was a ludicrously common agent of death. The sombre end of the Somme battle, Major-General Jack Seely found, was 'cruel to horses no less than to men':

> The roads were so completely broken up by alternate frost, snow and rain, that the only way to get ammunition to the forward batteries was to carry it up in panniers slung on horses. Often these poor beasts, who were led forward in long strings with three shells on each side of them, would sink deep into the mud. Sometimes, in spite of all their struggles, they could not extricate themselves, and died where they fell.

Wading through the Somme mud brought on exhaustion, for both beast and man.

The suffering of the horses caused anguish in men entirely inured to human tribulations. On the Somme Private Norman Gladden saw German bombs wound men and horses. One of the horses 'dashed across the field with its entrails hanging down. Its awful bellow of pain, in protest against man's inhumanity, was more shocking than all the rest of that afternoon's nightmare.' Marching up to the same battle with the Royal Welch Fusiliers Lieutenant Robert Graves was 'shocked by the dead horses and mules; human corpses were all very well, but it seemed wrong for animals to be dragged into the war like this'. Callow Second Lieutenant Stormont Gibbs, fresh from Radley and still young enough for whisky to make 'me feel sick', entered the trenches at Fricourt on 6 August 1916: 'That night we couldn't sleep because a wounded mule was screaming in the valley.'[36]

Private Thomas Hope, 5th King's Liverpool Regiment, considered the plight of the equines an indictment of their masters:

Standing near the debris of guns and limbers is a solitary horse gently cropping leaves from a low-lying hedge. At our friendly words it trots toward us as if pleased to have our company, but not sure of its welcome – poor faithful beast, how ill you are repaid for your staunchness.

I have long since become accustomed to wounded humanity. Their plight evokes pity and the desire to help, but a wounded animal leaves me with a feeling of loathing, loathing towards myself and the civilised humanity which I represent. Too often have I seen reproach in the eyes of a dying horse, and outraged frailty in the flutterings of a wounded carrier pigeon.[37]

Lieutenant Alan Hanbury-Sparrow, a Regular officer in the Royal Berkshires, thought the decree by which draught horses unable to make the retreat from Mons in 1914 were to be put down 'perhaps the most senselessly savage order ever issued by the staff'. The depth of his admiration for the horses was evidenced by a choice noun: Hanbury-Sparrow declared their shooting 'martyrdom'.

The sheer toil expected of the beasts of burden in winter aroused almost as much sympathy as did their injuring. Cyril Lomax was chaplain to the 8/Durham Light Infantry:

Everybody too hates mud, but we bathe in it, wade in it, sleep in it and clods of it adorn the most secret recesses of one's clothes, books and papers. To see the poor brutes of horses straining through axle deep mud with the food for the hungry guns goes to my heart even more than seeing the unfortunate men coming out of the front line. The poor beasts have such a pathetic droop, look so patient, and miserable, and respond so bravely to some tremendous effort to suck a limber out of the mud.[38]

Another priest in uniform, Methodist Thomas Tiplady, found his heart most affected by the plight of the mules in the Battle of Arras, which came hard on the terrible winter of 1916–17. With an understanding that a priest's duties extended to creatures as well as men, Captain Tiplady organised mercy killings for the most severely wounded mules:

One night, alone, I got three dying mules shot. The road was crowded with traffic, yet it was difficult to find either an officer with a revolver or a transport-driver with a rifle. I had to approach scores before I could find a man who had the means to put a mule out of its misery; and we were within two miles of our Front. So rigid is our line of defence that those behind it do not trouble to take arms. Even when I found a rifleman he hesitated to shoot a mule. There is a rule that no horse or mule must be shot without proper authority, and when you consider the enormous cost of one the necessity for the rule is obvious. I had therefore to assure a rifleman that I would take full responsibility for his action. He then loaded up, put the nozzle against the mule's forehead and pulled the trigger. A tremor passed through the poor thing's body and its troubles were over. It had come all the way from South America to wear itself out carrying food to fighting men, and it died by the road when its last ounce of strength was spent.

In a veritable paean of praise for the mule, Tiplady continued:

The mule knows neither love nor offspring. Apart from a few gambols in the field, or while tethered to the horse-lines, it knows nothing but work. It is the supreme type of the drudge. It is one of the greatest factors in the war, and yet it receives scarcely any recognition and more of whipping than of praise. Only too often I have seen their poor shell-mangled bodies lying by the roadside waiting till the battle allowed time for their burial. Yet what could be more innocent of any responsibility for the war?[39]

Tiplady was one of ten children born to Methodist parents, and had started his working life aged ten in a cotton mill, before taking private academic lessons, then attending a technical school and finally Richmond Theological College in London. He served five years in London's East End, at the Old Ford Mission in Poplar and Bow. He went to war as chaplain with the Queen's Westminster Rifles in the Somme and Arras campaigns.

Methodism was a working-class religion; Tiplady saw in the 'drudge' mule his own proletarian congregation of 'ordinary' Tommies.

While Tiplady's faith in God never wavered, others found that the suffering of the horses was a factor in the questioning of religious certainty. 'The amazed heart cries angrily out on God,' wrote the ever eloquent Private Ivor Gurney, in the ultimate line of the poem 'Pain'; part of Private Gurney's soldierly 'pain unending' was witnessing the distress of

horses shot, too tired merely to stir,
Dying in shell-holes both, slain by the mud.

Gurney ambivalently cries *on* God, not to God, neither quite accusing nor beseeching. Was God responsible for the pain of men and equines, or was He their salvation? That dilemma exercised many a soldier from August 1914 to November 1918.

If soldiers were upset by the hurt which befell horses, they were also uplifted by their nobility and courage. Much to Major-General Jack Seely's amusement, Warrior was his 'passport' to popularity. While men were chary of seeing 'the general', they were enthusiastic to pet Warrior, the cynosure of all eyes wherever he went:

As I rode along, whether it was in billets, in reserve, approaching the line, or in the midst of battle, men would say, not 'Here comes the general', but 'Here's Warrior'.[40]

The horse's 'vivid personality' helped Seely 'to gain the confidence of thousands of brave men'.

Short-legged, independent-spirited, always kindly, Warrior was a symbol of indomitability for soldiers to follow.

Warrior was a survivor. In September 1914, his groom Jack Thompson had to gallop him ten miles across country to escape encirclement by the advancing enemy. In 1915, a shell cut the horse beside Warrior clean in half, and a few days later another destroyed Warrior's stable, seconds after he had left it. Two years later, only frantic digging extricated him from mud in Passchendaele, and a bare three days before his galloping gallantry at the battle of Moreuil Wood in 1918[41] he survived a direct artillery hit on the ruined villa in which he was housed.

Soldiers like animals; and they like lucky animals most of all. The talismanic Warrior was the 'Horse the Germans Could Not Kill', according to his *Evening Standard* obituary.

Seely always maintained that Warrior made him the warrior he was: 'No, my stout-hearted horse not only kept his own fear under control, but by his example helped beyond measure.' Indeed, Seely attributed his crucial victory at Moreuil Wood to Warrior's 'supreme courage', since the horse seemed to lead him on:

> He was determined to go forward and with a great leap started off. All sensation of fear had vanished from him as he galloped on at racing speed. There was a hail of bullets from the enemy as we crossed the intervening space and mounted the hill, but Warrior cared for nothing.[42]

Like Seely, Captain The Honourable Julian Grenfell was a horseman to the tip of his polished boots, being commissioned into the Royal

Dragoons in 1910. He once described being separated from his horse as 'horrible ... It feels like leaving half oneself behind, and one feels the dual responsibility all the time'. Grenfell too understood the morale-raising capability of equines. In Grenfell's most famous poem, 'Into Battle', published in *The Times* on the day he died in May 1915, Grenfell pictures horses as the models for soldiers to imitate:

In dreary doubtful waiting hours,
Before the brazen frenzy starts,
The horses show him nobler powers
O patient eyes, courageous hearts!

There is a knowing, recondite allusion to Ancient Greece and its equine warrior culture in the line 'dreary doubtful waiting hours', which intentionally echoes Homer's 'And the horses, champing white barley and oats, stood by their chariots and awaited Dawn' from *The Iliad*.[43] Just as the horse itself was inspiration, so was the military, equine culture of the Hellenes. At a leading Edwardian public school such as Eton College, Grenfell's alma mater, a boy might spend half of his week studying the Classics, which forged an enduring mental template of heroism as an ideal. Less cryptic, but no less earnest in invoking the spirit of Ancient Greece for the Great War soldier was Second Lieutenant Ford Madox Hueffer (University College School) in his poem, 'Antwerp':

For the white-limbed heroes of Hellas ride by upon their horses
Forever through our brains ...

*

But it was the simple, pathetic illusion of the day that great things could only be done by new inventions. You extinguished the Horse, invented something very simple and became God! That is the real pathetic fallacy. You fill a flower-pot with gunpowder and chuck it in the other fellow's face, and heigh presto! the war is won. All the soldiers fall down dead! And You – you who forced the idea on the reluctant military, are the Man that Won the war. You deserve all the women in the world. And . . . you get them! Once the cavalry are out of the way!

*Captain Christopher Tietjens, Glamorganshire Regiment,*
*on cavalry, in* Parade's End *by Lieutenant Ford*
*Madox Hueffer, 9/Welsh Regiment*

What role could cavalry have in the science fiction age of H.G. Wells? A cartoon in the magazine *Punch* in 1892 had a meaningful joke; a young cavalry officer, Mr Bridoon, is asked by a general to define the role of horse warriors in war: 'I suppose to give tone to what would otherwise be a mere vulgar brawl!' answers Bridoon. Even before the turn of the twentieth century cavalry were becoming an expensive ornament. Seeing the writing on the wall, the Imperial German Army in 1909 revised its regulations to accommodate the actualities of modern warfare, abandoning the set-piece, three-wave cavalry charge and proposing the cavalry instead as scouts and raiders. So disastrous, indeed, were early cavalry actions on the Western Front that Germany raised no additional mounted divisions.

The Germans had a point. Trooper Benjamin Clouting rode at Audignies on 24 August 1914, where his regiment, 4th (Royal Irish) Dragoon Guards, together with 9th Lancers and 18th Hussars were ordered to attack across open fields to stop the enemy advance:

It was a proper melee, with shell, machine-gun and rifle fire forming a terrific barrage of noise. Each troop was closely packed together and dense volumes of dust were kicked up, choking us and making it impossible to see beyond the man in front. We were galloping into carnage, for nobody knew what we were supposed to be doing, and there was utter confusion from the start. All around me, horses and men were brought hurtling to the ground amidst fountains of earth, or plummeting forwards as a machine gunner caught them with a burst of fire.

Ahead, the leading troops were brought up by agricultural barbed wire strung across the line of advance, so that horses were beginning to be pulled up when I heard for the one and only time in the war a bugle sounding 'troops right wheel'. I pulled my horse round, then with a crash down she went.

Dazed, Clouting struggled to his feet. In the mayhem and dust a riderless horse came careering in his direction. Collecting himself, Clouting raised his hand in the air and shouted 'halt!'

It was a 9th Lancers' horse, a shoeing smith's mount and wonderfully trained, for despite the pandemonium, it stopped on a sixpence.[44]

And so Clouting rode to safety on a trusty steed. But behind him, 128 men and as many horses lay dead. A Victoria Cross, the first of the war to be officially listed in the *London Gazette*, went to Captain Francis Grenfell of the 9th Lancers for his part in the charge against unbroken German infantry (plus his role in the saving of 119th Battery's guns, although badly wounded, on the same day). Yet even the citation for Grenfell's VC was forced to acknowledge that the Lancers' charge at Audregnies 'was as futile and as gallant as any other like attempt in history on unbroken infantry and guns in position', though there was comfort in the proof 'that the spirit which inspired the Light Brigade at Balaclava ... was still alive in the cavalry of to-day'.

By 1917 the Germans had nearly abandoned cavalry – for any role – on the Western Front, and the British Prime Minister Lloyd George pressed the British army leaders to do the same. They demurred.

Many senior officers on the Western Front suffered a love of cavalry; indeed, both the commanders of the British Expeditionary Force, Sir John French and Field Marshal Douglas Haig, were cavalry men.[45] Look at a full-length photograph of French and you will see the evidential bow-legs of the mounted soldier; an X-ray of his brain would have found E-Q-U-U-S imprinted on the hippocampus. He notoriously, prehistorically, praised the lance as a battlefield weapon, the cavalry charge as the true way of war even as the cloudlets of conflagration gathered. (He was not alone in such sentiments; *The Cavalry Journal*, the organ of lobbyists in the horsed regiments, stated in 1909: 'The charge will always remain the thing in which it will be the cavalryman's pride to die sword in hand.') Regardless of their antiqueness, British cavalrymen were only too anxious to deploy their squadrons on the battlefields of the Western Front. So many cavalrymen wanted to get into action that by the close of 1914 nearly a third of the combat divisions comprising the British Expeditionary Force were cavalry, a much higher proportion than France or Germany.[46]

The addiction to cavalry is routinely presented as evidence of the cobwebbed minds of British generals. But the love of horse in the British army, especially in its officer corps, is explicable, even laudable. Neither should it be supposed that cavalry were wholly obsolete in the Great War. They had not yet passed into the dump of history alongside the pike and the bow.

The horse was central to the self-image of the upper class, and the officer corps of the British cavalry was nothing if not upper class. The British aristocracy was a warrior class, albeit in attenuated, civilianised garb. (The Great War offered them a last hurrah, and they seized it with avidity; no socio-economic group suffered a greater death rate.[47]) Blood sports, especially fox hunting, irrespective of the entertainment they offered were means by which military skills and physical courage were taught, maintained, brushed-up.

Class and horse went together like . . . horse and carriage. When young Dennis Wheatley tried to enlist in the Westminster Dragoons – a socially exclusive regiment – he failed the horse riding test, so tried instead to get into the Royal Fusiliers. A family acquaintance, a Territorial colonel, on hearing this cried, 'But my dear boy you cannot possibly go into the Fusiliers – they walk!' So Wheatley took horse riding lessons with Mr King who kept a dozen horses next to a stable attached to a pub near Streatham Hill Station and joined the altogether acceptable Royal Field Artillery.[48]

The novelist Ford Madox Hueffer (aka Ford Madox Ford) gives literary testimony of the importance to the aristocracy of the horse in his novels *The Good Soldier* (1915) and the *Parade's End* tetralogy (1924–28). Ford was more than a novelist; he was a soldier in the Great War and the high priest of the last days of High Toryism. Captain Ashburnham, the eponymous 'good soldier', might be a covert libertine and Christopher Tietjens, the protagonist of *Parade's End*, an emotional cripple but both men unstintingly do their duty by their estate staff and the troops under their command. Their ability with horses is a metaphor for their *noblesse oblige*. And both men are *excellent* with horses. The general tells Tietjens in *Parade's End*: 'You're the most wonderful hand with a horse.' Significantly and symbolically, in his reduced post-war circumstance as a smallholder in Kent Tietjens is horseless. Old style feudalism was belly up, finally finished off by four years of bloodletting war. The parade was truly at an end.

But before the fall the cavalry had days of glory in the Great War. The first action by the BEF on the Western Front? A cavalry engagement. On 22 August 1914 C Squadron 4/Dragoon Guards encountered a group of German Uhlans east of Mons. Corporal Edward Thomas fired the first shot by the BEF and Captain Hornby led the first charge, scattering the Germans, sabring several and taking others prisoner.

And the last action of the BEF on the Western Front? A cavalry attack. On 11 November 1918, 7/Dragoon horsemen galloped for ten miles to capture Lessines in Belgium and the crossings over the River Dendre, suffering no casualties themselves, but taking four German officers and 167 men prisoners. As was required by higher command this action was completed as the clocks were striking 11 o'clock, when hostilities had to stop in accordance with the terms of the Armistice.

The British cavalry on the Western Front were not entirely fancy ornaments. Unlike the French and German cavalry who, with their breastplates and polished steel helmets seemed dressed for a rerun of the Franco-Prussian War of 1870, the British cavalry wore khaki uniform, the plain service cap, and if sentimental about the lance and the sabre also carried the rifle. The 1907 edition of *Cavalry Training* emphasised that 'thorough efficiency in the use of the rifle and in dismounted tactics is an absolute necessity'.[49]

Along with brutal-but-cowardly generals, the uselessness of the British cavalry has become an immovable myth of the First World War. Suffice to say, the Germans at Gueudecourt on the Somme on 26 September 1916 found the British cavalry had a point. On that day Captain Fitzgerald of D Squadron 19th Lancers was ordered 'to seize the high ground some 600 yards east of the village and establish a strong point there'. Fitzgerald fast-trotted round behind Flers, crossed two British trenches, borrowed a troop of South Irish Horse and was in Gueudecourt before the Germans could react.

*Speed.* Horses had speed. Fitzgerald held the village until relieved by infantry. He lost just three men killed.

Then, on 30 March 1918, the British cavalry saved the day. As part of their great Spring Offensive or 'Kaiserschlacht', the Germans had captured Moreuil Ridge, which overlooked Amiens and, beyond the city, the railway line to Paris. Retaking the ridge was vital to the Allied cause, and the task was allotted to Major-General Jack Seely, fifty-one years of age, Canadian Cavalry Brigade. In a previous incarnation, Seely had been the British Secretary of State for War, a tenure which had ended in ignominy when he mishandled the refusal of Kildare-based army officers to march against the Ulster Unionists, the so called 'Curragh Mutiny'. Seely was surer with a horse's reins in his hands than he was with the affairs of state. He had the requisite characteristic of the successful cavalry commander. Dash.

He and the Canadian Cavalry sped to Moreuil Wood, quicker than tanks or men could have managed. At 9.30 a.m., astride Warrior, Seely led his twelve-strong signal troop in a gallop to the German position at the edge of Moreuil Wood, planting a red marker pennant for the Canadian Cavalry to aim for. Seely, his aide-de-camp,

Prince Antoine d'Orléans-Bragance, and six others made it through the bullets; five did not. Watching from the sidelines was Marshal Foch of France and Brigadier-General Maxime Weygand of his staff. 'Heroes, led by a lunatic' was Weygand's curt summary of Seely and his men.[50]

More supposed 'lunacy' came hot on the hooves of Seely's attack. The pennant planted, Canadian squadron after squadron thundered up the hill. They were supported by the Royal Flying Corps, which dropped 190 bombs and fired 17,000 rounds into the melee. The Canadians drove the Germans through the trees, and the heaviest fighting came at the northeastern tip of the mile-long deciduous wood, where Lieutenant Gordon Flowerdew's seventy-five-strong squadron of Lord Strathcona's Horse thundered up out of a hollow to find themselves confronted by 300 men of the Imperial German Army's 101st Grenadiers.

Born in 1885 in Billingford, Norfolk, Gordon Muriel Flowerdew had been educated at Framlingham College before emigrating to Canada, where he lived in the utopian colony founded for upper class English émigrés at Walhachin in British Columbia.[51] In 1914 Flowerdew had found the call of his old country too strong to resist and signed for Strathcona's Horse, rising through the ranks to a commission and finally into legend. On appraising the Germans before him at Moreuil Wood, Flowerdew ordered a troop under the command of Lieutenant Harvey VC to dismount and make a flank attack to the northeast of the enemy. While Harvey's troop were performing the diversionary movement, Flowerdew shouted 'It's a charge boys, it's a charge!' Flowerdew then led the three remaining troops of C Squadron in a full-scale, old-fashioned, sword-unsheathed cavalry attack.

It was terrible, but it was magnificent too, in the way that the Charge of the Light Brigade was magnificent and terrible. Despite fierce enemy fire Flowerdew's horsemen hacked their way through the defenders until they were clear of the enemy lines, then wheeled around for another charge. By this time Flowerdew had lost approximately seventy per cent of his force, and was himself severely wounded in both thighs and the chest. But the Germans were in disarray. Flowerdew ordered his surviving cavalrymen to dismount and engage the enemy in hand-to-hand fighting. The Germans broke. The Allies recaptured Moreuil Wood. No less a person than Marshal Foch declared that Flowerdew's charge at Moreuil Wood 'possibly deflected the whole course of history'.

Gordon Flowerdew did not live to receive the plaudits and garlands due him, succumbing to wounds on the following day at No. 41 Casualty Clearing Station. His Victoria Cross was awarded posthumously.

Only Western Front-centricity could even begin to entertain the postulate that cavalry were so many men sitting on white elephants. Out in the wide-open desert spaces of Palestine and Syria, it was horse-warfare good and proper. General Edmund 'Bull' Allenby's Desert Mounted Corps in Palestine comprised 20,000 men and horses, the largest cavalry force to operate under one commander during war. They overcame the Turks, but sometimes the desert overcame them. The Turks blew up wells, so the war in the golden wasteland was a battle for water. Devotion of man to beast could perform wonders; once the horses of the Worcestershire Yeomanry survived ninety hours without water without serious casualties. When the regiment's fatigued horses refused to eat their 'masters' kneaded dry grain into little balls moistened with the last drops of water and fed them by hand.[52] The dearth of water brought a desperate edge to the fighting. On 31 October 1917, after a twenty-four hour trek over unknown bone-dry country, it was essential Allenby's cavalry captured the Beersheba well to water the frantic horses. At 1630, bayonets fixed, two regiments of Australian Light Horse advanced at the gallop, half hidden by swirling dust, towards the Turkish trenches. The Turks' fire was largely ineffective: so amazed were they by the spectacle of the charge they omitted to lower their sights. After riding over two Turkish trenches the Australians dismounted and attacked with the bayonet. In ten minutes it was all over. Five hundred enemy were killed, and 2000 prisoners taken.

Allenby's cavalry then assaulted Jerusalem, in bitter icy winds and torrential rain, scrabbling up the rocky terraces of the Judean Hills. That was the quality of horses; they could do sandy desert, they could do stony slopes. The city fell in December 1917. After more than 400 years of Turkish rule, Jerusalem was once again under Christian control.

There were glories still to come for the Desert Mounted Corps and their immediate commander, Lieutenant-General Harry Chauvel, a former grazier. The Corps, in 1918, took Megiddo, then followed up this victory with one of the fastest pursuits in military history – 167 kilometres in just three days. That truly was the quality of horses: they had speed. The horsemen of the Desert Mounted Corps destroyed the Turks in the field. Damascus fell, then Aleppo, and on 30 October 1918 the Turkish nation indicated it had had enough, and surrendered.

Cavalry were not an irrelevance in the Great War.

On reaching the shores of the Mediterranean, according to Lieutenant-Colonel C. Olden, 10th Australian Light Horse, the horses:

> had not decently rested themselves for weeks, and what is much worse to a horse, they had not had a decent roll. Now they rolled and rolled and kept on rolling until it seemed they would never cease.[53]

Men thought they deserved it.

*

> But one of the finest things about the English soldier of the front line was his invariable kindness and, indeed, his gentleness at all times to the horses. I hardly ever saw a man strike a horse in anger during all the four years of war, and again and again I have seen a man risk his life, and indeed, lose it, for the sake of his horse.
>
> *Major-General Jack Seely, Canadian Cavalry Brigade*

Humans have a need to give and receive love. In war soldiers often find affection in animals, and the bonds between soldiers who work with animals and their charges can be especially deep. Lieutenant Charles Bennett was serving with a mule team when a shell landed, injuring a driver. The mule-driver was oblivious to his own pain because

> the death of his mule absorbed him: He kept on saying 'And he was my donkey, my donkey' poor fellow. They do love their animals.

Looking across at the Ypres battlefield, Private Christopher Massie, 76th Brigade, RAMC, noted the men and mules, broken in battle, dragging themselves towards the rear. Despite their own travails, men tried to succour the mules; 'Often the mules are bandaged with the men's first field dressings.'[54]

Gunner H. Doggett saw a shell kill the horse pulling an ammunition wagon. The driver fell to his knees stunned at the loss of his charge:

> A brigadier then came along, a brass hat, and tapped this boy on the shoulder and said, 'Never mind, sonny!' The driver looked up at him for a second and all of a sudden he said, 'Bloody Germans!' Then he pointed his finger and he stood like stone as though he was transfixed.
>
> The Brass hat said to his captain, 'All right, take the boy down the line and see he has two or three days rest'. Then he turned to our captain and said, 'If everyone was like that who loved animals we would be alright'.[55]

When Captain Francis Clere Hitchcock MC, 2/Leinster Regiment, returned to the front line after a year and a half on Home Service he immediately went to the battalion's transport, where:

I went through the horse lines, and discovered a few old friends of '15 days still there, notably Matilda, who was badly blemished about the hocks, having got into barbed wire some months previously during an air raid.[56]

So attached was Lieutenant-Colonel John McCrae, surgeon in the 1st Brigade, Canadian Artillery, to his horse Bonfire, a chestnut gelding, that he had him transported from Canada to France. Bonfire, McCrae told his sister, is 'the dearest thing in horses that one could find'. Once, when officialdom tried to take Bonfire away, McCrae went over all heads in France and appealed to Sir Sam Hughes, Canada's Minister of Militia and Defence. Successfully.

As one would expect from the author of the poem 'In Flanders Fields', McCrae was a deeply sensitive man. In his own words he was 'unable to bear a horse scream', and contrary to orders administered to equines as well as men. (Dogs also received the benefit of his surgery and hospitality.) Near unrelieved work treating wounded soldiers and animals caused McCrae's health to deteriorate. His only real relaxation was to ride Bonfire. On 28 January 1918 McCrae died of pneumonia and meningitis, just after receiving word he had been appointed consulting surgeon to the British army, the first Canadian to be so honoured. He was buried with full military honours in Wimereux Cemetery, near Boulogne, France. In recognition of the bond between McCrae and his horse, Bonfire led the cortège, his bridle laced in white ribbon.

Sometimes men risked their lives for the love of their horse. In May 1918, while withdrawing under heavy fire, one officer recorded:

I was riding when one of the troop's horses was badly hit by MG [machine gun] fire. Horse and rider crashed down in front of me. The horse lay on its side and the trooper, unhurt, had rolled clear. Kicking one foot off the stirrups I ordered the trooper to mount behind me. Instead, he crawled towards his horse which raised its head and was looking at him. He reached the horse, gently lifted its head on to his knee, and stayed put. I again ordered him to mount, and drew my pistol, saying I would shoot the animal. He said nothing, just looked up at me, then down to the horse, and continued to stroke its head. From the look in the horse's eyes, I think it knew it was the end, and I also think it understood its master was trying to give it what comfort he could. I didn't shoot. Bullets were still smacking around me, and the squadron was almost out of sight. I said something to the effect, 'Well, it's your funeral' and trotted to regain my place. The trooper caught up with the squadron later; he had stayed with his horse till it died. By all laws of averages, he should have stopped one too.[57]

How is such devotion of man for a horse to be explained? Mutual aid, or symbiosis, is part of it. Man feeds, waters and grooms the horse; in return, the horse performs the duties of portage and haulage. Shared experience had something to do with it. On campaign, a soldier rides and tends the same horse, and together they endure the same hardships.[58]

Second Lieutenant Vernon Laurie, RFA, who accompanied his father and four of the family's horses (Cupid, Polly, Flashlight and Nimrod) to war noted how acquaintance with horses changed men's attitude to them, writing home:

> One splendid man, an ex-sailor, awful rough chap, always collects all the bread over from meals and gives it to his horses. Nearly all the men are careful and fond of their horses now.[59]

In taking his horse to war, Vernon Laurie was, of course, taking part of his home with him.

Charlie May of the Manchester Regiment likewise took his horse, Lizzie, to war. May desperately missed his wife and baby, and Lizzie became the object of diverted endearment:

Horses are always so companionable and knowing, but I think she is more than usually so. She seems to know exactly what I want and attunes herself to my moods in quite a wonderful way. She has little or no appearance, but she is a good, trusty, useful and sound old soul and I am very fond of her.[60]

Lizzie enabled May to maintain normalcy, his pre-war identity.

May was not anthropomorphising Lizzie in granting her personality. No less than Charles Darwin, beyond reproach as a scientist, had suggested in *The Expression of the Emotions in Man and Animals* that the higher animals enjoyed states of mind, the foundation of personality. Horses, moreover, are social animals, and forge friendship bonds with other equines. Or equine substitutes. Part of the success of the Man–Horse relationship is that the horse pals up with the man, as well as vice versa. (Like dogs, horses have emotional awareness and a 'functionally relevant understanding' of human facial expressions.[61]) One officer in the Royal Horse Artillery (RHA) wrote in the *Yorkshire Post* of mules following their drivers round like big dogs, 'nuzzling them all the time in friendship'. Four days were enough for machine gun officer Captain A.J.J.P. Agius to convince his freshly issued steed to bond with him: 'Ben (my horse) is getting to know me quite well. He'll follow me about anywhere,' he wrote home.[62]

Equines, as much as humans, are desirous of company.

Also, there was fun to be had with horses. A day at the Divisional Races was a standard recreational activity for soldiers at the front. On attending Mule Races arranged by the Army Service Corps on 16 May 1917, Lieutenant Henry Williamson watched a programme which consisted of:

1. MULE RACE (SADDLED)
2. MULE RACE (BARE BACK)
3. HORSE RACE (GROOMS)
4. JUMPING COMPETITION (CHARGERS)

5. INTER SUB SECTION WRESTLING ON MULES
6. V.C. RACE (DRIVERS & GROOMS)
7. JUMPING COMPETITION (MULES)
8. HARNESS STRIPPING COMPETITION
9. CIVILIAN RACE (MULES)
10. DRIVING COMPETITION (PAIRS)
11. DRIVING COMPETITION (TEAMS)
12. MULE RACE (PAIRS)

This was all good, light-hearted stuff.[63] At the other end of the horse-sports spectrum was the hazardous two-mile steeplechase in which Captain W.H. Bloor rode in 1917, organised by a colonel possessed either by madness or more probably the desire to cock a magnificent snook at war. Bellona could go hang herself, the British required country pursuits, and ex-German front line trenches made decent ditch jumps. From Bloor's diary:

**October 18th**
Fine with sunshine . . . walked round the course again with Captains Friend and Whistle (of the 5th Division). The more I see of it the less I like it. There are some yawning old trenches about 10 feet wide, which we all think will stop the whole field, but the Colonel is obdurate and won't have them made any more suitable.

**October 20th**
The day of the race. Fine and dry . . . There were 24 started in the first race, but by the time I got to the first ditch it was full, the second likewise – the water at the sixth took toll of three more, leaving about seven of us still up. About half way round were the worst obstacles – four ragged trenches a few yards apart; the last of them about ten feet wide. Here Lt. Oxley and the Colonel came 'smellers, but the Colonel was up again as I came up to it. I managed to negotiate this as the Major was full of heart and we were lucky. After this, the Colonel, Colonel Jelf of the 148th and

myself were all of a bunch, none of us racing for half a mile, but at a ditch – bank ditch – (the last before the finish) I took a toss but got up again and was placed third. It should really have been doubled up, but the others had the best spot so I chanced him 'flying it' and paid the penalty. It was a mistake on my part as the horse was done, and I was trying to 'come' too early. Very glad of the experience and learned a bit by it. Three others finished, all having fallen – Colonel Jelf in fact was the only one who did not.[64]

Given such mayhem, officers who were understaffed, under pressure or under-resourced might forbid juniors from joining equestrian sports, as did Captain The Hon. R.G.A. Hamilton, RFA, at Borre in July 1917. 'Yesterday evening,' he wrote in his diary, 'we had brigade sports for the men and races for the officers. I did not encourage any of my officers to ride, as I cannot afford to have them breaking limbs or their horses' legs, just at present.'[65] Hamilton himself had been injured at the front in October 1914 when his horse fell on him. Four years further on he was less lucky. On 31 March he was killed when a shell burst under his horse in similar circumstances. By then Ralph Hamilton was commanding 108th Brigade RFA.

But, generally, wherever the British went they organised equine games. Major Jack Fairfax-Blakeborough, 9th Hussars, worked at the convalescent depot at Roclincourt:

It was very hot in May 1917, there was little firing, and consequently little ammunition to take up to the line . . . I really did see horses improve here, and thoroughly enjoy life. We had a little steeple-chase course put up, and jumping competitions . . . the summer was really lovely.[66]

Even in the Palestinian desert in 1917 Allenby's cavalry stopped for a race meeting; events included the Promised Land Stakes, the Anzac Steeplechase and a Jerusalem Scurry, the latter for mules only.

Perhaps the greatest pleasure a horse could afford at the front was the opportunity to ride away into the unspoilt countryside. It was a privilege almost exclusively the preserve of officers. Lieutenant Bernard Adams, 1/Royal Welch Fusiliers recalled:

> I rode, as I generally did, in a south-easterly direction, climbing at a walk one of the many roads that led out of Morlancourt towards the Bois des Tallies. When I reached the high ground I made Jim gallop along the grass-border right up to the edge of the woods. There is nothing like the exhilaration of flying along, you cannot imagine how, with the great brown animal lengthening out under you for all he is worth! I pulled him up and turned his head to the right, leaving the road and skirting the edge of the wood. At last I was alone.[67]

In the clearings of the wood the ground was a carpet of blue hyacinths, whose sweet scent came along on the breeze; 'their fragrance lifted my spirit'. Across the valley, patches of white cherry blossom, 'like white foam breaking over a reef, in the midst of a great green sea'. He tied up Jim and threw himself 'down on the grass to dream'.[68]

Second Lieutenant George Atkinson, RE, even managed to go riding on a filly in pursuit of a 'filly', writing in his diary on 6 May 1918:

> Borrowed a horse from the Cavalry Depot and went for a ride with one of the nurses. Had a ripping lunch at a little cafe in Petit Couronne – omelettes and fresh butter (to say nothing of the nurse) are much nicer than bully and dry biscuit.[69]

A donkey was the steed of Eliot Crawshay-Williams, RHA, on a jolly with a girl in Egypt. He struggled to achieve the sort of posture likely to impress:

> I was on a beast little larger than Teresa's, looking far more foolish. The most graceful girl will find it hard to look statuesque perched

on a side-saddle atop of a small donkey; but for sheer want of dignity give me the male man who goes a-donkey-riding in the desert. Even if he does not have to sit on a bundle of rags placed immediately over the hind-legs of his mount (in which case he should be grateful if no one whose respect he values catches sight of him), he will find himself astride a grotesque mass of highly decorated leatherwork, terminating, forward, in an enormous sort of hump. His legs will dangle nearly to the ground, his way will be determined by the donkey, and his balance will be precarious. In my case, the fact that one rein had broken adrift at its mooring to the donkey's bit, and that I could in consequence steer him only one way, did not add to my safety or my dignity.[70]

Neither was there much dignity to be found in riding a mule.

*

In 1912 the British army bought one mule from America. After glacial deliberation, a further three were purchased the following year. Come the Great War, however, and the army's purchasing of mules rose exponentially. Between 1914 and 1918 some 250,000 mules were brought to Britain. The ever so humble mule, the offspring of a horse father and donkey mother, turned out to be a war-winning weapon. (Some animals defined as 'mules' were strictly speaking 'hinnies', the product of a male donkey and a female pony.) In the words of the equine historian Captain Sidney Galtrey of the Remount Service, the mule was 'probably the most serviceable and satisfactory animal used in the war'.[71] Even Galtrey underplays the value of the mule. Britain's secret weapon in the Great War was never the steel tank; it was the flesh-and-blood mule, shipped over in tens of thousands from America.

Possessed of hybrid vigour, the mule had outstanding stamina. Three-quarters of the ammunition at Passchendaele was delivered by mule, where only one mule for every four and a half horses became invalided by the mud, the rain and the cold. The mules' willingness to soldier on was admired by all men, whether they were private or general, rifleman or cook. Or chaplain, like Captain Thomas Tiplady:

> The mule is magnificent for war, and our battles have been won as much by mules as men. Haig could rely on one as much as on the other. The mule will eat anything, endure anything, and, when understood and humoured by its driver, will do anything. It works until it falls dead by the roadside. In the spring, hundreds died in harness. In fact, few die except in harness. They die facing the foe, dragging rations along shell-swept roads to the men in the trenches.[72]

Wherever mules served in the Great War, they attracted enthusiastic encomia. Out in Mesopotamia, Lieutenant Graham Mackay, RA, discovered mules to be:

> worth their weight in gold to the Army . . . There is not one Artillery officer who would ever again prefer horses to mules after this. Mules are much hardier and contrary to popular belief practically never jib . . . Six old mules would not look so well on the parade ground at Woolwich but on a dark night with a sea of mud all round you and the wheels sinking slowly you thank God if you have six ugly looking mules instead of 6 flashy looking horses in the team.[73]

No, the mule, with its etiolated ears, was never accused of majesty or beauty. On a night road at Courcelles, with the moon swimming in milkiness, a transport section passed Private Fred Manning, 7/King's Shropshire Light Infantry. Two grey stallions were as 'Beautiful as the horses of Hippolytus' but the mules were mere commas in the parade, admirable in their 'bitter patience' but 'grotesque'.[74]

Mules came in two physical classifications: 'Heavy', standing up to a height of 16 hands 2in and weighing 1300lb; 'Light' mules, by contrast, were 15 hands and 1100lb. But they were never labelled 'handsome'.

Sergeant E. Miles would have demurred at Lieutenant Mackay's opinion that mules never jib. To get rations from reserve up to the trenches at Gallipoli's Suvla Bay, his pack mules needed to ascend a narrow cliff path bounded by a steep precipice with the sea a hundred feet below. All was going 'fairly well', until one of the mules started to mutiny. The fun commenced:

> One mule turned around (goodness knows how he done it) and bolted. Another one who attempted the same trick was not so fortunate and he slipped down the precipice, rations and everything with him. We heard a splash in the distance far below as he dropped into the sea, and that was the last we heard of either.[75]

Other soldiers would have nominated the donkey for the quirkiest beast among the army equines. Although the donkey saw service on the Western Front (where soldiers cuddled it in winter dugouts: warmth for beast, warmth for humans; a donkey, unlike a horse, will stand for any amount of petting), its main theatres of war were Palestine, East Africa and Gallipoli. That the donkey, Christ's animal, should be part of Allenby's march on Jerusalem was not without poignance. The worth of the 12,790 donkey reinforcements sent out to Palestine at the end of 1917 came, not least, when they ported ammunition up the mountain track to the British position at Es Salt in May 1918. Camels had been found to be too noisy, and horses insufficiently strong, so the donkeys of the Cavalry's cooks and batmen were loaded up for the forty mile trip. Donkeys could standardly carry panniers of up to 200lb.

The Great War donkey was also crucial in forging the foundation legend of Australia. Australia landed at Gallipoli in April 1915 as a British Dominion and left the peninsula's beaches in December 1915 as a de facto independent state. More than 8000 Australians died on that barren Turkish promontory, their blood to become the ink in which the Antipodean *Iliad* was written. The 'Digger' values of valour and sacrifice at Gallipoli became symbolised in twenty-two-year-old Private John Simpson Kirkpatrick (also known as John Simpson), a stretcher-bearer with C section of the 3rd Field Ambulance, 1st Division Australian Infantry Force, who used an abandoned water-carrier donkey, found in a hut, to carry wounded from the shooting ground above Anzac Cove to the beach hospitals. For three and a half weeks 'The Man with the Donk' traversed Monash Valley up to fifteen times a day, until he was killed by Turkish machine gun fire on 19 May. By the 1960s Simpson had become so intrinsic to the Gallipoli epic, so immutably imprinted on the Australian mind, that the Anzac Medallion issued to the battle's veterans carried his graven image, along with that of his ass.

The legend of 'The Man with the Donk' is laden with problems. Far from being a patriotic Australian, Simpson was a socialistic 'Pom' from South Shields who had washed up on Australia's shore as a merchant seaman; there lurks a suspicion that Simpson joined the AIF merely to get a free passage home. Although Simpson had worked as a donkey-lad for Murphy's Fair, taking children for rides on Herd Sands beach in South Shields, the idea of using donkeys as stretcher-bearers belonged to someone else, Private William Henry. The discipline and order of military life were hardly to Simpson's liking, and in transporting the wounded he was actually deserting his proper duties. And there was no single donkey used by Simpson; there was Murphy, Abdul, Duffy, Queen Elizabeth. Gallant donkeys all.

If Simpson was other than his legend, he was still a brave man. Colonel Monash, commander of the 4th Brigade, who was an eyewitness to Simpson's work, sent a lengthy submission to Australian and New Zealand Divisional Headquarters on 20 May.

I desire to bring under special notice, for favour of transmission to the proper authority, the case of Private Simpson, stated to belong to C Section of the 3rd Field Ambulance. This man has been working in this valley since 26th April, in collecting wounded, and carrying them to dressing stations. He had a small donkey which he used, to carry all cases unable to walk.

Private Simpson and his little beast earned the admiration of everyone at the upper end of the valley. They worked all day and night throughout the whole period since the landing, and the help rendered to the wounded was invaluable.[76]

From 1916 onwards there have been periodic but futile attempts to secure a Victoria Cross for Simpson. In 2013 the Australian Defence Honours and Awards Appeals Tribunal concluded that 'Simpson's initiative and bravery was representative of all other stretcher-bearers of 3rd Field Ambulance and that he was appropriately honoured with a Mention in Despatches'.

Simpson's donkey Murphy did better, being posthumously awarded the RSPCA Australia Purple Cross Award by deputy prime minister Tim Fischer, at a ceremony at the Australian War Memorial on 19 May 1997. The award was made to Murphy as a representative of all the donkeys used by Simpson, in recognition of 'their exceptional performance in helping humans while under continual fire at Gallipoli during the First World War'.[77]

In the East African campaign the donkeys had no opportunity to prove their ability to help humans, because the tsetse fly bit them first. A blood-sucker, the tsetse or tik-tik transmits the disease nagana, a form of trypanosomiasis.

East Africa witnessed the worst equinicide of the Great War. When the campaign ended German veterinary officers admitted that the German commander-in-chief, General von Lettow, had intentionally made a line of retreat through jungly country most deadly to equines. In one instance, between August and October 1916, von Lettow withdrew along the Korogwe–Morogoro road into the tsetse fly area. A British mounted brigade, consisting of 4000 horses and donkeys, went in pursuit and within three weeks all the equines were dead. Whereupon 8000 donkey and horse reinforcements were dispatched on the same route and also perished.[78] Small doses of arsenic in food enabled donkeys to continue working for up to six weeks after tsetse fly attack. Unfortunately, since the chemical was often improperly administered the donkeys died of arsenic poisoning. Out of 34,000 donkeys employed during the campaign only 1042 were alive at the end.

The death of donkeys from tsetse fly attack should hardly have been a surprise; in his 1899 novel *Heart of Darkness*, Joseph Conrad – a sometime captain of a steamer on the Congo – had written, 'In a few days the Eldorado Expedition went into the patient wilderness, that closed upon it as the sea closes over a diver. Long afterwards the news came that all the donkeys were dead.'

East Africa was always singular. Generally, care of animals in the British army during the Great War was of a higher standard than in any other combatant army. The Germans lost four horses for every one the British did, the French almost two. The British army valued its donkeys, its mules and its horses. Indeed, as junior officers would be told ad infinitum, the descending order of importance in the army was first horses, then men, with the subaltern a very poor and distant third.

The British had learned the hard way, in war itself, that mistreatment of, or at least heedlessness towards, animals was militarily ineffective.

In the eighteenth century more British army horses were lost to illness and poor farriery than to enemy action. Simultaneously, the public expressed concern over the welfare of the army's horses. In 1796 the Committee of General Officers took positive action and founded the Army Veterinary Service (AVS) 'to improve the practice of Farriery in the Corps of Cavalry'. This was a step forward, albeit a small one. During the Crimean War, the *Illustrated London News* declared the army horse to be: 'A skeleton covered with an old hide, no mane, no tail and lips shrunk away from their long, bare and hungry teeth.' Once again public outrage obliged the army to improve its equine professionalism, and in 1880 the Army Veterinary School was founded at Aldershot; in 1887 the Army Remount Department was established.

Another war, another tide of justified public outrage. According to an RSPCA pamphlet issued after the Boer War (1899–1901), one of the most painful recollections of the soldiers was 'the heavy moaning of the injured horses, and the sorrow of having to abandon these creatures in their suffering'. There was a great deal of suffering. Of the half million or so horses supplied to the army during the South African War 326,073 died – most from exhaustion and communicable diseases such as glanders, epizootic lymphangitis and mange. (The 'wastage rate' worked out at 7.8 per cent per month.) To assuage an angry public, a Parliamentary Committee was set up, which in turn improved and expanded the AVS into the Army Veterinary Corps.

As a result of lessons learned in Victoria's little war in South Africa, the British army entered the Great War as the best army – in terms of its veterinary services, as well as its infantry lethality.

In the Great War the treatment of wounded or sick horses mirrored precisely the casualty system for men. Initial emergency treatment was at a small mobile unit near the front, before passage to a veterinary evacuation station, and from there to an equine hospital at base, and from there to a convalescent remount depot. It was a chain of care. In the Colony there were 60 divisional AVC Mobile Sections and 20 horse hospitals, the latter catering for between 1250 and 2000 patients each. (Since 3000 camels were enlisted in the Middle East, they too had their hospitals, four in total.)

Naturally, the number of veterinary officers rose vertiginously in accordance with the expansion of the horse welfare system. On 4 August 1914, the number of officers in the Army Veterinary Corps, including the Special Reserve, was 197. On 11 November 1918, the total number of officers in the corps was 1356.

Surgery and first aid were the AVC's strong suits. Treatment of disease tended to be rudimentary, if not useless. One soldier recalled:

One AVC treatment for mange was to put horses in sealed stables with their heads sticking out through a canvas screen. Sulphuric acid gas was then pumped in.[79]

Such quackery was not the fault of the AVC, it was a failure of science. Antibiotics were still a pipette dream.

With no antibiotic cure, the AVC relied on early diagnosis (diseases respond better to treatment and therapy in their first stages) and prevention. The Veterinary Corps also went to great prophylactic pains to educate those who were responsible for the care of the animals. A ten-day course of lectures for both infantry and artillery transport officers was made, as far as it was possible, obligatory. At its peak, the course was attended by up to 50 officers and 300 NCOs a month. Transport officers, NCOs and men were bombarded with official how-to booklets. Lieutenant Henry Williamson, a transport officer with the Machine Gun Corps before he became the author of *Tarka the Otter*, was issued with, inter alia, *The Mounted Officer's Book of Horses and Mules for Transport*, subtitled 'The care of the Horse and Mule and how the harness should fit'.

What strikes the eye about the pamphlet is the depth of advice on the proper treatment of equines. Effectively, humane treatment of – and kindness towards, indeed – animals had become institutionalised in the army:

The object of this book is to assist those whose duties are with the machine Gun Transport. It should also be found useful to all officers who are to be mounted.

As it is considered a point of honour for the Machine Gunner to keep his Gun firing under all circumstances, so it should be a point of honour for the Driver to keep his animal always in a fit condition and ready for any emergency.

This can only be done by the utmost attention to the animals: watering, feeding, grooming and correct harnessing.

Very often the animal is put down as lazy or bad-tempered when the fault really lies with the man in whose care it is . . .

Harsh treatment should never be meted out to mules or horses, and this applies particularly to mules, who strongly resent any beating and refuse to be worked as a consequence. But by kindness, coupled with a firm hand, much good work will willingly be done by these invaluable assistants of the Machine Gun Corps.

The book contained sections (with fold out illustrations) on:

The Horse, points of
The bridle and how it should fit
The saddle and Blanket
The Correct Position of Rider in the Saddle
Officer's Charger Fully Equipped, marching Order
Girt Galls, How to keep from
The Draught Harness for the Mule or Horse
Grooming
Position of various injuries of importance
The Yorkshire Boot for Horses that Brush
How to Kill a Horse Humanely (handing it a handful of food whilst
    you shoot it with a pistol at an exact point on the forehead)
Watering
Feeding
The Duties of a Transport Officer
March Routine
RSPCA

During the four and a half years of total war the Army Veterinary Corps hospitals received 725,216 horses and successfully treated three-quarters of them. Because of the Veterinary Corps' efforts, a British army horse and mule, should it be taken out of line, had a 78 per cent chance of a recovery and return to active service. Given the infant state of veterinary science and the naivety of some handlers, this was a shining achievement. Field Marshal Haig believed that if the German equine force had been as good as the British one the Germans could have won the war. Certainly, the German army paid the khaki-clad horse carers a most backhanded of compliments: during the German Spring Offensive of 1918 General Erich Ludendorff reputedly ordered his advancing soldiers to capture, then utilise, the British army's horses, because their own were inferior.

In December 1918, the victorious British marched in parade ground order over the Rhine to Cologne. Among them was Captain T.H. Westmacott, who recalled that: 'A German looking on said that the Division must have come fresh from England.'

Westmacott's division had been at the front for three years. With a discernible touch of pride Westmacott went on:

> The horses were all fit and hard as nails, and the buckles of the harnesses were all burnished like silver. The mules were as fit as the horses, and went on wagging their old ears as if they crossed the Rhine every day of the week.[80]

Aside from the praise of Haig, Ludendorff and German civilians the AVC received another accolade for its work 'in mitigating animal suffering, in increasing the mobility of the mounted units and for reducing animal wastage'. On 27 November 1918 the prefix Royal was added to its name.

The AVC, the Remount Service and the army's soldiers were far from alone in supporting Britain's war horses.

Charity for horses began on the home front. At the start of the war the RSPCA offered its services but was turned down, somewhat sniffily, by the War Office. Three months later the burden on the AVC was so great that the Army Council climbed off its moral high horse and wrote to the RSPCA asking for staff to join the AVC (about 50 per cent did by 1915). The War Office also indicated that if the RSPCA would start up a fund to provide hospital equipment for sick horses that would not be unwelcome. The tragedy and the valour of the war horses was not lost on the nation of animal lovers, who emptied their pockets and purses. The total money raised by the RSPCA amounted to £250,000 (about £12 million in today's prices). The King was among the donors. Haig was among the applauders, writing to the RSPCA that:

> Animals have been exposed to very severe trials and hardships and have suffered heavily, not only as battle casualties, but through the exhaustion and loss of health consequent on the severe stress of work. Their lot has, however, been greatly lightened, and their comfort in sickness materially added to by the assistance, which the RSPCA Fund has been able to give.[81]

The RSPCA Sick and Wounded Horse Fund provided, by the end of the war, 13 tented hospitals in France (with room in total for 13,500 horses) 180 horse ambulances, 28 motor ambulances (costing more than £1000 each), 50 mechanised corn crushers for veterinary hospitals, electrically-driven apparatus for clipping and grooming, and much veterinary equipment.

Horses were helped in Egypt, Salonika, Italy, Mesopotamia as well as the Western Front. So invaluable did the RSPCA become to the war effort that it was made an official auxiliary of the AVC.

People gave to other animal charities too, notably Our Dumb Friends League, which had set up a Blue Cross Fund – a Red Cross for animals – in the Balkan War of 1912. With the outbreak of the Great War the Blue Cross Fund was revived, and like the RSPCA used its donations to send veterinary supplies and ambulances to the front. One grateful commanding officer in France wrote to the charity: 'I heartily thank you for the liberal supply of the veterinary stores received this morning, every article was in splendid condition … believe me your work is fully appreciated by everyone who has charge of the poor dumb animals doing their part in this great war.'

By the close of 1918 the Blue Cross Fund had raised about £170,000 (£6.5 million) from the concerts and carnivals and collecting tins. *A Book of Poems for the Blue Cross Fund (To Help Horses in War*

*Time)*, published in 1917, with all proceeds to the fund, went through three editions in that year alone. But the Blue Cross's most inspired idea was to commission the Italian artist Fortunino Matania to paint *Goodbye, Old Man*. Together with Kitchener's accusing finger in 'Your Country Needs You', Matania's scene of a Tommy saying farewell to his mortally wounded horse became one of the enduring images of the Great War, and sold in its tens of thousands as a poster, postcard and print.

Matania's *Goodbye, Old Man*, subtitled 'An incident on the road to the battery position in Southern Flanders' is habitually labelled as saccharine sentimentality, although detractors should be aware that Matania, an official war artist and a painstaking proponent of 'illustrated realism', visited the front several times, and that the painting is possibly based on an event on the Aisne when a Gloucester soldier stayed with, and died beside, a hideously injured horse during a German advance. Yet it hardly matters whether *Goodbye, Old Man* portrays a specific happenstance; the painting is not baseless romanticism. Time and again, men had to say goodbye to animals who were more to them than dumb beasts. Touchingly, William Parr, who served with the Canadian Field Artillery, heard a driver say that should he 'go west' he hoped he would not be separated from his horses. A few days later a shell killed the soldier and his horses. William Parr buried the driver, and wrote the poem 'His Two Horses' in commemoration. Parr too, if he suffered a warrior's death, wanted to be interred with his equine comrades:

> And when the grand, great, final roll call comes,
> To be the first upon parade we'll try,
> Oh Lord of All please grant my only prayer,
> To take my horses with me when I die.

The great Goodbye between Man and Horse would come in 1918.

# *Interstice 3*

# *Poems about Horses Written by Serving Soldiers*

## Gun-Teams

Their rugs are sodden, their heads are down, their tails are
    turned to the storm;
(Would you know them, you that groomed them in the sleek fat
    days of peace,
When the tiles rang to their pawings in the lighted stalls, and
    warm,
Now the foul clay cakes on breeching strap and clogs the
    quick-release?)

The blown rain stings, there is never a star, the tracks are rivers of
    slime:
(You must harness-up by guesswork with a failing torch for light,
Instep-deep in unmade standings; for it's active-service time,
And our resting weeks are over, and we move the guns to-night.)

The iron tyres slither, the traces sag, their blind hooves stumble
    and slide;
They are war-worn, they are weary, soaked with sweat and
    sopped with rain:
(You must hold them, you must help them, swing your lead and
    centre wide
Where the greasy granite pave peters out to squelching drain.)

There is shrapnel bursting a mile in front on the road that the
    guns must take:
(You are thoughtful, you are nervous, you are shifting in your
    seat,
As you watch the ragged feathers flicker orange, flame and
    break):
But the teams are pulling steady down the battered village street.

You have shod them cold, and their coats are long, and their
    bellies stiff with the mud;
They have done with gloss and polish, but the fighting heart's
    unbroke . . .
We, who saw them hobbling after us down white roads flecked
    with blood,
Patient, wondering why we left them, till we lost them in the
    smoke;

Who have felt them shiver between our knees, when the shells
    rain black from the skies,
When the bursting terrors find us and the lines stampede as one;
Who have watched the pierced limbs quiver and the pain in
    stricken eyes;
Know the worth of humble servants, foolish-faithful to their gun.

*Captain Gilbert Frankau, RFA*

## Horse-bathing parade

A few clouds float across the grand blue sky,
The glorious sun has mounted zenith-high,
Mile upon mile of sand, flat, golden, clean.
And bright, stretch north and south, and fringed with green,
The rough dunes fitly close the landward view.
All else is sea; somewhere in misty blue
The distant coast seems melting into air —
Earth, sky, and ocean, all commingling there —
And one bold, lonely rock, whose guardian light
Glistens afar by day, a spire snow white.
Here, where the ceaseless blue-green rollers dash
Their symmetry to dazzling foam and flash,
We ride our horses, silken flanks ashine,
Spattered and soaked with flying drops of brine,
The sunny water tosses round their knees,
Their smooth tails shimmer in the singing breeze.
White streaks of foam sway round us, to and fro,
With shadows swaying on the sand below;
The horses snort and start to see the foam,
And hear the breaking roar of waves that come,
Or, pawing, splash the brine, and so we stand.
And hear the surf rush hissing up the sand.

*Corporal W. Kersley Holmes*


## Robin-a-tiptoe

Robin-a-Tiptoe is sixteen hand,
And carries his head and his tail in air;

He seems to step to a silver band
That he alone listens to everywhere.

Robin-a-Tiptoe is chestnut bright,
With a dainty blaze on his silken nose;
On every leg is a stocking white
That flickers in time as he lightly goes.

Robin-a-Tiptoe's rippling mane
Flames in the wind when he gallops out,
Yet the smallest touch on the tightened rein
Will check him or stop him or turn him about.

Robin-a-Tiptoe's eyes are bright,
And his nostrils quiver with pride to live;
His speed and strength are his heart's delight,
And the willing gifts that he loves to give.

Robin-a-Tiptoe, the Colonel's steed,
He'll gallop the wind, and win, unspurred;
He'll gallop as straight to the death, at need,
At the call of a touch and a whispered word!

*Corporal W. Kersley Holmes, Army Remount Service*

## A mid-day halt

All morning we had ridden in the heat,
Amidst the dust that floated from the beat
Of trotting horse-hoofs on the sun-baked road:
Our skins, our clothes, the saddles we bestrode
Were hot as if to burning, and the eye
Ached from the glare of parching earth and sky.

At noon we walked our horses round a turn,
Where the bleached highway dipped to cross a burn,
And found a little valley hidden there
A cup of green and gold, brimmed with blue air.
Here we drew rein, dismounting by the stream
That cooled already with its limpid gleam,
And led our horses to the dusty brink.
Eased of their bits, with slackened girths, to drink.
How eagerly they pressed to quench their thirst!
(How enviously we watched them drinking first!)
Some drank with dainty lips; some in their turn
Sucked noisy mouthfuls from the troubled burn;
Some raised their dripping muzzles, then again
Drank as if endless rivers they would drain.
Each hot and eager creature satisfied,
We led them from the water, and untied
The bag of oats on every saddle borne,
And soon the cheerful sound of crunching corn
Told every horse was happy; then at last
The troopers took their soldierly repast,
Lounging at ease upon luxuriant green,
With eyes at leisure for the radiant scene.

*Corporal W. Kersley Holmes*

### Transport (Courcelles)

The moon swims in milkiness,
The road glimmers curving down into the wooded valley,
And with a clashing and creaking of tackle and axles
The train of limbers passes me, and the mules
Splash me with mud, thrusting me from the road into puddles,
Straining at the tackle with a bitter patience,

Passing me . . .
And into a patch of moonlight,
With beautiful curved necks and manes,
Heads reined back, and nostrils dilated,
Impatient of restraint,
Pass two gray stallions,
Such as Oenetia bred;
Beautiful as the horses of Hippolytus
Carven on some antique frieze.
And my heart rejoices seeing their strength in play,
The mere animal life of them,
Lusting,
As a thing passionate and proud.


Then again the limbers and grotesque mules.

*Private Frederic Manning*


### The Silent Volunteers (To the horses that have fallen)

No less, real heroes than the men who died
Are you who helped the frenzied ranks to win;
Galloping heroes – silently – side by side,
Models of discipline.
You, too, had pals from whom you had to part –
Pals rather young to fight, or else too old –
And though the parting hurt your honest heart,
You kept your grief untold.
Thus in the parting have you proved your worth,
As you have proved it time and time again;
You, the most human animal on earth –
Nobler perhaps than men.
Nobler, perhaps, because in all you did –

In all you suffered you could not know why;
Only, you guessed – and did as you were bid –
Just galloped on – to die.
Unflinchingly you faced the screaming shell
And charged and charged, until the ground was gained
Then falling mangled – suffered simple hell –
And never once complained.
There, where your life blood spilled around you fast –
Lying unheeded by the surging van,
You closed your great big patient eyes at last.
And died – a gentleman.

*Lieutenant Leonard Fleming, Queen Victoria's Rifles*

## The Conscript

SAW him to-day, with the A.S.C.
And I knew at once what his brand would be,
That noble head, and those hoofs, tough and blue.
Is the kind they raise on the old 'Bar U'.
As I patted his neck, I said, 'Old son,
How long is it since you had a run
On the bunch-grass hills by the rushing Bow
Where the coyotes howl and the cotton-woods grow?'
'Can't you hear the wind roaring through the grass
As it licks all the snow off the prairie grass?
And the prairie chicken exclaims 'Cluck, cluck
I'll be eating grasshoppers soon . . . with luck.'
'And in summer time when your flies were bad
Often I've watched your noble old dad
Leading his mares at a rattling pace
Over the hills, with the wind in his face.'
And, believe me, that horse quite understood

And would have answered me if he could.
For he shoved his muzzle in under my coat
With a sigh that brought a lump to my throat.
Then I questioned his driver, said he, 'Old Dan
Is the best of the bunch, sir. Every man
In the corps wants to drive him, but, so far,
I've managed to keep him, and here we are.'
'Off to France to-morrow, it do seem a shame
To send horses to war. Thanks all the same,
I don't drink, sir, if you like, you can
Give a bob to the "Blue Cross" Fund, for Dan.'

*Horace W. Warden, 24th Reserve Batt., CEF*

## Dumb Heroes

There's a D.S.O. for the Colonel,
A Military Cross for the Sub,
A medal or two, when we all get through,
And a bottle of wine with our grub.
There's a stripe of gold for the wounded
A rest by the bright sea-shore.
And a service is read as we bury our dead,
Then our country has one hero more.
And what of our poor dumb heroes
That are sent without choice to the fight.
That strain at the load on the shell-swept road
As they take up the rations at night.
They are shelling on Hell Fire Corner,
There's shrapnel just burst in the Square,
And their bullets drum as the transports come
With the food for the soldiers there.
The halt till the shelling is over.

The rush through the line of fire.
The glowing light in the dead of night.
And the terrible sights in the mire.
It's the daily work of the horses
And they answer the spur and rein.
With quickened breath, 'mid the toll of death.
Through the mud, and the holes, and the rain.
There's a fresh treated wound in the chestnut,
The black mare's neck has a mark.
The brown mule's new mate won't keep the same gait
As the one killed last night in the dark.
But they walk with the spirit of heroes,
They care not for medals or cross,
But for duty alone, into perils unknown,
They go, never counting their loss.
There's a swift painless death for the hopeless,
With a grave in a shell-hole or field,
There's a hospital base for the casualty case.
And a Vet. for those easily healed.
But there's never a shadow of glory,
A cheer, or a speech, in their praise.
While patient and true they carry us through
With the limbers in shot-riven ways.
So here's to 'Dumb Heroes' of Britain,
Who serve her as nobly and true.
As the best of her boys, 'mid the roar of the guns
And the best of her boys on the blue.
They are shell-shocked, they're bruised, and they're
broken
They are wounded and torn as they fall,
But they're true and they're brave to the very grave,
And they're heroes, one and all.

*Captain T.A. Girling, Canadian Army Veterinary Corps*

## Old Bill of the RFA (The story of a faithful friend)

*Founded on a true incident.*

Old Bill, they used to call me,
Bill, of the R.F.A.
And a fine and easy time I had.
Till the 'other Bill' found his 'Day'.
A little artillery driver.
Looked after me, day and night.
And he spoke with joy in his voice and heart
When he said, 'We're off to fight!'
They took us across to Flanders,
And there in the mud and wet,
I'd think of the stall in 'Old Blighty'
And the care I used to get.
I'd think of the little driver,
Who never would drive again,
He'd done his bit for the dear old Flag,
And the thought would ease the pain.
They sent me soon to Egypt,
The land of the blazing sun,
Where the heat would blister the very skin
Of the shining breech of a gun.
The heat and sand soon put me
In the lines reserved for the 'cast',
With nothing to do but to pine away
And dream of the days long past.
To dream of the days when I galloped,
In the lead, at the 'Right of the line',
Ah! Those were the days worth living,
The days of Auld Lang Syne.
And now in a native stable

I tremble and start at each sound,
Five hundred piastres bought me,
And humbled my soul to the ground.
My little artillery driver
Loved me with fond caress.
But now I am tortured, day after day,
By a fiend, in woman's dress.
He's a brutal, cruel master.
He bought me for five pounds.
And if 'he' knew, who sleeps in France.
His rage would have no bounds.
For 'he' loved me like a brother,
'He' loved me like a wife.
And if it lay within my power.
For 'him' I'd give my life.
Thank Heaven, I'm quickly dying
(There's a heaven for horses too),
And, Tommy, lad, I'll shortly come
To take my rest with you.
And the 'powers that be' in England
For five pounds, break and still
The hearts of the friends whom Tommies love,
The horses like 'faithful Bill'.

*Driver Harvey J. Greenaway, RFA*

## The Offside leader

I want not praise, nor ribbons to wear
I've done my bit and I've had my share
Of filth and fighting and blood and tears
And doubt and death in the last four years.
My team and I were among the first

Contemptible few when the war-clouds burst.
We sweated our gun through the dust and heat,
We hauled her back in the Big Retreat,
With weary horses and short of shell
Turning our backs on them . . . that was hell.
That was Mons . . . but we came back there
With shine on the horses and shells to spare!
And much I've suffered and much I've seen
From Mons to Mons on the miles between,
But I want no praise nor ribbons to wear –
All I ask for my fighting share
Is this: That England will give to me
My offside leader in Battery B.
She was a round-ribbed blaze-faced brown,
Shy as a country girl in town,
Scared of the gangway and scared of the quay,
Lathered in sweat at the sight of the sea,
But brave as a lion and strong as a bull,
With the mud to the hub in an uphill pull.
She learned her job as the best ones do
And we hadn't been over a week or two,
Before she would stand like a rooted oak,
While the bullets whined and the shrapnel broke,
And a mile of the ridges rocked in glee
As the shells went over from Battery B.
One by one our team went down
But the gods were good to the blaze-faced brown,
We swayed with the battled, back and forth
Lugging the timbers back and forth
Round us the world was red with flame,
As we gained or gave in the changing game
Forward or backward, losses or gains
There were empty saddles and idle chains.
For Death took some on the galloping track

And beckoned some from the bivouac;
Till at least were left, but my mare and me
Of all that went over with Battery B.
My mates have gone and left me alone
Their horses are heaps of ashes and bone
Of all that went out in courage and speed,
There is left but the little brown mare in the lead.
The little brown mare with the blaze on her face
That would die of shame at a slack in her trace;
That would swing the team to the least command
That would charge at a house at the slap of my hand,
That would turn from a shell to nuzzle my knee –
The pride and the wonder of Battery B.
I look for no praise and no ribbon to wear,
If I've done my bit, it was only my share,
For a man has his pride and the strength of his Cause
And the love of his home, they are unwritten laws,
But what of the horses that served at our side,
That in faith as of children fought with us and died.
If I, through it all have been true to my task
I ask for no honours. This only I ask.
The gift of one gunner.
I know of a place,
Where I'd leave a brown mare with a blaze on her face,
'Mid low leafy lime trees in cocksfoot and clover
To dream, with the dragonflies glistening over.

*Captain Will Ogilvie, Army Remount Department*

[Will Ogilvie, born in Kelso in 1869, educated at Fettes; emigrated to Australia – largely because he wanted wide open spaces and horses – at the age of 20 where he worked on remote sheep stations and counted among his friends the legendary horseman, Harry 'Breaker' Morant. Worked in the Outback for twelve years, where he started writing poetry for the *Sydney Mail* and other newspapers, including the much anthologised 'Fair Girls and Gray Horses'. He wrote an account of his time in Australia, *My Life in the Open*. On his return to Scotland he settled into life as a countryman and journalist, and married Margaret Scott Anderson, daughter of the Master of the Jed Forest Fox Hounds in 1908. He volunteered for the Army Remount department as he was too old for active service.]

## The Remount Train

Every head across the bar,
Every blaze and snip and star,
Every nervous twitching ear,
Every soft eye filled with fear,
Seeks a friend and seems to say:
'Whither now, and where away?'
Seeks a friend and seems to ask:
'Where the goal and what the task?'

Wave the green flag! Let them go! —
Only horses? Yes, I know;
But my heart goes down the line
With them, and their grief is mine! —
There goes honour, there goes faith,
Down the way of duel and death,
Hidden in the cloud that clings
To the battle-wrath of kings!

There goes timid childlike trust
To the burden and the dust!
Highborn courage, princely grace
To the peril it must face!
There go stoutness, strength, and speed

To be spent where none shall heed,
And great hearts to face their fate
In the clash of human hate!

Wave the flag, and let them go! —
Hats off to that wistful row
Of lean heads of brown and bay,
Black and chestnut, roan and grey!
Here's good luck in lands afar —
Snow-white streak, and blaze, and star!
May you find in those far lands
Kindly hearts and horsemen's hands!

*Captain Will Ogilvie, Army Remount Department*

## The Horse and the War

Many months at a time I was up on the Somme
In the rain and the mud and the mire:
We were 'packing' the shells to the various Hells
In the dips of the vast undulations and dells
Where the field guns were belching their fire.

It was very poor sport when the forage ran short
First to eight and then six pounds a day,
But we managed to live on the blankets they brought,
Though blankets I now think, and always have thought,
Are but poor substitution for hay.

I remember a week when we played hide and seek
With the shrapnel the Boches sent over:
I remember the night when they pitied my plight.
And pipped me, and put me clean out of the fight

With a 'Blighty' – then I was in clover.
For they dressed me and sent me quick out of the line
To a hospital down at the Base,
Where the standings were good and the weather was fine
And the rations were not a disgrace:
There, just within sound of the Heavies I found
La France can be quite a good place.
And now I've recovered – I'm weary and thin
And I'm out of condition and stale,
My ribs and my hips are too big for my skin
And I've left all the hair of my tail
On the middlemost bar of the paddock I'm in,
For they turned me out loose, as I'm frail.
Now the life in a paddock according to men
Is a sort of a beautiful song
Where animals wander around and can squander
The time as they wander along.
With nothing to worry them, nothing to do
Except for food intervals daily; but you
Can take it from me they are wrong,
For paddocks are places conducive to thoughts
That settle unbid on the brain.

And often I find them to follow a kind
Of a minor-key tune or refrain
As I doze for an hour in the afternoon sun
Or I stand with my rump to the rain
I dream of the barn on my Illinois farm
And I long to be back there again.

*Anonymous, Base Indian Remount Depot, BEF, France*

### His Two Horses

Oh Lord, to Thee I want to make my prayer,
My soul is troubled sore from day to day,
I never had the chance to know Thee Lord,
Nobody ever taught me how to pray.

So if my prayer is not as it should be,
Is not as padre prays on church parade,
Please pardon me, forgive what I've forgot,
For at thy feet my naked soul is laid.

If in the roster kept by Thee above
My name is next to cease this life fatigue,
And I must fall in with my fallen pals
A clean life's page behind I want to leave.

Grant that I die where bursting shrapnel sings,
My team upon a gallop toward the foe,
And when my soul at last reports to Thee,
Please let me take my horses where I go.

If it is true what our old padre says,
That there are horses in the land above,
Are there not some spare stalls to hold my two,
My Black, my Brown, the horses that I love,
They're only common field artillery plugs,
And I am just a common soldier man.

We've fought and starved together side by side,
I'd like to take them with me if I can.

I know my saddle Black is pretty mean,
And kicks and bites at everyone but me,
Still when I'm with him he is always good,
Just let me bring him up for you to see.
He'd be ill-treated if I left him here,
Be kicked and cursed and starved until he died,
Please can't I ride him through the golden streets,
The gentle old Brown Off-horse at his side.

They've carried me on many a weary ride,
They've been my pals, my everlasting joy,
I've nursed them both when they were sick,
And kept their harness burnished like a toy.

I've gone with them into the jaws of death,
Gunners and drivers killed on every trip,
Their panting hides have dripped with mud and sweat,
My horses needed neither spur nor whip.

Oh Lord, if heaven has no stable room,
With greatest reverence this I'd like to tell,
And if the fiery regions have some stalls,
Then let me ride my horses down in hell.

And when the grand, great, final roll call comes,
To be the first upon parade we'll try,
Oh Lord of All please grant my only prayer,
To take my horses with me when I die.

*Private William Parr, Field Artillery, 1st Canadian Division*

## The Battery Horse

He whinnied low as I passed by,
It was a pleading sort of cry;
His rider, slain while going back,
Lay huddled on the muddy track.
And he, without a guiding hand,
Had strayed out on the boggy land;
And held there by the treacherous mire,
Lay exposed to shrapnel fire.

He was a wiry chestnut steed,
A type of good Australian breed;
Perhaps on steep Monaro's height,
He'd followed in the wild steer's flight,
Or out beyond the great divide
Roamed free where salt bush plains are wide
Or, through the golden wattle groves
Had rounded up the sheep in droves,
Then shipped away to feed the guns,
And help the boys to strafe the Huns.

*Lance-Corporal E.R. Henry*

## My Beautiful

Before the sun has shown himself, for your complacent sake,
Obedient to the bugle, I reluctantly awake;
Though hurricanes may whistle and though drenching torrents
    fall,
I've got to sacrifice my ease and stumble to your stall

Is man creation's master, O my beautiful, my bay?
Yet I must do you courtesies with each returning day:
You stand – impatient frequently – impassive at the best,
While like a lazy potentate you're brushed and combed and
    dressed.

With rake and spade and haik and graip I serve you in the gloom;
For you I wheel the barrow, and for you I wield the broom;
That you may look your handsomest, I fling my tunic off,
And labour with a dandy-brush – you sybarite, you toff!

BUT
I'm only chaffing you, old hoss, you needn't mind my fun –
You pay me back a thousandfold for anything I've done.
I slip my saddle on your back-swing up myself, my own –
And every monarch on the earth is welcome to this throne!

*Corporal W. Kersley Holmes, Army Remount Service*

# CHAPTER IV

# Of Lice and Men

*Trench Pests, Vermin and Disease*

All trenches in the Colony heaved with rats, brown (*Rattus norvegicus*) and to a lesser extent black (*Rattus rattus*). Although the Western Front is popularly imagined as Arcadia before the gun-holding hand of man turned it into Armageddon, the front line ran through towns and industrial areas, as well as farmland and woods. Cuinchy, near La Bassée, was dominated by thirty or so ziggurat-like stacks from the local brickworks. The town had that indispensable of rat life in abundance: water. Robert Graves, then serving with the Welsh Regiment, recalled:

> Cuinchy bred rats. They came up from the canal, fed on the plentiful corpses, and multiplied exceedingly. While I stayed here with the Welsh, a new officer joined the company ... When he turned in that night, he heard a scuffling, shone his torch on the bed, and found two rats on his blanket tussling for the possession of a severed hand.

Further ratty horrors awaited the young subaltern. On one of the Welsh Regiment's periodic attacks on German lines, Graves found that in rushing for cover from shell hole to shell hole:

> many of the craters contained the corpses of men who had been wounded and crept in there to die. Some were skeletons, picked clean by the rats.[1]

If Graves thought Cuinchy the worst place for rats on the front, he was sadly mistaken. On going into the trenches at Fricourt in March 1916 with the Royal Welch Fusiliers, he discovered that the excavations, cut into chalk, simply oozed rats:

> We always ate with revolvers beside our plates, and punctuated our conversation with sudden volleys at a rat rummaging at somebody's valise or crawling along the timber support of the roof above our heads.[2]

On the Western Front the rats were so multitudinous that they seemed to be the masters of the dominion, not man. Tom Kettle, the Irish nationalist who joined the King's side, dubbed this new continent 'Ratavia':

> Ratavia, as one may designate it, resembles China in that there has never been a census of its population but that it approximates to the mathematical infinite. They are everywhere, large rats, small rats, bushy rats, shy rats and impudent, with their malign whiskers, their obscene eyes, loathsome all the way from over-lapping teeth to kangaroo tail. You see them on the parados and the shelter-roofs at night, slinking along on their pestiferous errands. You lie in your dug-out, famished, not for food (that goes without saying), but for sleep, and hear them scurrying up and down their shafts, nibbling at what they find, dragging scraps of old newspapers along, with intolerable cracklings, to bed themselves. They scurry across your

blankets and your very face. Nothing suppresses their numbers. Not dogs smuggled in in breach of regulations. Not poison, which most certainly ought not to be used. Not the revolver-practice in which irritated subalterns have been known to indulge. Men die and rats increase.[3]

While there was no census of *Rattus* in Ratavia, many soldiers tried an educated guess at population density. Amateur naturalist Private Norman Ellison did a back-of-the-envelope calculation at Wailly, just southwest of Arras, in 1916 and determined the rat population in the village at 250,000. 'Everywhere is honeycombed with their burrows until the whole place is one gigantic warren of runs and holes.'[4]

Fellow soldier-cum-amateur naturalist Arnold Monk-Jones concluded that at Thames Alley near Arras 'the only nature study possible there is rats!'

Man turned France and Flanders into the ideal breeding conditions for the rat. Unburied bodies of man and horse provided easy meat for the omnivorous rodent.

The sight of human cadavers being gorged upon by rats was not easily forgotten; Francis Hitchcock of the Leinsters inadvertently entered a house of horrors in the Salient:

Coming from the dressing station, I saw a very gruesome sight. I happened to go into a wrong house by mistake, and in front of me in the dim light I saw the body of an officer of the sappers stretched on a table awaiting burial. As I looked I was horrified to see a rat jumping down off the corpse. The house was being used as a mortuary by the R.A.M.C.[5]

Second Lieutenant George Atkinson walked into a painting by Hieronymus Bosch:

We were so tired last night that I tried the short way back again through the woods. Once we stumbled on a colony of rats, feeding on the sodden corpse of a Frenchman. I shuddered involuntarily as they scattered away, screaming, and then turned to watch us with beady, malevolent eyes. The last time I was home on leave I remember my mother asked me why the trench rats were so big. I nearly told her, but then it occurred to me that I might be 'missing' myself and the thought would have driven her mad – so I said it was because of the food we used to throw over the top. God help the mothers who really know these things.[6]

Actually, Atkinson told his mother the truth, albeit unwittingly. Discarded rations, rather than uninterred bodies, were the real causative factor in the population boom of *Rattus* in the trenches. Captain Philip Gosse, one of the 10,000 civilian doctors who joined the RAMC for the duration, was the rat specialist of the Western Front. His elevation to such an exalted position had come about in typical military fashion. Lying in his billet at Steenwarde ('with the unwonted luxury of sheets in the bed') Gosse had been disturbed by a small but fierce staff officer who, after determining that he indeed had Captain P.H.G. Gosse before him, breathlessly informed him 'You are appointed Rat Officer to the Second Army.' News of Gosse's interest in zoological activities had reached the ears of General Porter, Second Army Director of Medical Services, and it was evidence enough for Gosse to be decreed 'GOC Rats'. Gosse's batman, Bob Church, was delighted they were heading for 'a cushy job'.

On the basis of experience Gosse concluded:

But probably the most important reason for the increase in rats was food: The British army was supplied with a vast surplus of rations, much more than could be consumed. Food, stale bread, biscuits and particularly cheese, littered the ground. Some quartermasters, to save themselves trouble and to guard against the risk of being caught without enough would indent for greater quantities of rations than they required or were entitled to. This surplus was disposed of in different ways. Much of it went to feed hungry Belgian and French children, at which nobody could complain; as much again was thrown on the rubbish heap, burnt in the incinerators, or buried in pits when a battalion moved from its camp.[7]

As Gosse was acutely aware, static warfare, as well as providing provisions, provided rats with habitation. Trenches were a form of bank, a landscape feature much in demand by rats, a highly fecund creature; female rats in the wild live for approximately two years, during which time they produce batches of up to twelve young every six weeks, winter, spring, summer and autumn. Which in turn beget young. Gosse considered that in ideal conditions a pair of rats would produce a 'staggering' 880 offspring in one year.

Soldiers lamented the rain trapped in trench bottoms; rats literally lapped it up. War was rat heaven in earth.

Connoisseurs of the murine postulated that the rats of the front, as well as being multitudinous, grew to uncommon proportion. The rats of Vimy Ridge, Francis Hitchcock swore, were of 'colossal size', 'almost as big as dogs'.[8] Private Thomas McIndoe, 12/Middlesex, encountered rats so big that 'if they were put in a harness they could have done a milk round, they were that big, honest'.[9] Private Ellison, being of scientific inclination got out the ruler. At Vaux Wood in October 1915 he 'strafed' rats with a stick, one of which was 'twenty-three inches from nose to tip of tail, as big as a rabbit'.[10]

A soldier's first night in a rat-infested dugout was a memory for life: Second Lieutenant Guy Chapman, 13/Royal Fusiliers, later author of *A Passionate Prodigality*, one of the 22-carat memoirs of the conflict, and husband of novelist Storm Jameson, was shown into his Houplines dugout, a cell-like six by four foot hole, half of which was taken up by a wire bed. A stump of a candle guttered in a niche in the wall:

I lay down and blew out the light. Mysterious rustlings became audible, grew louder; there was a scamper of little feet. Rats, I guessed and shuddered. I relit my stump. The rustling abruptly ceased, and I dozed off . . . I came back to the surface with a jerk. I could hear something scrabbling beside my ear. I turned my head and caught a glimpse of what looked like a small pink monkey, clambering up the wall. With a spasm of disgust, I threw myself off the bed and bolted into the mess, where I sat shuddering and retching until the subaltern on duty pushed his head in and called 'Stand-to'. I was not yet hardened to rats.[11]

Major Patrick Butler, cavalryman transferred to Shanks' pony at Ypres, recalled:

My dug-out was a very deep one, down a steep flight of steps. It was simply swarming with enormous rats, who looked upon man as an intruder, and would scarcely make room for him at all. When I went into that dug-out and struck a match, a sort of black dropscene would ascend the walls. It was rats climbing up behind the brushwood lining of the dug-out.[12]

Driver James Reynolds, 55th Field Coy, RE, wrote home:

I've laid down sometimes of a night with just the candle burning to have a read, and on looking up seen as many as ten or a dozen pairs of bright eyes watching me, no doubt waiting for me to put the light out before going on the scavenge.[13]

Stuart Cloete, a nineteen-year-old serving as an acting captain, thought rats 'quite fearless, their familiarity with the dead having made them contemptuous of the living'. He was bitten on the face by an over-familiar rat in a dugout. Far from being silky, healthy specimens trench rats, according to Cloete, tended to be 'piebald, blotched with pink, where they had lost great patches of hair'.

Men tried everything to keep their food protected from rats, normally to no avail. Captain Anthony Eden, King's Royal Rifle Corps, set his dog, Con, a wolfhound, to guard a Christmas treat of peppermint creams; the sweets were eaten. The future prime minister concluded that Con had been too sated by eating rats ('the size of buck rabbits') for effective sentry duty. Rats were fantastically indiscriminate in their dining. Officers of dandyish inclinations ('knuts', after the swell in the musical hall song 'Gilbert the Filbert', the 'Knut with a K') soon learned to mend their ways. In the trenches at Annequin in June 1917, Lieutenant Alexander Stewart was 'much troubled by the rats coming and licking the brilliantine off my hair; for this reason I had to give up using grease on my head'.[14] Corporal A.H. Roberts, a signaller with 13/Gloucestershire Regiment, recorded in his diary that on 2 October 1916: 'Rats eat Divisional Orders during night'; in July 1917 he 'Woke up to find the rats eating the Daily Mirror'. Major Sladen, birdwatching in Palestine, secured what he took to be a desert bullfinch but before he could make a positive examination 'a rat took this skin from my dugout'. Corporal Arthur Cook, 1/Somerset Light Infantry, suspended food in sandbags from the dugout roof only to awake to find the rodents 'having a swing on the bags, cheeky rascals'.[15] He and his pals had to cover their heads at night, because the rats regarded their faces as convenient comestibles, live food in the larder. Sometimes the rats got through the blankets, or men forgot to cover their heads. Lieutenant Roe, sleeping in a billet behind the lines (where there was no shortage of rats), woke at night to see:

Corporal Arthur Major [who had been asleep] was sitting up in the straw with a fully grown rat swinging from his nose with his teeth in the cartilage. We had already experienced rats nibbling away at the back of hair . . . The lighting was elementary, a couple of hurricane 'butties' and a torch or two and I was momentarily taken aback. Clearly I could not shoot the rat with my 0.45 inch revolver in such a confined space and equally clearly I could only open the teeth and free them from the cartilage if the rat was first killed. There was only one solution, so I borrowed [Sergeant] Appleford's bayonet and got on with the job.[16]

Canadian Will Bird was awake when someone in his company kicked off a rat and it landed in the open mouth of a snoring soldier: 'The creature squealed as it sprang away and into the wall. Thornton sat up and spit for an hour afterwards and I rolled in mirth.'

The sleep-deprivation caused by nocturnal rat activity was one of the true banes of Ratavia. Captain Bill Murray reported to his family in 1915 that the young of the five rat families in the roof of his dugout liked to 'practise back somersaults continuously through the night, for they have discovered that my face is a soft landing when they fall'.[17] Charlie May, billeted in the stables at Mesnil chateau in the same year, wrote home to Maude, his wife:

I see that last evening I boasted that it would take more than rats to disturb us. I was badly mistaken. They beat us – easily. The trouble was that Bunting [Charlie May's batman] had laid my bed across a favourite run of theirs and they did not intend being put off it by a mere intruder like myself.

They ran over my legs, body, chest and feet, and I was adamant. But when they started on my face I must own that I slavishly surrendered, fell to cursing horribly and finally changed my lying place. Thereafter I fared better but Murray dropped in for it. They ate his iron ration [. . .] which incidentally proves that they are but lowly people. Knawed [sic] through Prince's pack and ate his also. I can tell you they are some rats, these.[18]

If humans were awed by the rats, the rats were absolutely unafraid of humans, as gunnery officer Lieutenant Richard Talbot Kelly discovered at Plugstreet:

One morning, up at the Observation Post, a very large black rat came and sat right in the middle of my loophole, completely blocking my view of the enemy lines and obstructing the observation I was supposed to be carrying out. It sat just out of arm's reach and washed. I shouted at it, flicked mud at it, threw pebbles at it and not the slightest heed was taken.

Eventually in desperation I fetched my stick and, measuring the distance carefully, was able to give it a very violent jab in the middle. It then moved to one side and continued to wash. But I was determined that next time I went up to the OP I would bring my revolver and deal with it more thoroughly. This I did, shooting it through the throat.[19]

Rifleman Alfred Read, 1/18th London Regiment, met an equally obdurate rodent:

Another night while walking along the duckboard track, another orderly and myself saw two rats just in front. Being only room enough to walk in single file we could not pass, so made a noise to frighten them. They were both about a foot long and too fat to run. This is because they used to feed on our dead, excuse enough for us to detest them. Well, one flopped into the water, but the other became bold, turning round and making a hissing noise. I, being the nearest, had visions of my throat clawed, so bringing my rifle down, I took aim from about five feet and fired. I hit him fair and square, but the noise brought plenty of chaps running from dugouts.[20]

Walking along a communication trench Lieutenant Cyril Drummond, 135th Battery, Royal Field Artillery, met a brown rat toddling towards him;

He was enormous, with ferocious and venomous eyes, and I freely admit I flattened myself against the trench wall and let him go past, which he did without turning his head.[21]

Eric Rees, an officer with the Durham Light Infantry, resorted to a method of rat-control popular with officers and men alike; it involved using the bayonet on a rifle in a manner unimagined by Colonel Ronald Campbell in his famous 'The Spirit of the Bayonet' talks back at base: 'A great trick with these rats is to put a bit of cheese on the bayonet and rest it on the parapet and when a rat starts nibbling pull the trigger – result no rat'.[22]

There were many ways to kill a rat, aside from shooting them from point blank range with a cheese-tipped Lee Enfield .303 rifle. Officers plugged away with revolvers, outside the dugout, as well as within. Captain Charles McKerrow RAMC, attached 10/Northumberland Fusiliers (and dugout comrade of Philip Gosse), informed his people at home:

> I go rat-hunting with my automatic pistol in the evenings, but with little success, as much practice has made the rats of the neighbour-hood very wily.[23]

On the Somme in September 1916, Captain A.E. Bundy also got out his sidearm:

> The rats on the level ground in front of my trench are larger and more numerous than I have previously seen. At dusk (when we were not visible by the Boche) we dug the rats out of their holes and had good practice with our revolvers.[24]

Officers on their nightly round in the Armentières sector in 1917 would, recorded Private Stuart Dolden, fire on the rats 'and in the morning it would be a common sight to see disembowelled rats lying amongst our barbed wire'.[25] Officially, shooting rats was discouraged in order to save ammunition (and to prevent accident), but the injunction was only honoured in the breach. Dolden himself waited for rats to emerge from the sumps at the bottom of the trench then gave them 'a mighty kick and there would be one less to batten on us'.[26] So 'nauseatingly plump' were the Armentières rats that they could barely move.

At Ypres Patrick Butler encountered an officer in the Duke of Cornwall's Light Infantry whose method of rat-dispatch had a quasi-knightly aura about it; the DCLI officer had fashioned a lance from 'a long pole and knife' and stabbed the rats that ran across the doorway of the dugout. Butler, like Dolden, settled for the blunter method of the boot:

> Sometimes one would meet a dozen of the creatures in a narrow trench, as they lolloped along, clumsy with gorging on recently-buried dead. One used to kick them along the trench like sodden footballs. Often, as I sat by night in some part of my long trench-line, I would see a string of rats moving along the top of the para-pet or parados against the sky. Their evil heads were down, and one saw nothing but their rounded backs, making them look like a row of skulls of the dead arisen from beneath the trenches for a veritable dance of death. It was an orgy of rats.[27]

During heavy nocturnal shellings, rats would wail outlandishly. Sapper officer George Atkinson was shelled at night in July 1918 near Mount Kemmel, and took refuge in a shell hole next to a ruined farm:

> The shells were coming just round us in solid masses so close that we could feel the earth heaving, and once or twice we were half buried. I had lost my bearings completely, and McDougall was still blind and apparently dazed, for he wouldn't answer when I shouted in his ear. Then I felt alone and I thought I would go mad – there were rats in the same hole with us, screaming with terror, and all the time those blasted shells, crash, crash, crash . . . God, in Thy mercy, let me never again hear any one speak of the Glory of War![28]

Daylight was always relief from a night overrun with rats. Patrick Butler:

Yes, the nights in those trenches were horrible, and we preferred the days. You had the blessed sunshine then, and although the appearance of calm was deceptive, it was impossible not to take pleasure in the singing of the larks, and in the vivid poppies that nodded bravely along the edges of the communication-trenches.[29]

Rats disturbed slumber, ate rations, destroyed equipment, as well as transmitting infections via their urine and bites; their habit of micturating on food surplus to requirements spread Weil's disease, notably in Gallipoli.[30] Pest control became a military necessity. Newspapers reported that 'train-loads' of terriers were being sent to France for the purpose of exterminating rats.[31] So in demand were ferrets for ratting in 1915, that their price in Ashford – close to the embarkation ports – gazumped from 1s to 5s per animal. (The problem of rampant rats at home also pushed up the price of ferrets: with rat-catchers away at war, the UK rat population grew unchecked; by 1918 the native population of rats was estimated by the zoologist W.P. Pycraft to be forty million. The rat's partiality to grain, plus the depredations of U-boats on shipping, threatened starvation.[32]) As the war wore on, the export of animals to France became frowned upon; when Major A.G.P. Hardwick wanted to take a pair of ferrets over to France in 1918 he needed to sneak them across, which led to pantomime moments; on the boat train the ferrets stank so much he had to put the pair out in the corridor for fear of self-asphyxiation, which somewhat ruined his attempted smuggling. In the fresh air of France, the ferrets were let loose on a trial run amid the shell holes:

The old buck is dashed good and almost immediately got first blood. He killed a decent-sized rat in a blind hole and we had to dig them out. It was only a trial run, as they had had a huge breakfast, but it shows that they are alright![33]

Killing rats also made for sport in the trenches. One of the appeals of 'ratting' was that it offered the chance to kill time – and to be the primeval hunter, rather than be the wartime hunted. Ratting was a bonding exercise too, a team game. Driver Reynolds recalled:

> One of our great sports consisted of ratting in the evening, just as it was getting dusk. Then they were about like kittens and with two or three of the stray dogs that always seemed to be hanging around the camp we would have fine hunts. Armed with sticks we sometimes accounted for as many as twenty in an evening.[34]

Richard Talbot Kelly and his fellow artillery 'subs' spent many an hour in candlelit rat-shooting competitions (with revolvers) in the vast cellars of the deserted Festubert brewery, a venue which happened to be a favourite target for German gunners; as Talbot Kelly and his pals potted away downstairs, shell splinters and bullets whined through the windowless rooms above them.

To the delight of Trooper Benjamin Clouting, the increase in British artillery shells delivered to the front meant that more cordite could be filched for trench-time ratting:

> A whole afternoon could be taken up, packing cordite into holes before the rats were smoked out in their dozens. Earlier in the war, ratting had been something of a laborious exercise, as cartridge cases were emptied from hundreds of bullets to get enough cordite to prove effective.
>
> By 1917, when more shells were available, it was possible to get hold of a shell case, or, better still, the cordite that was packed separately to fire the big guns. Howitzer cordite gave off a nasty green gas and was packed into a hole from which a trail of cordite was drawn. Once the trail was lit, a clod of earth was quickly packed around the cordite in the hole, forcing fumes down the tunnels and the rats out. There was a great deal of excitement as we laid into the rats with sticks and clubs, scattering them squealing in all directions, as we killed just as many as we possibly could.[35]

Brer Rat had a virtue beyond being sport for trench sportsmen. Canny soldiers realised that the rat could be used as the excuse for misdemeanours. When Lieutenant Bernard Adams, 1/Royal Welch Fusiliers, sat down in his Somme dugout for tea, there was bully beef and bread and butter, but no sugar:

> Richards [Adam's batman] smiled and said the rats had eaten it. Whenever anything was missing the rats had eaten it. Just as they were responsible for men's equipment and packs getting torn, and their emergency rations lost.[36]

This was Brer Rat as scapegoat.

Yet the prize for the imaginative use of a rat in wartime must go to Captain James Bell Foulis's company of the 5/Cameron Highlanders. Having killed a rat with a spade, they put the dead rodent into the trench mortar 'and threw it all the way into the German trench'.

This was Brer Rat as ammunition.

In war, every gas cloud had a silver lining. German attacks with gas, of the chlorine and phosgene and mustard varieties, destroyed rats as well as men. Second Lieutenant John Gamble, 14/Durham Light Infantry, remembered:

> I had just been bandaging up a couple of wounded when one of them called my attention to a couple of big rats which were staggering about on their hind legs as if drunk. It really was one of the funniest sights imaginable . . . They were half-gassed of course, but strangely enough it was one of the things I remembered best after the show was over. One good thing the gas did was to kill a lot of the least beasts . . .[37]

Gas was indiscriminate in its culling of course. Those 'least beasts' included, according to Major-General Foulkes, 'ants and caterpillars, beetles and butterflies. I found a hedgehog and an adder both killed by gas.'

Arthur Empey was an American who had signed up for the cause of democracy, following the sinking of the *Lusitania*. He was serving in the trenches with the Machine Gun Corps when 'a new man at the periscope' remarked: 'There's a sort of greenish, yellow cloud rolling along the ground out in front . . .' Empey banged, with his bayonet, the empty shell case that served as the gas alarm. There was pandemonium as gas helmets were put on and men roused from dugouts to man the fire step, because the Germans often attacked behind the cloud. One man, too slow with his helmet, died, 'clutching at his throat'. The company's little pet dog also died, 'paws over his nose'. There was sympathy for the dog but not for the rats affected, because 'Tommy does not sympathize with rats in a gas attack.'[38]

Alas, German gas, British revolvers, boots and bayonets barely dented the numbers of rats in the cross-Channel Colony. Set the task of controlling rats in the area of the Second Army, Captain Philip Gosse wanted to employ poison, but this was judged too dangerous to the men. So instead he ordered in hundreds of rat traps and beseeched quartermasters to protect stores better. It was this preventative measure, concluded Gosse, that brought 'a great improvement' in the rat situation:

Every food store was now protected by wire-netting, and in many places where rats used to swarm, scarcely one was to be found.[39]

His talk on rats, 'A Lecture on Zoology and its Relation to Sanitation', was one of the fixtures on the curriculum of Second Army schools.

Such was the caprice of the British soldier, though, that on occasion the detested rat could engender pity. Lying in his dugout ('three battered sheets of corrugated iron, a wagon cover, and the back of a hen shed, reared miraculously against a bank of earth') at Messines, Lieutenant George Atkinson was disturbed 'by an old brown rat [who] wanted to keep me company'. Atkinson 'turned him out three times, but the poor devil was so persistent and so pathetic that finally I let him stop'.[40] One platoon found a three-legged, one-eyed rat; clearly a fellow sufferer in adversity, 'Albert' became their pet.[41] The manufacturers of Abdulla cigarettes, a popular wartime brand, considered a Tommy and a rat having a 'tête-à-tête' a sufficiently engaging proposition to use it to advertise their wares: the advert's rodent is 'so cheery and calm and fat/That Thomas banished all lurid dreams of slaying his pet Trench Rat'. Private Isaac Rosenberg, 11/King's Own Royal Lancaster Regiment, hated the war, and only signed up for money to help his family. The working-class Jewish boy and the reviled rat were both outsiders. In 'Break of Day in the Trenches' Rosenberg encounters a rat on the parados at dawn stand-to:

> The darkness crumbles away.
> It is the same old druid Time as ever,
> Only a live thing leaps my hand,
> A queer sardonic rat,
> As I pull the parapet's poppy
> To stick behind my ear.
> Droll rat, they would shoot you if they knew
> Your cosmopolitan sympathies . . .[42]

*

Mice, despite being close cousins of the rat, never raised the same feelings of loathing. Mice were never so corpulent as to be gross or threatening, nor were they associated in the soldier's mind with the eating of human flesh, nor did they pluck a psychic memory as the agent of the Black Death. On the contrary, mice could be triggers for comforting childhood memories, since Beatrix Potter's *The Tailor of Gloucester* (1903) had been a staple of Edwardian nurseries and bedrooms.

Mice evoked sympathy for their very smallness. Captain Philip Gosse, the unwilling Rat Officer for the Second Army, was invited by a battery commander to his dugout for a drink. A mouse appeared; the major became red-faced, and cursed the mouse. Gosse offered to come back with a baited trap. The trap worked:

> I went and picked up the trap and showed the major the little soft body, quite warm, the cheese still between its minute, sharp teeth. I felt a curious feeling of pride that in my own ingenuity I had outwitted it. But this sensation did not last long, and began to ebb away while I held the little limp thing in my hand. After all, I reasoned with myself, it's only a mouse, and it annoyed the major. But all the same I wished I had not killed it. Bother the major, why on earth had I told him I had a mousetrap; why had I not told him to catch the mouse himself if he wanted to? But it would never do to let him see how I was feeling about it; he would despise me for a sentimental fool. I finished off my whisky and turned to say goodbye. The major was holding the little mouse in his hand, and surprised me by saying, 'I wish now we hadn't killed the little chap. I believe I had grown quite fond of him.'[43]

Charles Douie sitting in his dugout at Thiepval, where the trenches ran through the garden of the chateau ('a shell trap of the worst description'), witnessed a 'strange little comedy':

> I was nearly asleep when my eye was caught by a most unwarlike scene in the entrance to the dug-out. A dud shell lay partly embedded in the dry mud. A mouse with his head on one side peered at me, then took refuge behind the shell, reappearing a moment later on the far side. This was repeated several times. Then, emboldened, the mouse departed and brought back a friend. A game ensued, and whenever I blinked the two mice fell over each other in a ludicrously human way as they sought the security of their strange haven.[44]

In the middle of Third Ypres, Edmund Blunden saw a family of twenty field mice, with a 'tame and curious look about them (these calmed me, on these depended my salvation)'.

Writing from the Reserve trenches opposite Hohenzollern Redoubt in October 1915, Rowland Feilding informed his wife;

> Last night, while we were dining, our food being spread upon the floor, a mouse ran about among the plates, and was not at all abashed by the burning candles, or ourselves. They run up and down the earth walls of the dug-outs and at night have violent scuffles overhead, shaking the earth into our eyes and ears as we lie beneath. The amusing thing is that we all take care not to tread upon them or injure them in any way. In some mysterious way the war, while making one more callous to the sufferings of men, seems to increase one's sympathy with the lower animals.[45]

Captain C.P. Blacker's dugout comrade, Lieutenant Bird, a sapper who kept his canary on the table, enjoyed feeding the mice in their four and a half foot high chamber: 'Indeed, he had named two of them which would almost take food out of his hand.'[46]

Mice did, however, disturb sleep. Sergeant Hector 'Saki' Munro noted that the war brought 'a partial mobilization of owls, particularly barn owls' which made a laudable effort to thin out the mice of the front, yet 'there are always sufficient mice left over to populate one's dug-out and make a parade-ground and race-course of one's face at night'.[47] This was no laughing matter. The Great War soldier was tired for much of the time. Somnambulance affected the combat efficacy of the soldier to the point of psychiatric collapse.[48]

*

It was a lovely war for microbes, but then the Great War provided a perfect trifecta of conditions: vectors such as rats, huddled humanity, insanitary conditions. Although, on the Western Front, lead bullets took the greater toll of deaths, the incidence of disease was Dark Age. In 1918 in France hospital admissions for sickness in the British army were 980,980 (with 8988 deaths).

Disease lessened the army's fighting capability. On average a sick soldier in France–Flanders spent 42.5 days in a base hospital or, put another way, absent from service. For the soldier himself disease was unpleasant, enervating, sapping of morale and sometimes fatal. Disease left Tommy toothless, figuratively and practically.

The men who fought the Great War were frequently lacking teeth. Lieutenant Siegfried Sassoon, before the 'Big Push' of July 1916, worried less about mortality than the irritating mud ('I was always trying to keep squalor at bay, and the discomfort of feeling dirty and tickly all over was almost as bad as the bombardment') and his acute necrotising ulcerative gingivitis. The initial symptom of the disease was painful bleeding gums, the last symptom was loss of teeth. Due to its commonality on the front line acute necrotising ulcerative gingivitis was known simply as 'trench mouth'. Lucky, and rare, was the Tommy free of 'trench mouth', caused by the bacterium *Bacillus fusiformis* and the spirochaete *Borrelia vincenti*.[49] Stressed men were unusually susceptible, and there were plenty of stressed men in the channels and holes of the earth that stretched from Sea to Somme.

When soldier's mouths were not hurting, their feet were. In the winter of 1914 troops began to report that the flesh of their feet was peeling away. The obvious explanation was the waterlogged condition of the trenches; only later did it become apparent that the true causes were fungal infection and, infrequently, gangrene caused by the bacterium *Clostridium perfringens*. 'Trench foot' sent 20,000 troops to hospital that first winter of the long war; in 1917 trench foot still accounted for 3294 admissions to Casualty Clearing Stations on the Western Front. Like trench mouth, trench foot subtly eroded morale.

But nothing in the Colony reduced the soldier's spirit like the insect enemy dressed in grey. Lice were an attack on bodies already worn down by war, and to trenchland tyros they were the unwelcome introduction to personal squalor. Private Henry Gregory of the 119th Machine Gun Company had barely stepped foot in France when he met the body louse:

We got a shock after tea: the 'old sweats' in the hut had their shirts off. They were catching lice, and were all as lousy as cuckoos. We had never seen a louse before, but they were here in droves. The men were killing them between their nails. When they saw us looking at this performance with astonishment, one of the men remarked, 'You will soon be as lousy as we are, Chum!' They spent the better part of an hour in killing lice and scratching themselves.[50]

The four millimetre-long female body louse lays quotidian batches of six or more eggs in the seams of clothing, the choicest sites being the creases at the back of shirts and the seams in the fork of trousers. In evolutionary terms the body louse is a downwards-travelling mutation of the head louse, one which finds the new habit of humans to dress in fur, wool and cotton to its advantage. When hatched the offspring of *Pediculus vestimenti*, looking curiously like miniature scuttling lobsters, feed off the blood of their human host, biting into the skin and causing irritation. Their progress is marked, as well as by red blotches, by a distinctive sour smell.

In the Colony visible lice were known as 'coots', or more commonly as 'chats'. This derived from 'chattel', meaning something which is carried about (soldiers as early as the Napoleonic wars referred to lice as 'chats', although the Hindi word for a parasite, *'chatt'*, is another etymological contender). The Canadians called lice 'seam squirrels'.[51] Companionable talking among Great War soldiers while lice-hunting is the origin of 'chatting', as in neighbourly talking. The eggs or 'nits' of *Pediculus vestimenti* could be killed by running a candle, lighted cigarette or heated bayonet along the seams of shirts and trousers, the incineration of the pests making a satisfying crackling noise. The problem with the running candle method was, as Corporal Arthur Empey put it, 'you are liable to burn holes in the garments if you are not careful'. The ritual of 'Louse Hunting', in all its camaraderie and vulnerability and mania, was painted in verse by Private Isaac Rosenberg:

Nudes – stark and glistening,
Yelling in lurid glee. Grinning faces
And raging limbs
Whirl over the floor on fire.
For a shirt verminously busy
Yon soldier tore from his throat, with oaths
Godhead might shrink at, but not the lice.
And soon the shirt was aflare
Over the candle he'd lit while we lay.
Then we all sprang up and stript
To hunt the verminous brood.
Soon like a demons' pantomime
The place was raging.
See the silhouettes agape,
See the gibbering shadows
Mixed with the battled arms on the wall.
See gargantuan hooked fingers
Pluck in supreme flesh
To smutch supreme littleness.
See the merry limbs in hot Highland fling
Because some wizard vermin
Charmed from the quiet this revel
When our ears were half lulled
By the dark music
Blown from Sleep's trumpet.[52]

'Yon', 'Godhead', 'Smutch': Rosenberg used antique words for an antique practice, the ridding of lice from the human body.

There were other counter-attacks to be made against the body louse, aside from candles and fingernails. Veterans made wooden scratchers, about eighteen inches long and 'rubbed smooth with a bit of stone to prevent splinters'.[53] A good bath brought welcome, if temporary respite, as Lance Corporal Cook, 1/Somerset Light Infantry, discovered after the Mons Retreat of 1914. His 'bath' was a vat in a brewery, with ten men per vat:

> on discarding shirts and boots we clambered up into the vats like a lot of excited kids ... By this time we were a very lousy crowd, the lack of washing facilities had bred lice by the thousand, and the surface of our bath water had a thick scum of these vermin. But we didn't care, we helped scratch each others' backs (which already looked as if a lot of cats had been scratching them) to ease the itching.[54]

Letters home frequently pleaded for a tin of bug-killer. 'Vermijelli', 1/- a tin, was a 'preventative and remedy for lice and fleas' which was mixed with water. The promising-sounding 'Maxem Belt No. 2 or Vermin Destroyer (Medicated)' was worn next to the skin and claimed not only to kill vermin but 'render the wearer immune from further attacks', as well as protecting against chills. Lieutenant Edwin Campion Vaughan, who became infested after sleeping in a former German dugout where the lice dropped on to his face at night, wrote home for 'naptha'; Naphthalene, derived from coal tar, was a Victorian and Edwardian scatter-gun for anything with six legs that crawled, crept or flew. But it was another household favourite, Keating's, made from crushed chrysanthemum (pyrethrum), that was the commonest insecticide dispatched to the boys at the front. Keating's, costing, depending on size, 3d, 6d or 1s a tin, came with a devil on the label and the promise 'EVERY ONE KILLED' of 'Bugs, Fleas, Mosquitoes, Gnats and Beetles'.

In truth, the efficacy of most commercially available insecticides was minimal (Keating's only killed live lice, at best), which was an irritant in itself.[55] Some soldiers swore that insecticides only *attracted* the six-legged enemy. Private Anthony French managed to remain cheerfully louse free for three whole months – until he applied anti-louse ointment:

Almost immediately they found me. They thrived and multiplied and gorged themselves on the pomade, and then turned their attention to me. I was never alone. I became louse-conscious. And I joined my colonel and my comrades in the daily hunting routine.[56]

Arthur Empey confirmed the uselessness of proprietary insecticides:

Recruits generally sent to Blighty for a brand of insect powder advertised as 'Good for body lice.' The advertisement is quite right; the powder is good for 'cooties,' they simply thrive on it.[57]

Officers wore silk pyjamas in the hope that the material was less welcoming to lice. Shorts, apart from giving comfort in summer, reduced lice infestation purely because there was less material for the lice to inhabit.

Lice observed neither rank nor class. Lieutenant John Reginald Reuel Tolkien served as a signals officer in the Lancashire Fusiliers, sharing a dugout with the Reverend Mervyn Myers. According to Myers, he and the future author of *The Lord of the Rings* lay down for a night's sleep only to find 'hordes of lice got up':

So we went round to the Medical Officer, who was also in the dugout with his medical equipment, and he gave us some ointment which he assured us would keep the little brutes away. We anointed ourselves all over with the stuff . . . instead of discouraging them it seemed to act as a sort of hors d'oeuvre and the little beggars went at their feast with renewed vigour.

Corporal Arthur Empey was amused to see his commanding officer writing a letter, but 'every now and then he would lay aside his writing-pad, search his shirt for a few minutes, get an inspiration, and then resume writing'. The letter was to Miss Alice Somebody, in London, the major's sweetheart. 'Just imagine it, writing a love letter during a "cootie" hunt; but such is the creed of the trenches.'

On first contracting lice, Lieutenant Stuart Cloete was embarrassed. Later, he became so desperate for relief from his lice-infested trousers that he bought a pair from a passing artilleryman, and put them on, still warm from the previous wearer. In war, Cloete concluded, one 'loses daintiness'. The public communal louse-hunt was a trial for the sensitive and those of a sheltered upbringing.[58]

It was an offence under army regulations to be lousy. By 1915 there were divisional baths once a fortnight, and while the men bathed their clothes were boiled or passed through 'thresh steam disinfectors' or, late in the war, sterilised in a hot air delouser called 'the Russian Pit'. Hair was cut short, and Driver Rowland Luther was not alone in having his 'cut off by a machine which was used to clip the horses'. Lice, declared Luther, were 'an enemy we could not destroy'.

These official measures were little better than sprinkling with the Keating's sent from home. Private George Ashurst lamented:

the fumigation had killed the lice all right and we had some relief from the itching and scratching, but the seams of our pants and coats still held thousands of lice eggs and we soon discovered that the warmth of our bodies hatched them out again.[59]

In anything approaching an emergency, bathing routines, understandably, went out of the window. Private W.H. Harris RAMC was in the trenches with the 9th Division from the middle of January to 31 March 1918, and thus got caught up in the German Spring Offensive:

I myself had only left the trenches once in that time, March 11th, for a few hours for a bath, and had only had too [sic] changes of underclothing. All our spare time was taken up 'chatting'. They grew as fast as we could kill them, and by the time we'd gone over all our clothes once it was time to start again.[60]

For Driver J. Reynolds RE it was the very routine of war which made him lousy; he was attached to a Guards unit that 'went in for

the regimental biz' of spit and polish, and his horses and their tack
needed to gleam as bright as mirrors:

> Then every man's shirt walked, for the simple reason no one had
> time to wash his personal kit after spending hours on his harness
> and brasses and attending innumerable parades.

Men cramped together in a trench, lying body-by-body in a dugout
while unable to wash, made ideal conditions for lice infestation. The
egg to egg cycle could be as little as sixteen days. And so, men were
lousy, all the time. When one unit checked the shirts of its soldiers,
only 4.9 per cent were louse free.[61] The old sweats who had informed
Private Henry Gregory he too would soon be running with lice did
not lie. He spent an hour a day lice-hunting: 'Every day brought a
new batch; as fast as you killed them, others took their place.'

In his year of service for His Majesty, Private Frederick Hodges
noted: 'I do not think I was ever entirely free from lice, and I found
this a great trial. On more than one occasion I rubbed the skin of
my legs just below the knees until I was sore and bleeding, and then
I had to ask the corporal at the First Aid Post to treat them.'[62] Men
could become so sensitised that they could feel each louse, each bite.
Lice drove men into a frenzy, especially when it was time to sleep. As
Private J.M. Harkins of the Australian Infantry Force versed in 'The
Chat's Parade':

> When the soldier, fagged and weary,
> In surroundings that are dreary,
> Aside lays he his rifle and grenade,
> Seeks solace in forgetful slumber,
> From shell-crash and battle's thunder,
> 'Tis then the 'chats' are mustered for parade.
> At the double about his back
> In a most irregular track
> They make for the parade-ground on his spine.

When there they will never keep still,
Undisciplined they stamp at will,
And up and down they march in ragged line.
Round his ribs they do manoeuvre,
Curses issue from the soldier,
There's divisions by the score, he declares,
Doing artillery formation
Without his approbation,
He wriggles and he twists and loudly swears.
Through long, dark night they carry on,
At the charges they become tres bien,
The soldier to disperse them madly tears
With savage fingers at his skin,
As he prays for the morning glim,
In darkness, though, the victory is theirs.[63]

Harkins signed off his poem with a couplet matching the crimes of the lice with those of the Germans: 'They are almost like the Hun/ Their foul deeds are performed behind the back.'

Lice were a fact of war far beyond the Western Front. Harkins's fellow Australian poetaster Lance Corporal T.A. Saxon fought at Gallipoli, where:

It ain't the work and it ain't the Turk
        That causes us to swear,
But it's havin' to fight at dark midnight
        With the things in our underwear.
To-day there's a score – tomorrow lots more
        Of these rotters – it ain't too nice
To sit skin-bare in keen morning air
        Lookin' for bloomin' –

They're black an' grey an' brindle an' white,
        An' red an' big an' small,

They steeplechase around our knees –
    We cannot sleep at all! –
They're in our tunics, and in our shirts,
    They take a power of beating,
So for goodness sake, if you're sending us cake,
    Send also a tin of Keating.[64]

Lice undermined the wholesome sense of self, because lice made men feel dirty; lice were the prerogative pest of the tramp and the slum-dweller. For a 'respectable' man of the working, middle or upper classes to find the little grey legion upon him was simultaneously to be unclean and de-classed. ('Lousy' as a figurative for 'bad' or 'dirty' had been around since medieval times.) The new Georgian age was a time when godliness was next to cleanliness. Lice bit at the mind. Lieutenant Alec Waugh, brother of the more famous Evelyn, who served as a Royal Artillery officer at Passchendaele, considered that 'there are few conditions that demoralize one more than being verminous with lice'.

Lice were more than inconveniences affecting dignity and spirit. In the unsanitary trenches, scratching at affected areas risked disease.

*

In mid 1915, physicians in the British Expeditionary Force in France and Flanders began to notice an unusual feverish sickness among the troops. Major J.H.P. Graham of the RAMC recorded in 'A Note on a Relapsing Febrile Illness of Unknown Origin' in September that:

> A private belonging to an infantry regiment was admitted to a casualty-clearing station from a field ambulance where he had been detained suffering from a febrile illness of three days' duration and of sudden onset.

The symptoms of the condition were unlike anything Graham had previously encountered:

*Top* The power of nature to reclaim. The battlefield of Contalmaison, Somme, today. British soldiers considered the Somme to be heaven on earth.
*Above* Men called it Hell. The devastation of nature at Passchendaele, 1917.

British Cavalry Scout, Flanders, 1914. The horses were there at the beginning, and at the end. The last British action on the Western Front was a cavalry dash on 11 November 1918.

Britain's secret weapon was never the tank – it was the mule. A mule team struggles through mud, Potijze Farm.

GOLDEN ORIOLE.

*Clockwise from top left* The (much-loved) goat mascot of a Royal Garrison Artillery battery, Pilckem Ridge, 1917; a golden oriole, the holy grail of bird-watching on the Western Front; Red Cross nurses with cages of canaries on a British ambulance train near Doullens – the canaries were kept to cheer up the wounded; loot as good as gold – a British soldier with a cage of canaries salvaged from a ruined house in St Venant, 15 April 1918.

A messenger dog, the fighting man's best friend on the Western Front.

Swords into ploughshares, battlefields into gardens. A soldier of the Directorate of Agricultural Production tends celery in the bottom of an old communication trench, Vimy Ridge, 1918.

A vet tends a wounded British horse hit by shrapnel. Between 1914–18 Army Veterinary Corps hospitals received 725,216 horses and successfully treated three-quarters of them.

A billet flower garden, Proven, Flanders, 1917.

Cats had numerous occupational lives on the Western Front: mouser, gas-detector and, as with this gunner officer, companion to humans.

RFC personnel with their pet rabbits, Western Front.

Feeding time for 'Dulcie', the pet duck of an officer of the Royal Field Regiment, Salonika. Dulcie lived in the barrel by the entrance to the dugout.

Sport in self-defence. British soldiers go ratting in the trenches with the aid of bayonets and a terrier.

'Serve to lead', the ethos of the British Army 1914–18 in a single snap. A British officer gives his dog a lift on his horse on the Amiens–Albert road, 25 August 1916.

A-hunting-we-will-go. Army officers chasing partridges near the frontline, France, c. 1915.

Gone fishing. Two Tommies try their luck with rods made from sticks at Aveluy, the Somme, August 1916.

Commonwealth cemeteries on the Somme, architected to be English gardens and parks of remembrance abroad. The dead are not buried in France; they lie in English scenes.

the patient's condition on admission was marked by frontal head-
ache, dizziness, severe lumbago, a feeling of stiffness down the
front of the thighs, and severe pains in the legs referred chiefly to
the shins.[65]

By 1916 cases of the new disease, termed 'pyrexia of unknown origin'
(PUO) by the medical profession and, with all the acuity of first-hand
experience, 'trench fever' by the troops, reached epidemic proportions; between 1915 and 1918 some 520,000 British troops contracted
trench fever. Rarely, if ever, did trench fever kill, but commonly it
incapacitated; it also blocked up to 10 per cent of the beds in military
hospitals in the Colony. The fever was at its worst for five days (hence
'five-day fever' being another of its common names), and a minority
of patients recovered immediately following the medical officer's
standard prescription of 'M & D' (the Medicine of a No. 9 laxative
pill, and Duty), but around 80 per cent of the infected were ill for up
to three months.

A significant number of soldiers were so chronically affected by
the disease that they became long-term casualties, among them the
twenty-four-year-old Second Lieutenant J.R.R. Tolkien, the battalion
signalling officer with 11/Lancashire Fusiliers during the battle of the
Somme. In and out of the trenches for three months, Tolkien saw
war's extremes: the resilience of the ordinary British soldier – the
inspiration for Samwise Gamgee in *The Lord of the Rings* – and the
grimness of a battlefield fought over for three months. By rainy October, when 11/Lancashires were sent to Ypres, corpses were afloat in
shell holes. (In *Lord of the Rings* Tolkien has Frodo Baggins recount a
scene straight out of the Somme: 'They lie in all the pools, pale faces,
deep deep under the dark water. I saw them: grim faces and evil, and
noble faces and sad. Many faces proud and fair, and weeds in their
silver hair. But all foul, all rotting, all dead.') Taken ill with 'PUO' on
27 October 1916 at Beauval, Tolkien was hospitalised at Le Touquet,
before being repatriated to Birmingham University's wartime hospital. Tolkien was never fit for front line service again and spent the rest

of the war either convalescing or on garrison duties before eventually being discharged as unfit for military service. It was during his spells in hospital that Tolkien began writing the Middle Earth fairy stories which would eventually become *The Hobbit*, *The Lord of the Rings* and *Silmarillion*.

With soldiers dropping ill by the thousand, the government set up no less than two committees to investigate trench fever and advise on remedies: the British Expeditionary Force Pyrexia of Unknown Origin Enquiry and the War Office Trench Fever Investigation Commission. As a result of the WO Commission's research *Rickettsia*, a small bacterium carried by the body louse, was eventually identified as the vector for trench fever. Infection was conveyed by the bite of the louse, or more usually by the rubbing of infected louse excreta into scratched skin. Under War Office sponsorship the entomologist A.W. Bacot at the Lister Institute developed, in 1918, the only really effective insecticide against lice, a paste of NCI (naphthalene 96 per cent, creosote 2 per cent, iodoform 2 per cent) which when spread on the seams of tunics killed lice within two hours.

More effective even than Bacot's paste in reducing trench fever was peace. With war's end, there were no more trenches. Trench fever all but disappeared in 1918.

But the body louse is the vector of more human diseases than trench fever; it is also the agent of relapsing fever and endemic typhus (caused by *Rickettsia prowazekii*). Typhus is on an altogether different register of deadliness to trench fever and relapsing fever. Fortunately, if mysteriously, typhus never took a grip on the Western Front. Typhus did, however, kill a hundred or so British prisoners of war held by the Germans, after they became infected with *Rickettsia prowazekii* carried by the body lice on fellow Russian PoWs. Sanitation in the Kaiser's PoW camps could be cruelly lacking; at Wittenberg Lager, which covered ten and a half acres on the bleak Klein Wittenberg plain, there were ten thousand prisoners, two taps and no soap. The inevitable happened; on Christmas Eve 1914 men started dying from typhus. Instead of devoting proper medical services, the

Germans abandoned the camp leaving the inmates to perish. Only when the '*Fleckfieber*' epidemic had been running amok for over a month did the German authorities bow to international pressure and allow in six British RAMC doctors, along with a number of doctors from other nationalities. According to the subsequent report by the British government entitled, aptly enough, 'The Horrors of Wittenberg', one of the doctors, Major Priestly, entered a wooden barracks hut and 'in the half-light he attempted to brush what he took to be an accumulation of dust from the folds of a patient's clothes, and he discovered it to be a moving mass of lice'.[66]

The camp authorities refused point blank the British request to be housed separately to prevent the spread of disease from the Russians. Effectively this was a death sentence for British, French and Belgian PoWs because the Russians had a level of immunity against typhus from childhood.[67] Only through tireless work and incessant seeking of supplies did the British doctors, aided by fifty volunteers from among the prisoners, eventually triumph over the disease, with cases dwindling to zero in late July 1915. By then 185 PoWs had died, 60 of them British. The British fatalities included three of the six RAMC doctors along with ten of the volunteers. The British Government Committee on the Treatment by the Enemy of British Prisoners of War was moved to write about the dead volunteers of Wittenberg:

> The Committee feel that every one of these officers and men has truly offered his life for the sake of others as any soldiers on the battlefield . . .[68]

Although Wittenberg caught the attention of the British public, typhus smote at least thirty other major German PoW camps between December 1914 and July 1915, including Gardelegen, Kassel (7000 cases), Cottbus (1765) and Schneidemühl (where every British prisoner except eleven was hospitalised). In the whole epidemic 44,732 PoWs in Germany caught typhus.

Typhus was virulent and habitual in Eastern Europe, but an epidemic in 1915 took on the scale and looks of the Black Death. At the start of the First World War Serbia numbered some three million people. Six months later, one in six Serbs – amounting to 500,000 people – had contracted typhus, and the mortality rate in some districts reached 70 per cent. Over 200,000 Serbs, 70,000 of them soldiers, died from the disease. The Serbs were unable to cope; Serbia had few doctors (400 for the entire country) and few hospitals. The country collapsed, and presented easy pickings for the Central Powers. But they could not enter the country because of the typhus epidemic.

Of all strange turnarounds, it was 'General Typhus' who held the line in Serbia.

*

The warming of the earth in spring on the Western Front brought the curse of flies.

For Lieutenant Will Harvey of the Gloucestershire Regiment, flies were the devil's work, just as they were in the Old Testament, where Beelzebub is the lord of the flies. Harvey considered the flies of the front worthy of a hate poem, 'Ballade of Beelzebub, God of Flies':

> Some men there are will not abide a rat
> Within their bivvy. If one chance to peep
> At them through little beady eyes, then pat,
> They throw a boot and rouse a mate from sleep
> To hunt the thing, and on its head they heap
> Curses quite inappropriate to its size.
> I care for none of these, but broad and deep
> I curse Beelzebub – the God of Flies . . .

In trenches near Ypres with 1/9th London Regiment (Queen Victoria Rifles), Captain Eliot Crawshay-Williams spent some idle hours pondering the soldier's eternal question: which of all the nuisances of the front was the worst?

Certainly one of the chief terrors of the Front is the flies. It is a question which is the worse the sudden pang of a bullet, and the torment of a wound, or the everlasting torture of a fly-ridden life. Surely something could be done, and ought to be. Unfortunately, there is no doubt where the flies that infest our food and crawl over our faces have been, and the horror of these fat and obscene creatures is a very real one.[69]

It was the buzzing of the flies that did for Lieutenant Lawrence Gameson, 45th Field Ambulance RAMC:

They swarm upon food, they buzz. Night and day this room resounds with their buzzing. The drone becomes a background, it even steals into one's sleep.

Dugouts in summer could swarm with thousands of 'fat and obscene' flies. (Flies, like rats, in the estimation of the British soldier, were always big, never small.) What produced revulsion was the knowledge of where the flies had hitherto been feasting. Francis Hitchcock considered the 'horrors' of the Somme to be 'colossal shell-fire', 'maddening thirst', 'lack of sleep', the 'heat of the days', 'the intense cold at night' and 'the enormous blue-black flies. How they crawled into one's food after they had been settling on some exposed piece of human mortality lying on No-Man's Land.' The flies in Gameson's dugout were so numerous that, 'This evening I killed fourteen flies with one swipe with a rolled-up copy of an ancient Times . . .' He added:

The neighbourhood is an incubator for them. Eggs are laid in corpses of Germans and horses, hatching in the rotting semi-liquid flesh . . .[70]

Flies were hated too because they attacked the notion of the honourable battlefield death. No soldier, if he fell, wanted to think of himself as a fly-covered unretrieved corpse, maggots coming out of the eye sockets. As carrion. 'There is none of the dignity of death – the flies and rats see to that,' Chaplain Cyril Lomax, 8/Durham Light Infantry, wrote to his family. Despite the horror, Lomax never doubted the goodness of God, or the durability of the DLI.

There was an official campaign, of sorts, against the flies of Flanders and the Somme. Wires dipped in a sugary, sticky solution were hung in cookhouses, and when coated black with flies were burned, then redipped and hung. 'It was a form of fly-paper without the paper,' remarked Lieutenant James McQueen, Sanitary Officer, 51st Division.[71] Meat safes, boxes with zinc mesh sides, played a prominent role, and were meant to stay in camp. According to McQueen, so popular were meat safes:

> that it would be more correct to say that in modern warfare battalions marched out of camp not with banners flying but with meat safes concealed, for there was a constant loss of these safes, which had to be replaced as they were stolen by units on the move.

Flies were a particularly unpleasant feature of the Gallipoli campaign. Trooper I.L. Idriess of the 5th Australian Light Horse was overwhelmed by flies immediately he opened a tin of jam:

> I wrapped my overcoat over the tin and gouged out the flies, then spread the biscuit, held my hand over it, and drew the biscuit out of the coat. But a lot of flies flew into my mouth and beat about inside ... I nearly howled with rage ... of all the bastard places this is the greatest bastard in the world.[72]

Gunner A.F. Hibbert, Royal East Kent Mounted Rifles, also found flies to be an inadvertent and disgusting addition to the Gallipoli menu:

After coming out of the trenches at night my comrade and myself went to the cookhouse and enjoyed a feed of which we thought was rice and currants, the next morning we were told by the cook it was plain rice & the lid had been left off the Dixie the feed, therefore, was rice and flies.

After complaining about the flies of France, Captain Eliot Crawshay-Williams on landing in Egypt with his new regiment, the Royal Horse Artillery, found the 'plagues' there infinitely worse. The flies drove him to something like madness, as is apparent from his missives home:

I have not yet touched on one element which, literally, enters into all our meals. I mean the flies . . . I can scarcely trust myself to write about the flies. One tends to lose control. I have seen men almost go off their heads under the actual infliction of flies. I have heard them address the flies with a concentrated fury of hatred and disgust of which I had never suspected them capable. I have seen others gradually, day by day, give up the struggle and resign themselves to be crawled on. I have felt myself that, if I had an enemy deserving of the uttermost agony and torture, I would desire him to be cursed with flies. And the most horrible, the most maddening part of it is that all the time you hate, and loathe, and rave, the flies are not only generally immune, but also serenely unconscious and uncaring. You cannot communicate your feelings to the fly. Even if you kill it, blasting it with curses as you do so, it merely perishes an innocent and surprised victim of an unknown sudden doom. There is no sense of sin, of just retribution, of defeat. And there are millions more.[73]

As it was in Egypt, Gallipoli and the Western Front, so it was in Mesopotamia, where the flies played a loathsome role in spreading disease. Born in Burma in 1874, Gustavus Perreau was a career soldier (and amateur naturalist) serving with the 2/4th Gurkha

Rifles in Mesopotamia. He informed his 'Dear Old Mater' that:

> Flies are simply appalling, almost impossible to eat, each morsel
> was black at once. They're baddish now as a nuisance and
> tickly ... I was skinning a bird, and bird and hands were black,
> felt like tepid water being poured gently over one's hands and
> face ...

There were also mosquitoes, sandflies ('awful') and locusts ('a beastly
nuisance') and ants. 'It was most annoying,' wrote Perreau, 'to hastily
shove onto a damp skin a shirt simply swarming with minute red or
blackish ants (skin always damp except in sun or wind) which bite
far worse than big ants.'

The heat was 121 degrees Fahrenheit. The battalion was awaiting
action, and action would at least have taken the mind off the heat and
the insectoid torments. As the battalion camped in the sandy, stifling
desert it dissolved into disease. In a letter of July 1916 Perreau reports
on the health of the battalion officers; it is a roll call of sickness. 'Col
Hutchie and myself are really about the fittest of our lot and he gets
occasional bad goes of pneuralgia [sic] and his tummy is practically
permanently out of order.' Bill Kingsley, the adjutant, 'had had a
good deal of fever and tummy troubles'; Denys 'has been convalescing about a month'; Barrowman 'has been sick a good deal'; 'Thomas
a stout lad to look at joined us from Quetta as a war baby has just
been returned (sick) to India'; Wilson 'Has had quite a lot of fever but
he takes it well (has had more since)'; Nye 'previously in a bank, very
good chap, been keeping fairly fit bar boils, got jaundice'; Robson,
'our doctor, a rotter of the worst, has just gone off sick'; Walton, 'another war baby (Sandhurst) a bit of a knut and pretty young, of real
good stuff when you get at it. Is now away for a change, got boily and
run down'; Dewar was 'mostly sick'.

Perreau added, 'I should not call this country a health resort.'
Tents, he explained to the Mater, gave some protection from the
wind, sand and sun but were unbearably humid 'and one sweats and

sweats'. He signed off, sorry for harping on this unsavoury subject 'but it obtrudes itself'.

In his next letter home, written a fortnight later, he reported that: 'Massy and Wilson have gone to Amara sick, fever and dysentery.' Perreau himself had sores, though 'really sores don't count'. He told his mother not to worry about cholera, despite the fact 'our Brigadier died of it the day before I joined', which was unlikely to assuage her worries. As for his own relative hale and heartiness, he attributed it to drinking a bottle of beer per night; 'all the beer drinkers seem to be keeping pretty fit'.[74]

\*

Like lice, mosquitoes seemed to benefit from chemical measures intended to eradicate. On the Somme near Morlancourt, Private Norman Ellison noted in his diary:

> The mosquitoes ('skeeters') here are persistent devils; they positively thrive on anti-fly creams and such things. Our faces are swollen with bites, we can scarcely recognise each other.[75]

Private G.W. Broadhead, an orderly with 18th Battalion West Yorkshire Regiment[76] at Givenchy, noted in his diary on 19 September 1916:

> Trenches. Very heavy strafing to our left just on the ridge but fairly quiet in our sector. Usual worry with mosquitoes.

Lieutenant George Scott Atkinson was, in his words, 'tortured to death in the evening by mosquitoes . . . after dusk they fed on us in millions – there is no respite, you grow tired of killing them and dawn finds you on the edge of insanity, swollen like a long-dead mule. It is these things which constitute the horror of war – death is nothing.'[77] Flies annoyed, but female (principally) mosquitoes bit, inserting a serrated proboscis into the skin; enzymes in the mosquitoes' saliva cause the human body to produce histamine, resulting in weals and swelling.

In spring and summer, there was little relief from the whining, biting mosquitoes. Since the female mosquitoes tracked their human prey by smell, as well as sight, even going underground provided no relief. In the Ypres Salient, Lieutenant C.P. Blacker recalled:

> The dug-outs and cellars in which we messed and slept were heavily infested by mosquitoes which bred freely in the damp ground . . . When your platoon lined up in the dark their faces were blotched and swollen by insect bites. I have a mental picture of CSM Luck appearing on parade one evening scarcely recognisable. Both his eyes were closed and his temper was atrocious.[78]

The Ypres Salient was wonderful for mosquitoes, as were the watery margins of the Somme river and the Ancre, not omitting the Yser *marais*, near Saint Georges, where Lieutenant Charles Douie was posted in 1918:

> My wrists, for which the mosquitoes had a particular predilection, were so covered by bites that they became swollen and shapeless. The immediate result was to reduce my vitality and to make me easily tired.[79]

At the end of a march he collapsed. His morale remained standing, as did that of his Dorset fellows. Regardless of the 'failure of the 1917 offensive and another winter in Flanders', when a dangerous enterprise was planned 'every subaltern in the regiment submitted an application to be placed in charge of' it. The successful applicant pulled a technical detail to achieve the honour:

> His claim was upheld, but he became the object of as much dislike on the part of the other subalterns as if he had cheated at cards.

On the Western Front mosquito bites were irritating, perhaps temporarily disfiguring, and certainly no aid to patience. There were some limited outbreaks of malaria – of which the mosquito genus Anopheles is the vector – in France and Flanders during 1914–18, but these were, the medical experts postulated, introduced malaria, courtesy of the movement of troops there from malarial colonial countries in Africa and Asia. For once modern warfare worked in the soldiers' favour; the ground of the Western Front was so torn up and 'sterilised' by munitions and poisonous gases that potential breeding places for Anopheles were destroyed.

In other theatres, the malaria-spreading mosquito caused havoc. In 1917 malaria rates per 1000 of strength on the Western Front were 0.48 – in Macedonia (Salonika) they were 353.18, in Mesopotamia 94.20, in Egypt 94.20 and in East Africa an apocalyptic 2880.9, meaning that individual patients were readmitted several times per year.

Over 160,000 British soldiers were hospitalised with malaria. Two million man days were lost to the British army because of the disease. Even the aridity of official documents moistened into sympathy when discussing the plague that was malaria. The War Office's *Statistics of the Military Effort of the British Empire during the Great War 1914–1920* declared:

> Our forces at Salonica have consequently suffered greatly, both from malaria and the tedium of monotonous and uncomfortable surroundings, where billets are unknown, amusements few and leave rare.[80]

The *basic* malaria rate in Salonika was 325 per 1000. Of the 300,000 British troops in Salonika in 1917, around 120,000 (40 per cent) became unfit for service due to malaria.

And malaria killed. There were 693 malaria fatalities at Salonika, known to all British troops who served there as 'The Bird Cage', which was generously surrounded with lakes and marshes. One French general in Macedonia, with 80 per cent of men struck by malaria, telegrammed his superiors: 'Regret that my army is in hospital with malaria.' Desperate British soldiers resorted to primitive anti-malarial measures, beating the air with leafy branches in an attempt to reduce the swarms of mosquitoes. Effectively, on the Macedonian front from 1916–19 both the Allied and belligerent armies were im-mobilised by the disease.

Although the British army and its allies only occupied the Gal-lipoli peninsula for nine months, this coincided lucklessly with the entire 1915 malarial season. Of the 480,000 Allied troops on Gallipoli, 90,000 were evacuated due to sickness, many because of malaria.[81] In Palestine, by the end of 1918, half of the Australian-led Desert Mounted Corps were incapacitated with malaria and a hundred died. Malaria was a permanent scourge of Mesopotamia, the land between the rivers. As for sub-Saharan Africa, it lived up to its reputation as 'The White Man's Grave'. In the forests and savannah, malaria trans-mission occurred throughout the year. The disease-wracked white British became increasingly dependent on black soldiers and porters, who were, by and large, immune to malaria. In East Africa alone the British employed over a million porters.[82] In the jungle of East Africa black troops were particularly heavily committed, and in this 'side-show' diseases were diabolical. The troop returns of the Gold Coast Regiment make sobering reading. From a force 3800 strong 215 died in action, whereas 270 died from disease. A further 567 men were invalided out of service because of disease. Of the 105,000 who died in East Africa the majority did so from disease. As one NCO put it pithily, the war in East Africa involved having to fight nature in a mood 'that very few have experienced and will scarcely believe.' One young British Caucasian officer, well versed in the horror of trench warfare on the Western Front before being transferred to the dark continent, was equally concise. 'I would rather be in France than here,' sighed Lieutenant Lewis.[83]

Malaria and the British army were old familiars. Indeed, the role of Anopheles mosquitoes in transmitting malaria had been discov-ered by a British army surgeon, Ronald Ross, working in Calcutta, India in 1897. Quinine, a crystalline extract obtained from the South

American cinchona tree, was an effective anti-malarial drug, usually taken daily dissolved in gin. Army officers got so used to the astringent taste of their daily prophylactic dose of quinine dissolved in gin that they replicated the taste by adding quinine to soda water when social drinking – hence gin and tonic. During the Great War British troops in malarious countries were dispensed 300mg of quinine per day. The great problem for the Germans was obtaining quinine, since the Cinchona tree is mainly limited to South America, the Dutch East Indies, India and East Africa, all Allied-controlled areas. Faced with this supply problem, the German East African army synthesised its own quinine at its Research Institute at Amani in northern Tanganyika. One of the reasons for the supremacy of the German pharmaceutical industry post-war was that necessity in wartime forced it to be inventive.

Malaria never won or lost a theatre of war. But in East Africa, Mesopotamia and Salonika it lengthened the casualty list, and consequently lengthened the campaign and the misery of fighting it.

There was no end to the insects and creepy crawlies of trenchworld. 'Funk holes' or dugouts were lairs for spiders, which made them places of dread for arachnophobes like Signaller Cyril Newman. 'There is a nasty, black, jumping tribe of spiders – I kill any who come near me', he informed the folks at home.[84] Neither did his tolerance extend to other things 'with umptun legs', notably the ants which crawled all over him, all the time. But he did take pity on a large green beetle which kept falling while attempting to scale the trench side; he enticed it on to an envelope, then helped it go over the top. The self-identification was obvious. Naturally, wee beasties were bigger and badder in Africa and the Middle East. Lieutenant-Colonel Perreau found 'a loathsome huge spider' inside the anti-mosquito curtains of his cot in Mesopotamia late one night: 'And I hate spiders.' Then he realised the spider 'really gorged himself' on flies, so Perreau decided to adopt a benign live-and-let-live approach, and refrained from slaying.

Sleeping bags were infamous for breeding fleas, so infamous indeed that in trench argot they became 'flea bags'. All bedding seemed a magnet for unpleasurable company. On putting his hand into his valise in Mesopotamia to get some kit Lieutenant Birkett Barker unveiled 'a small viper's head'. With the sanguinity of the time-served, he observed: ' It is perhaps just as well I had decided not to sleep on my valise tonight.'[85] Any soldier south of the Somme who failed to check sleeping quarters or boots for scorpions was simply asking for trouble.

Some of the insect annoyances of the front line were oddly wondrous. Major Ynyr Probert was the son of Mary Badcock, the little girl whose photograph Lewis Carroll and John Tenniel took as their inspiration for the original illustrations of *Alice in Wonderland*. In the lead up to the Somme, Probert recorded in his diary a troubling danger: 'One of the hazards of returning from the Observation Post in the evenings walking across the open was the crowd of heavy, noisy Maybugs which lived in the oak woods. They struck with considerable force, necessitating carrying something like your tin hat in front of your face.'[86] Maybugs are flying beetles, which can reach up to twenty miles an hour. Polished, brown, they look like small chips off an inlaid mahogany table.

Probert encountered the Maybugs around May 1916. Five weeks later he was dodging bullets. Despite wounds of a severity no Maybug could inflict he survived the Somme to win an MC on the Hindenburg Line in 1918.

There were still more insect species on the Somme able to make an aerial attack. At Beaumont Hamel the date for Edmund Blunden's battalion of the Suffolks to go over the top had been changed, yet they still took fire. Resting in a wood, the battalion dug trenches:

These, however, could not protect us from a plague of wasps, and the engineers had to add to their varied service that of clearing some monstrous nests with gun cotton![87]

Meals and drinks in the trenches always seemed to come with added insect protein. There were flies in water, as well as soup. Most smaller insect fry, explained Lieutenant Kenneth Blair, were ignored and one 'just boils it up with the tea and swallows the lot'.

Only an entomologist like Blair, though, could get excited about large fry in the provisions:

> Cooking occupies a good deal of one's off time, as all water has to be boiled before it is safe to drink it. It may be taken from the pump of some ruined farm near the lines, often approachable only by night, or more often it is from some shell hole. Yesterday I nearly got a fine female of Dytiscus marginalis [Great Diving Beetle] in my canteen for tea.[88]

One man's beastie is another man's beauty. In the Vardar sector of Macedonia, Lieutenant Amos, taking an al fresco bath, was caused 'no little anxiety' by a swarm of bees. The rest of the mess, recalled Lieutenant Birkett Barker, sensing the opportunity of improving the larder, grabbed shell-fuse boxes to 'make a rough hive' and captured the swarm.[89] Glow worms were universal objects of wonderment, although stories that Tommies gathered them and used them as lanterns are apocryphal. One comedic Tommy did try to recruit a glow worm as a 'lucifer', or match, as Lance Corporal R.M. Kirke jotted in his diary on 24 September 1914:

> One of our Tommies being without a light and being unable to procure one, picked up a glow worm and placed it upon his pipe with the remark 'I'll get a light somehow'.[90]

And everybody enjoyed the butterflies, a species which flourished amid the uncut weeds, crops, and flowers of no man's land. One soldier, Captain W. Bowater, wrote home in the summer of 1917:

The crops here are barbed wire, thistles and nettles; I don't know what the first produces, but the last two have brought out great lots of painted ladies, red admirals, peacocks, and a positive swarm of small tortoise-shells.[91]

Captain W. Bowater was elected a Fellow of the Entomological Society in 1913, the year he turned thirty-three. Born in Birmingham, he had qualified in both medicine and dentistry, and during the First World War he served in the RAMC in France and Italy, commanded 143rd Field Ambulance and was awarded the MC and bar. On departing for war he left his wife Irene in charge of his original research into Mendelism, which resulted in the hybrid moth which bears his name.

All the kit and caboodle associated with butterfly collecting – the long nets, the killing jars, the setting boards – made collecting on the front impossible, but Bowater, in his own words:

kept an eye open for Lepidoptera whenever possible; although when out of doors, I was usually riding a horse or in an ambulance car.

Insects flying, or at rest, or larvae, to be noticed under these circumstances must be fairly prominent, so that although I can record no varieties, I desire to testify how valuable to me an interest in Lepidoptera has been, especially when feeling the need for something on which the mind could dwell, exactly opposite to war and its horrors.[92]

Butterflies, so closely associated in the British mind with sunny days in gardens, were a beautiful divertissement from war. They offered a touch of Heaven in Hell. Bowater was lucid on the benefit of 'good' nature in war:

Thus, on a certain rather trying occasion, when all that could be done was 'to stand and wait,' the flight of Limenitis Sibylla (a fresh experience for me) served admirably to please the eye and calm the thoughts.

*Limenitis sibylla* is the White Admiral, a woodland dweller, velvet black with white bars, and among the handsomest of butterflies. Such relief provided by nature was ongoing, a drip, drip of honey. Bowater:

> Again after many hours of continuous work, the dashing arrival of Cosmotriche potatoria [Drinker moth] at the lamp made a moment's distraction, and reminded one that there were other better things on earth than man slaughtering man, so graphically typified by the brave fellows filing through the dressing station.

On another occasion:

> I have seen the lordly Apatura iris [Purple emperor] in flight here, a pleasure denied to me in England.

Entomologists were never bored in war. How could they be? Flying things and creepy crawlies were ubiquitous. Billeted in a Somme house which 'enjoyed out of doors temperature, as it lacked furniture, windows and window frames', Captain Bowater found among the internal bareness three hibernating small tortoiseshells: 'I noted that they moved their position slightly twice during this period.' He managed to reach and secure, with the aid of a packing case and a rifle fixed with a bayonet the chrysalis of a herald moth. One small tortoiseshell hibernating on the stairs had to 'be listed as "accidentally killed" by a despatch rider who leant against the banister'.

The charm of butterflies and insects extended to the magazines which featured them. Captain Bowater wrote to *The Entomologist's Record*:

> Finally, what a welcome sight the entomological magazines afforded! In what curious scenes and abodes have their leaves been

scanned by some of their readers in the years 1914–16 of the Christian era!![93]

In the 'entomological magazines' a certain pride in the resolution of the bug-men under fire, as scientists and as soldiers, is detectable. The 'Current Notes' of *The Entomologist's Record* 1915 declared that 'the staff of the Entomology Department S. Kensington is well to the fore in this mighty struggle'; the same magazine reported in 1916 a minute from the 2 February meeting of the South London Entomological Society:

Ants from the Front. – Mr. Donisthorpe exhibited two ants taken at the front – *Myrmica rugulosa*, Nyl., fem, taken by Mons. Bondroit at Ramscapelle (Yser), December 14th, and *Messor barbara* var., winged Fem. taken in the fire trenches at Gallipoli on December 21st, 1915, by Lieutenant Noel S. Sennett.

Another butterfly man at Gallipoli was Private Denis Buxton RAMC, whose diary vividly evokes the days of butterflies and bullets in a great land for lepidoptera.

2 June: Below me the Indians are washing (themselves, each other, and their turbans and shirts). A female Greyling appeared, and I caught the Sibylla in my helmet, a great triumph. Someone also found a large Hawk. M. Carva Euphorniae I imagine, as it seems to like a rank kind of spurge. One female Janira (fresh).

7 June: Last night we were again shelled from Asia: one of our Drivers was hit in the jaw ... The Gully was full of butterflies. V. Atalanta common. Cardui. Brassicae. Semele (Greyling). One Marbled White. The usual Thecla. Lycaenids. Limenitis Sibylla. One male 'janira'. Edusa common.

18 June: I saw a large and quite strange butterfly today in our dusty camp, stopping to drink where some water had been spilt. It seemed like L. Sibylla, though bigger and browner: and

underneath sandy brown with a darker bar across H-W.

20 June: I had one entomological expedition into the middle of the land we occupy. The land near the ASC Bakery (Between Cape Tekeh and X Beach) was dusty and covered with various prickly plants. There were a few Edusa, Belia, etc, and some young Wheatears just hatched in a trench. From there we turned to the Right on to scrub, and found Cardui (females) common on scabious, and a few 'Janira' and 'megaera' (both these are greyer on H-W underside than English), and also a 'Blue', some rather small 'Treble Bars' and a few 'Tros Incognitus' which I find is a very highly coloured *greyling*; in some cases the black band on the h-w underside is reduced or absent.[94]

Some days, Buxton noted, the sun was 'too hot for most butterflies'. There were days too when the war at Gallipoli was too hot for men.

# Interstice 4
## The Statistics of Disease

**Admissions to British army hospitals:**
**Proportion of wounded to sick in certain years**

| | WOUNDED | | SICKNESS | |
|---|---|---|---|---|
| | Total admissions | Total deaths (incl. killed) | Total admissions | Total deaths |
| France, 1918 | 574,803 | 46,084 | 980,980 | 8,988 |
| Egypt and Palestine, 1917–1918 | 32,255 | 9,451 | 359,855 | 3,360 |
| Macedonia, 1917–1918 | 12,552 | 2,843 | 331,753 | 3,031 |
| Italy, 1918 | 4,671 | 470 | 54,626 | 661 |
| Mesopotamia, 1916–1918 (white troops only) | 16,793 | 6,752 | 242,159 | 2,752 |

The figures show that admissions for disease in other theatres than France were 14.6 times as numerous as those for wounds (988,393: 66,271), while even in France, where the rate of fighting and profusion of weapons was greatest, admissions for disease were still the more numerous.

## Admissions to British army hospitals for enteric, dysentery, malaria, nephritis in the main theatres, 1915–18

| RATES PER 1,000 OF STRENGHT | FRANCE | ITALY | MACEDONIA | EGYPT & PALESTINE | MESOPO-TAMIA | EAST AFRICA |
|---|---|---|---|---|---|---|
| ENTERIC | | | | | | |
| 1915 | 3.1 | / | / | / | / | / |
| 1916 | 2.3 | / | 6.3 | 14.2 | 54.4 | / |
| 1917 | .7 | / | 2.5 | .7 | 14.2 | 4.76 |
| 1918 | .2 | 1.48 | .8 | .9 | 6.3 | 6.80 |
| DYSENTERY | | | | | | |
| 1915 | .03 | / | / | / | / | / |
| 1916 | 4.09 | / | 63.89 | 31.19 | 50.94 | / |
| 1917 | 3.76 | / | 28.89 | 23.13 | 60.34 | 486.56 |
| 1918 | .79 | 9.54 | 58.23 | 21.80 | 51.12 | 116.51 |
| MALARIA | | | | | | |
| 1915 | / | / | / | / | / | / |
| 1916 | .05 | / | 331.47 | 8.10 | 68.61 | / |
| 1917 | .48 | / | 353.18 | 44.66 | 94.20 | 2880.9 |
| 1918 | 1.77 | 2.90 | 369.29 | 134.40 | 95.79 | 1278.0 |
| NEPHRITIS | | | | | | |
| 1915 | 7.16 | / | / | / | / | / |
| 1916 | 8.46 | / | / | / | / | / |
| 1917 | 9.51 | / | / | / | / | / |
| 1918 | 4.17 | / | / | / | / | / |

In France patients averaged 42.3 days under treatment, while those which were transferred to England averaged 118.3 days.

Source: W.G. MacPherson, et al., *History of the Great Based on Official Documents. Medical Services. Diseases of the War*, Vol. 2. (London, 1923)

# CHAPTER V

## The Bloom of Life

*Trench and PoW Gardens, Flowers
and Botanists at the Front*

'We are all first class navvies now. We are getting quite proud of our muscular prowess. One result of this training will show itself when the war is over. We shall be lost without a garden so country houses will be in great demand. We shall all keep gardens, and they will be the best anywhere if turning the earth over and over will do any good.'

*Private J.W. Graystone, 10/East Yorkshire Regiment, May 1916*

On encountering Captain Siegfried Sassoon in the House of Commons in 1918, Winston Churchill informed him that 'War is the normal occupation of man.'

Sassoon, a private warrior, the winner of a Military Cross for bravery, was also a celebrated public pacifist, and challenged the Minister of Munitions. So, Churchill added a codicil: 'War – and gardening.'

In the Great War cultivation and conflict were sometimes practised in the same moment. 'Will you please send as soon as possible two

packets of candytuft and two packets of nasturtium seeds?' Captain
Lionel Crouch wrote to his 'Dear Old Dad' at home in Springfield
House, Chelmsford. Only, perhaps, in context was the request unusual for a Home Counties Englishman. Captain Lionel Crouch was
an officer in the 1/Oxford and Buckinghamshire Light Infantry and
his missive was penned from a chamber excavated from the side of
a war-torn Flanders trench in 1915. Crouch intended to start a flower
garden around his dugout HQ.

His men, part-time Territorials who had volunteered for overseas
service, had already planted up a section of the communication
trench. Crouch told his father: 'It is labelled "Kew Gardens – Do not
pinch the flowers".'[1] Later the men put two bones on top of 'Kew Gardens' and erected a sign: 'Here lieth all that remains of the last man
who walked on the L'Hawn.'

Crouch liked flowers. His batman, Wheeler, cut him flowers from
the garden of the abandoned chateau next door. Crouch knew the joy
of flowers, on eye and on nose. Narcissi, Lionel told the Pater, 'smell
ripping'. A few days later he was telling 'My Dearest Old Governor'
that in his dugout Wheeler had placed 'a large earthenware vase full
of beautiful peonies'.[2]

Bitten by the gardening bug, Crouch, along with another officer,
Young, made-over 'the beastly manure-heap' on the local farm by
planting it with flower bulbs shipped out from England. Six months
later, the muck heap was transformed into 'a grassy mound with
lovely daffodils and purple and white hyacinths'. And so, Lionel
Crouch's small corner of a barbed wire strewn, stinking foreign field
was turned into an English cottage garden.

Captain Crouch gave a fresh twist to the military expression
'trench raid', encouraging his company to infiltrate the gardens of
the nearby ruined village, where

we get potatoes, rhubarb, and spinach. This is very good for the
men, and I encourage them to go out at night to get garden stuff.[3]

In civilian life Crouch was a solicitor; it was a funny old war the First World War, it turned upstanding men into poachers.

A year later, Captain Lionel Crouch was killed leading his company on an attack on the enemy's trenches at Pozières on the Somme, in the usual sort of trench raid. Everything went wrong; there was moonlight and the British barrage intended to suppress German machine guns was ineffective. Three other officers were killed, along with eight other ranks.[4] The date was 21 July 1916. Crouch was twenty-nine.

Captain Crouch and his gardening Ox and Bucks 'Saturday Night Soldiers' were utterly ordinary in their turning of Hell into Heaven: there were trench gardens everywhere on the 150 miles of British front line. Touring medical facilities in the Colony in the spring of 1916, the journalist Carita Spencer saw the soldiers' gardens at La Panne (Ypres):

> So the soldiers portioned off the rough earth beside the board walk that ran parallel to the rampart, and first they had a little vegetable garden, and next to it for beauty's sake a flower garden, and next to that a little graveyard, and then the succession repeated. Five hundred yards beyond the main line, across the inundated fields streaked with barbed wire sticking up out of the water, was the front line trench, a rougher rampart, mostly of earth and when it rained, oh mud![5]

Douglas Gillespie, Argyll and Sutherland Highlanders, started his trench garden on 21 March 1915, with nasturtium seeds sent out by his parents. In May he was able to tell them: 'I watered our garden; the pansies and forget-me-nots are growing well.'[6] He also cleared a stream so it ran more smoothly; it then gave off 'a pleasant smell of warm mint and waterweed, which always remind me of the water meadows at Winchester, and the birds, too, are very much the same'. He had been at school at Winchester. A dutiful son, he wrote to his parents every other day. On 5 July he reported the latest garden news:

I started the day's work at 4 a.m. by watering the garden, a long
and muddy business, for I had to jump half the way down our wall
to fill the watering-can, and stand on a slippery cask. The well is
only a hole about six feet deep, which has been a trap to frogs and
toads, until it swarms with them, but since all kinds of flies and
moths and beetles tumble into it too, I expect they find a living.
We have mignonette and corn-flowers coming on well now, with a
lot of nasturtiums and canariensis to follow.[7]

To boost his floral range, Gillespie carefully transplanted wallflowers,
pansies and peonies from a nearby ruined village. He reassured his
parents that there were 'still plenty' of flowers left should anyone ever
come back to the houses.

Gardening was a natural cure for boredom. And it can hardly be
surprising that the nation of gardeners, when they went to war, in-
dulged in horticulture.

Trench gardens were invariably on the reverse side of the rear
parapet, though celery, it turned out, grew well in the dark dank of
the trench bottom. More often than not, trench gardens were edged
with stones, partly for aesthetic reasons, partly to indicate ownership. Rubbish which could be repurposed as flower containers and
pots abounded, and spent German howitzer shells were a popular
choice as flower pots. The irony of using German ammo for cultivat-
ing British flowers was relished. That was one over on Fritz.

As well as being something to do during the waiting game of war,
gardening was an expression of faith in the future, because the gardener expects to see his seeds grow. Gardening in the trenches was
always a belief in life over death. In planting a tree garden outside his
dugout Major Ronald Schweder, RFA, was perhaps expecting a long
existence. Or a long war.

More: Gardening gave the opportunity for beautification of dull,
scarred earth. Recreation as re-creation. At Givenchy-lès-la-Bassée
Irish guardsmen transformed the midden at 'The Keep' strongpoint
into an Italian style garden. Bulbs, box plants and other shrubs

looted from a nearby cemetery traced out the shapes of regimental badges. The Irish Guardsmen were wildly cosmopolitan in their Italianate design, because British trench gardens were invariably a mini English country garden abroad. They evoked and they preserved the rural idyll that men were fighting for.

Gardening was about control too. Soldiers were told to do everything, from reveille to dusk stand-to: gardening was something they could control themselves. Soldiers were uniform: gardening allowed self-expression. Although soldiers were always on the lookout for comestibles to add to their diet, vegetable growing was a lower priority in trench gardening than flower cultivation. The soldiers of the Great War turned sociologist Abraham Maslow's hierarchy of needs (where basic physiological requirements must be satisfied before 'higher' wants are addressed) on its head, or at least laid it on its side. Troops in the trenches required the soul as well as the guts satisfied. The religious among them might have remembered too Genesis 2.9, that when God planted His garden in Eden, He propagated 'every tree that was pleasing to the sight and good for food'. Beauty before butter. If it was good enough for God it was good enough for Tommy.

The Colony was gardened all over, from battle line back to base via billets. On arriving at Harfleur Captain Rowland Feilding noted that:

> The officers passing through have, in their spare time, made flower beds which now glitter with daffodils and other flowers. The coats of arms of all the Guards regiments have been planted in flowers. It makes the camp, which is on the side of a steep hill, very pretty.[8]

No self-respecting British soldier would pass up the opportunity of emblazoning the countryside with the regimental colours. Tommy (and his regiment) Was Here.

Captain Philip Gosse considered gardening was 'all the rage' at the base camp at Poperinge for the RAMC and Army Service Corps (ASC), while Private Broadhead, on the orderly room staff of 18/West

Yorkshire Regiment, was delighted when ill with flu at Mailly-Maillet on the Somme to be put in a billet hut 'amongst daffodils'. Broadhead had just arrived from Egypt and the change in temperature had done him 'no good'.

Billets offered most scope for gardening. The garden made by 2/Scots Guards amid the ruins of Cartigny, near Péronne, in 1917 was legendary. After first erecting some wooden barracks, the men, led by Private Armstrong, a gardener on the estate of a Scottish laird, began clearing away rubble and planting up gardens.

Private Stephen Graham, who served with Armstrong, wrote of him:

> He was the genius of Cartigny, and in his quiet, sweet way one of the strongest men in the battalion, an expert wrestler, but also one of the most gentle, one of the few men in our care-less, violent crowd who did not use bad language. Of course he found kindred spirits, and the other gardeners of the battalion shone out through their camouflage of khaki. 'Gardeners camouflaged as soldiers', I hear the hard voice of the R.S.M. a-saying. But before long every man had become a gardener, and was co-operating to work the miracle amid the ruins. And since they worked in mid-April, a month beyond the equinox, they had one greater than all co-operating with them, the great god of gardens breathing radiant life and energy over their bended backs.[9]

Armstrong then began lining the pathways with white bricks, before devising some rockeries 'so that the place might not seem so bare'. Flower borders with transplanted narcissi, tiger lilies, auriculas, pansies, violas and a rose followed.

Watching Armstrong's formal garden grow, the admiring officers in the battalion encouraged the men to make gardens throughout the camp. The CO offered prizes for the best gardens the various companies could produce. Cartigny hummed with 'work and happiness'. Private Graham:

Each company has marked out the pattern of its formal garden, each platoon has its special care. A platoon of A Company has enclosed a tent in a heart; a border of boxwood marks out the pattern of the heart the plan is that the crimson of many blossoms shall blend to give a suggestion of passion and loyalty and suffering. Another platoon endeavours to embody in floral contrast the blended patterns of the regimental crest the cap-star. Armstrong produces wonderful thistles, the green part of which he obtains by just cutting the pattern in his turf, and the blue heads by thickly sown lobelia. One thistle is on each side of his gentle rose. F Company makes an elaborate and ambitious figure, an imitation of the floral clock that is to be seen in Princes Street Gardens in Edinburgh. Each man has found or improvised trowel and basket, shovel or hoe. The bayonet is for ever in use, cutting lumps of chalk to right sizes, making holes in the earth, cutting and slicing wood. Petrol-tins with holes in the bottom serve as watering-cans. How eager the men are seeking the plants and then in watering and tending them. Cheerful water-fatigue parties are to be seen every evening going to and from the river. Primroses and daffodils and narcissi are soon blossoming in plenty. Lilies followed, arums and Solomon's-seal, and then forget-me-nots, pansies and violas. At the same time the perfecting of the designs of stones and glass, bricks and chalk, goes on. Armstrong's rockeries became the wonder not only of the battalion but of our many visitors and guests in this time of qualified rest. The work also on the railway still goes on; the garden is only the expression of a leisure which might otherwise have been spent in card-playing and noisy gregariousness; on the horizon, we must off to the wars again.

On judgement day the CO awarded first prize to those who made the floral clock. Armstrong, ruled out of the competition because of his genius, received a special prize. The CO, sole judge and arbiter was, said Armstrong, 'delighted beyond words at what the men have done, and he thanks them'.

Gardening was one of Britain's genuinely cross-class hobbies. On settling into his townhouse billet in Péronne, Lieutenant Edwin Campion Vaughan determined to make a garden by clearing out the waist-high rubbish behind the house and planting it with flowers. Vaughan had trained at Hare Hall camp in Essex at the same time as Edward Thomas and Wilfred Owen, before being commissioned in the Royal Warwickshire Regiment. After an uncertain start as an officer he matured, and would eventually be decorated for his part in capturing a bridge over the Sambre (in much the same circumstances that Owen won his Military Cross). Vaughan was one of the army's secret diarists:

Sunday. No work today so I finished off the garden, Really finished it! Every bit of rubbish burnt, paths swept, rose trees cleared and beds weeded. I was planting flowers scrounged from other gardens when Ewing came out and I stood pointing at my handiwork with pride. He stood for a bit sneering slightly then said, 'Well, Vaughan, you know it's labour in vain don't you?' 'Why?', I asked. 'Because we're moving north tomorrow.' And with that he left me. Gazing round at the result of my many hours of hard work, I felt inclined to cry, but consoled myself with the thought that someone would get the benefit of them . . .'[10]

It is certain they did. Two years before, tramping through the Pas-de-Calais town of Laventie, Lieutenant The Honourable Edward Wyndham Tennant had been lifted from disconsolation purely by the sight of a garden:

Green gardens in Laventie!
Soldiers only know the street
Where the mud is churned and splashed about
By battle-wending feet;
And yet beside one stricken house there is a glimpse of grass.
Look for it when you pass.

Beyond the church whose pitted spire
Seems balanced on a strand
Of swaying stone and tottering brick
Two roofless ruins stand,
And here behind the wreckage where the back wall should have
    been
We found a garden green.
The grass was never trodden on,
The little path of gravel
Was overgrown with celandine,
No other folk did travel
Along its weedy surface, but the nimble-footed mouse
Running from house to house.
So all among the vivid blades
Of soft and tender grass
We lay, nor heard the limber wheels
That pass and ever pass,
In noisy continuity until their stony rattle
Seems in itself a battle.
At length we rose up from this ease
Of tranquil happy mind,
And searched the garden's little length
Afresh pleasaunce to find . . .[11]

The experience left Tennant's soul 'dancing'.

The garden by the church with the needle spire still exists, and has long outlived Tennant, who died by a sniper's shot on the Somme on 22 September 1916. 'Bim' Tennant is buried at Guillemont Road Communal Cemetery, in the same row as his friend Raymond Asquith, the son of prime minister Herbert.

The officer's ideal billet was the one which came with a ready-made flower garden. Lieutenant Bernard Adams was in luck:

I lit a pipe and strolled out into the garden. This was undoubtedly an ideal billet, and a great improvement on the butcher's shop, where they used always to be killing pigs in the yard and letting the blood run all over the place. It was a long, one-storied house, set back about fifty yards from the road; this fifty yards was all garden, and, at the end, completely shutting off the road, was a high brick wall. On each side of the garden were also high walls formed by the sides of stables and outhouses; the garden was thus completely walled round, and the seclusion and peace thus entrapped were a very priceless possession to us.

The garden itself was full of life. There were box-bordered paths up both sides and down the centre, and on the inner side of the paths was an herbaceous border smelling very sweetly of wallflowers and primulas of every variety. Although it was still May, there were already one or two pink cabbage-roses out; later, the house itself would be covered with them; already the buds were showing yellow streaks as they tried to burst open their tight green sheaths. In the centre of the garden ran a cross path with a summer-house of bamboo canes completely covered with honeysuckle; that, too, was budding already. The rest of the garden was filled with rows of young green things, peas, and cabbages, and I know not what, suitably protected against the ravages of sparrows and finches by the usual miniature telegraph system of sticks connected by cotton decorated with feathers and bits of rag ... 'The worst of this war,' said I to Edwards, puffing contentedly at a pipeful of Chairman, 'is this: it's too comfortable. You could carry on like this for years, and years, and years.'[12]

For the 9/Devons nature provided the billet garden. When the battalion set up their canvas billets at Treux Wood during training for 1 July 1916 they found bluebells growing in the bottom of the tents, and some of the officers 'arranged for the space to be fenced off as a sort of indoor garden'.[13] Lieutenant John Upcott so worried about crushing the bluebells he slept outside, though this was not entirely successful; a fox or badger nuzzled up to his head, then stole his air pillow.

At Neuve Chapelle in 1916, Captain Raymond Hepper dwelt in a poor ruined farmhouse. It did not matter: 'There is quite a good garden to this billet and we spend our time reading amongst the flowers.' In being billeted in a house by Ypres' ramparts in May 1915, Corporal Garnet Durham drew the accommodation short straw; the 'Shells came over in pairs', and the window glass was blown out. The one compensation? 'We have a nice garden – lilacs in bloom, and cherries, quite large but ripe.'[14]

For off duty soldiers in the Ypres Salient, there was a permanent garden open to them at Talbot House, on the main street of Poperinge. Founded in December 1915 by Phillip 'Tubby' Clayton and Neville Talbot, Talbot House was, as a sign proclaimed, 'EVERY MAN'S CLUB', the one place where men and officers could mix. 'Toc H.', as Talbot House was universally known, had a garden; the sign in the conservatory beckoned visitors: 'COME INTO THE GARDEN AND FORGET THE WAR'. Tubby Clayton was aware that the significance of the garden for soldiers was in the aesthetic delights it offered, as well as in the sense of escape; and 'how far a little beauty went amid such surroundings as ours'.

The environs in which Lieutenant-Colonel Perreau and his Gurkha Rifles battalion were quartered were as desolate as the Salient in winter. In the mouth-drying aridity of the Mesopotamian desert, the desire for vegetables and fruit was great. Looking at the monotonous treeless landscape around him, Lieutenant-Colonel Perreau eyed up the 'low scrub out of which I can't help thinking that a botanist might get some sort of "sag" [spinach] for the men'. Sag was any green stuff cooked like spinach. He wrote to his mother, 'any green stuff would be most acceptable . . . I've been meaning to ask for M and C seeds for ages'.[15]

Given the difficulties of supply in Mesopotamia and elsewhere, the army did the sensible thing and grew its own food. The beginnings were small and casual. A pamphlet was produced telling soldiers what to grow and how two acres could grow veg for 200 men, and to concentrate minds gardening competitions were sponsored, often with medals issued as prizes. (It was possible to come home from the Great War with a gong for 'First Prize Tomatoes,' as well as service and valour medals.)

As the war progressed, however, army vegetable gardening in the war zones turned into a vast enterprise, which was eventually (in January 1918) brought under the control of an army agricultural committee. In Mesopotamia alone 750,000 acres were cultivated by the army and civilian helpers;[16] Lieutenant Graham Mackay's RA battery had a farm at Tekrit:

> I was out at the battery farm the other day – about five miles away. We have about 20 acres under cultivation chiefly barley and stuff called juwari. All our ex-ploughmen etc in the battery live out there and we send out horse teams to do the work of ploughing and harrowing etc. we have the latest American agricultural implements to use – they have done this farming in the spring ever since the Army first landed – there were Battery farms etc behind sumnn-yatt [lunn-y-att?] even before Kut was recaptured. The barley is coming on well, as will anything in this country with its wonderful soil. The only trouble is the birds – we keep Indians out at the farm all day to drive them off.[17]

The Indians' bird-scaring tactic, Mackay thought, was 'very effective'; they threw 'lumps of earth from a long cloth used like a sling'.

By the end of 1918 in France, the army was practically self-supporting in vegetables, and was producing significant amounts of grain and forage for horses. Many soldiers spent the war, or at least part of it, farming. Some 15,000 Australian soldiers were diverted to agricultural work in the Somme region in 1917 alone. A soldier was most likely to swap his rifle for a pitchfork at harvest time, working either on army farms or aiding local farmers, in the spells out of the trenches. In August 1918 Captain Francis Hitchcock and his company of Leinsters were at Strazeele:

The countryside had a most peaceful aspect on this lovely evening, and the peasants were all busily employed attending to their crops. We received a great welcome from these poor people (composed of old men, women, and children), as on the previous tour officers and men had helped them to gather the harvest. They would have been in terrible difficulties over the saving and cutting of their crops but for the British Army.[18]

From its bases near Abbeville and Montreuil the British Cavalry helped with ploughing and threshing and transported large quantities of manure to the fields nearby. In 1917 in the Somme 15,000 Australian troops and 3300 horses were involved in agricultural tasks. Farm work in the Colony was risky. Sometimes the fields to be harvested were under observation by the Germans and sometimes under fire, meaning that harvesting took place at night with the men wearing gas masks.

*

Twenty-fifth September 1916. A letter from one Thomas Howat arrives at the Royal Horticultural Society's offices in the suitably leafy Vincent Square, London. The letter formally announces the foundation of the Ruhleben Horticultural Society, and asks for affiliation with the august RHS.

'Under the circumstances,' Howat's letter explains, 'we are unable to remit the usual fee but trust this will be no hindrance to our enjoying the privileges of affiliation.'

In minute red pen the RHS Secretary, William Wilks, annotates the letter: 'certainly not'.

The circumstances referred to by Tom Howat were unusual. He sent his missive from Ruhleben internment camp, six miles outside Berlin, where, since the outbreak of the war in 1914, 4000 or so British civilian men had been incarcerated. The men, who were all aged between seventeen and fifty-five, were the luckless individuals working in or travelling around Germany when the conflict commenced. They could not be allowed to return home in case they signed up to fight the Reich; they could not be let free in Deutschland in case they sabotaged her. And so, these 'Enemy Aliens' were detained for the duration in 'Ruhleben Gefangenen Lager für Engländer'.

The internees were a miscellaneous lot. Aside from a large contingent of sailors, there were professional footballers, academics, tourists, at least one composer (Edgar Bainton), plus Wagner-lovers who had chosen 1914, of all years, to attend the Bayreuth Festival. There was also a handful of professional and amateur gardeners, among them Henry Martin, who had been working as gardener to Prince Friedrich Karl of Prussia.

In the beginning life at Ruhleben, a former horse trotting course, was grim. The internees slept in the stables, where raw manure still clung to the walls. Washing facilities in each barrack consisted of two stand-pipes and fifteen bowls. Food was conspicuous only by its absence. One captive, Burton, lamented to his diary: 'Cabbage soup again, third time in seven days . . .'[19]

In 1915 the hungry men rioted.

The German authorities were not quite blind, however, to the plight of their internees. Since the camp was so close to Berlin, it was easy for neutral governments to check on conditions. There was also the matter of self-interest: 26,000 German nationals were interned in Britain, and the Germans feared tit-for-tat reprisals. Felicitously Ruhleben also had, in the distinguished shape of Count Schwerin, a seventy-year-old landed gentleman from Mecklenburg-Strelitz, one of the more humane camp commandants in Germany. If Schwerin made no great effort to reform the prisoners' lot, at least he was no obstructer of improvement. Effectively, Schwerin allowed the PoWs to found what was a self-governing colony run upon communal lines; a little Britain in Germany. The guards retreated to the perimeter fence around the oval arid acres. With the receipt of private and Red Cross food parcels from Britain, food became adequate. There were also shops set up on 'Bond Street', selling groceries purchased from German suppliers. One enterprising prisoner, who was always referred to as 'Mr. W.H. Smith', managed to sell *The Times* newspaper, proving the truth of one British genius, that for shopkeeping.

Another British genius soon raised its head. The first gardens, grown in biscuit tins, window boxes or the strips of earth under barracks windows, appeared in early spring 1915. Within a year gardening was everywhere at Ruhleben. In March 1916 the first issue of *The Ruhleben Camp Magazine* (cost: 30 pfennigs) came out, complete with a horticultural advice column, 'The Garden', penned by the pseudonymous 'Forget-Me-Not'. He signed off:

Perhaps some may think that gardens are superfluous in the Camp, but whether we be in our own land, or in someone else's, a pretty, well cared for garden, however small, reflects credit on those who provide it.

These few remarks will, I trust, be useful to those who have not had the opportunity of taking up gardening as a hobby – but are nevertheless willing to try their hand in making their present domicile as much like 'Home sweet Home' as possible.[20]

What seems to have stimulated organised gardening in Ruhleben was a gift of seeds from the Crown Princess of Sweden (formerly Princess Margaret of Connaught, the daughter of Prince Arthur, an Honorary Fellow of the Royal Horticultural Society), and urgings by the imprisoned botanist and geneticist Michael Pease that:

No self-respecting Town Council in England is without its Parks and Gardens Committee; surely in Ruhleben, too, some public energy, and public funds, could be devoted to beautifying the Camp? With such a body in existence, some organised effort could be made with the happiest results, in the direction of utilising the spaces available for floral decoration. Some bright colour, for example, introduced round the arc lamps in the compound, and by the gateways, and in that dismal waste between the 'village pump' and the dentist's surgery would be a source of untold joy to all, throughout the summer and autumn, and would be one of the few beautiful things to which we could look back in Ruhleben.

The twenty-four-year-old Pease was also a mover and shaker behind the founding in September 1916 of the Ruhleben Horticultural Society. The annual subscription was fixed at one mark. Membership reached 943 – just under a quarter of the entire camp population. Fittingly the membership card had art nouveau twirling creepers; the nature designs in art nouveau always spoke to nostalgia for innocent times and an escape from dehumanisation. Art nouveau was Romantic verse in pen and paint and sculptor's clay.

Like the solo gardeners in the barracks, the priority of the Ruhleben HS was beauty. Ornamental plants were propagated for barrack gardens and camp thoroughfares (which were christened patriotically: the largest open space was called Trafalgar Square); public gardens were created in front of the YMCA house and the invalids' barrack; long flowerbeds were dug alongside barbed wire partitions, circular beds around lampposts. Proud of their efforts, the RHS Committee noted: 'Few can have failed to appreciate the patches of brightness and colour which the Society's effort have brought into the camp.'

Colour there most definitely was. Internees grew lobelia, pyrethrum, bedding begonias, antirrhinums, godetia, clarkia, petunias, summer chrysanthemums, balsam, brachycome, sweet peas, marigolds, mallows, calliopsis, asters, stocks, nicotiana, dimorphotheca, convolvulus, *Humulus japonicus*, nasturtiums, chrysanthemums, dahlias and hollyhocks.

There were greater gardening wonders to come. The Ruhleben HS built a nursery of about 600 square yards on waste land behind Barrack 10, where they cleared the plot and improved the soil with composted drain refuse and tea leaves. Cold frames and a greenhouse were erected. Eventually a second-hand boiler was located and installed, using a loan from the German camp authorities. (A 'black economy' ebbed around civilian and military PoW camps in Germany, which was under a trade blockade by the Allied powers.

Almost anything could be bought in a PoW camp, from mynah birds to escape kit, for money or for soap.)

One pressing reason for the requested affiliation with the other RHS was that the Ruhleben flower shows could then be held and judged on the gold standard of horticulture: the rules laid down by Vincent Square.

Ruhleben HS held its first flower show on 7 April 1917, in the camp's YMCA Hall. Howat described the result to the other RHS, the one in Vincent Square:

> You will be interested to know that we had our first flower show last month, when we staged some 200 pots of spring flowers, which had been grown in frames in the nursery. The exhibition was in every way successful, and was much appreciated by our fellow-prisoners.

The RHS was suitably impressed with its initialsake, and on 3 July 1917 Council 'decided to make a free gift' of medals and certificates for the forthcoming Ruhleben Camp Summer Flower Show and Competition. This was held on 3–4 August, with a special competition for the sweet pea, which was effectively the national flower of Edwardian England; eighty-three varieties of the flower were grown at Ruhleben. The Ruhleben Camp show also included miniature, or 'table', rock gardens, just as the RHS shows in London. The numerous other competition categories included table decorations, best private garden, individual plant, cut flowers, button-hole, window box. There was also a barracks garden category. As photographs show, barracks gardens at Ruhleben had reached zeniths of elaborateness; Barrack 7 boasted flower borders, rustic fencing and trelliswork incorporating a gateway, climbing plants draping the uprights.

As internee E.L. Wright, observed, entirely accurately, the show 'would not have disgraced a country flower show at home'.[21]

Gardening at Ruhleben, despite its intended facsimile of English rural and suburban life, despite its satisfying of a human need, could never escape the torturing shadow of the barbed wire walls. The Rules and Standing Orders of the 'Ruhleben Horticultural Society' contained an appendix:

> The Committee meet every Thursday afternoon from 3 to 5 p.m. in Mr Lazarus' Summer House behind Barrack 7 where members may apply for information.

Gardening clubs in dear old Blighty did not meet behind barracks.

It was not until the winter of 1916–17 that a serious programme of food cultivation commenced at Ruhleben. The British blockade of German ports hit the food supply badly, while frost devastated the native crops of Germany, particularly the potato. Germany was starving. Since less food could be bought in by Ruhleben inmates, they did the sensible thing and decided to grow their own. In January 1917 the Ruhleben HS asked to use the central part of the racecourse as a large vegetable garden (the other half of the course was taken up by the sports pitches). The camp authorities were likely happy to encourage the cultivation of green stuff in order to avoid disease in the camp. They also pocketed a rent of 100 marks per month.

Digging on the vegetable garden began on 29 March. Some poor quality pig manure, basic slag, 'eight cwts. of Bone Meal' and potash salts was spread over the five acre site. Fertilising, even stabilising, the loose, fine soil of Ruhleben was always a trial; a sandstorm wiped out many rows of the first seedlings. The gardeners of Ruhleben won through. Vegetable growing at Ruhleben was more than a hobby; it was market garden scale horticulture. The garden had sections devoted to beetroot, brassica crops (including Brussels sprouts, cauliflowers and spring cabbage in individual beds), runner beans, dwarf beans, radishes, turnips, spinach, lettuce, carrots, beets, parsnips, onions, leeks and potatoes. Vegetable seeds and bulbs, as with flowers, were largely obtained from British nurseries, following an appeal by the London RHS, which were then forwarded to Germany in Red Cross parcels.

At peak production Ruhleben HS grew 33,000 lettuces and 18,000 bunches of radishes. By the end of the war, the camp was more or less self-sufficient in fruit and vegetables, and the diet inside the perimeter fence was superior in all respects to that outside it. Fresh produce went on sale to internees at nominal prices. Edward Stibbe, who spent four years at Ruhleben, was delighted that 'every man was able occasionally to have fresh vegetables with his tins of meat'.[22]

Outside Ruhleben, the citizenry of Berlin were so ravenous that when a horse dropped dead in the street crowds rushed to butcher it. Towards the end at Ruhleben, a German officer, Captain Amelunxen, demanded with Prussian arrogance that fifteen red cabbages were donated to the camp's officers' mess, and the outer leaves handed over as cattle fodder. The Horticultural Society laid the matter before the captains of the barracks; and the captains decided unanimously that supplying the red cabbages to Amelunxen would aid the German war effort. So, the officers' mess went without its *Rotkraut*. As for the leaves, Amelunxen was told that he could have them in exchange for manure from the cattle. According to the camp captain, Joseph Powell, the leaves 'were duly handed over; but I have reason to believe that they were intercepted on their way to the cattle, and eaten'.[23]

By the end of the war the gardeners of Ruhleben had achieved their own victory, over the Germans, over fate. They had fed the soul and the body of their fellows for four long years.

The gardeners of Ruhleben had definite advantages over British military prisoners held at the Kaiser's pleasure because they were, aside from being self-governing, sedentary. The lot of PoWs in khaki was to be endlessly shifted from pillar to post, A to B; other ranks, especially from 1916 onwards, were enrolled in slave labour schemes, of which working on the land was the popular choice (in so far as the process was voluntary) since it was seen as healthy and not directly contributing to the German war effort. When prisoners became acquainted with the long hours of self-exploitation of German peasant farmers and market gardeners, agriculture and horticulture usually lost their bloom.

By the conventions of the day, officers did not work and were incarcerated in separate camps. They were still subject to itinerancy though, because camp authorities worried that the idle hands of officers made devilish escape plots, and to forestall tunnels and breakouts moved them on periodically. Despite all handicaps, British PoWs, officers and other ranks alike gardened away. When Daniel McCarthy, a US doctor engaged as neutral camp inspector, entered Minden 'other ranks' Lager he found evidence of positive morale in the form of a 'few flowers . . . grown in the window tops of the barracks'. Friedrichsfeld, another Mannschaftslager, with 7500 British PoWs, was 'tastefully decorated with flower beds in front of each barracks'.

Conrad Hoffman from the YMCA on his visits to camps in Germany found gardens in many of them, with the hospital quarters at Worms especially catching his eye: at Worms 'every inch of ground about them [the barracks] was utilized for growing vegetables, and entering every door into a barracks was a hanging basket with blooming plants'. The nationals of other Allied powers gardened too, though the emphasis with them was on vegetables. Hoffman noted that at Darmstadt the French and Russians had gardened according to their particular national tastes:

In one compound vines had been planted along the entire side of the barracks and with a second row of sunflowers which incidentally furnished sunflower seed for the Russians who regard it as more or less of a delicacy, presented a really delightful aspect.[24]

True, the British were better provided with Red Cross and home parcels than the Russians certainly, and the French possibly, so the impetus for vegetable growing in the military camps was never great. But with the British it was flowers, for their own sake, for the sake of Anglicisation. At Gütersloh British officers created a complete

English cottage garden. Lieutenant Will Harvey, Gloucestershire Regiment, the poet laureate of the PoW camps, was among the prisoners who enjoyed this corner of Germany turned into England. Yet there was bitterness in the sweetness, a metaphorical maggot in the apple, for no matter how perfect a re-creation of a garden of deepest, quietest England, it was a copy. Harvey preserved the Gütersloh scene in 'English Flowers in a Foreign Garden':

> Snapdragon, sunflower, sweet-pea,
> Flowers which fill the heart of me
> With so sweet and bitter fancy:
> Glowing rose and pensive pansy,
> You that pierce me with a blade
> Beat from molten memory.
> With what art, how tenderly,
> You heal the wounds that you have made!
>
> Thrushes, finches, birds that beat
> Magical and thrilling sweet
> Little far-off fairy gongs:
> Blackbird with your mellow songs,
> Valiant robin, thieving sparrows.
> Though you wound me as with arrows,
> Still with you among these flowers
> Surely I find my sweetest hours.[25]

Around the camp were crested larks, leading a British orderly to remark that 'even the blinkin' birds wore spiked hats in Germany'.

*

> Where the parapet is low
> And level with the eye
> Poppies and cornflowers glow
> And the corn sways to and fro

In a pattern against the sky.
The gold stalks hide
Bodies of men who died
Charging at dawn through the dew to be killed or to kill.
I thank the gods that the flowers are beautiful still.

*Sergeant Leslie Coulson, France, 8 August 1916*

The year 1915 witnessed the first of the Western Front poppy fields. Captain Rowland Feilding arrived in the Cuinchy trenches in June 1915 in time to see soldiers rushing wildly across a no man's land 'ablaze' with scarlet poppies. Private Len Smith, later a war reporter, kept a diary; pressed between its pages was a corn poppy, with a scribbled caption: 'Actual Flanders Poppy from "No Man's land" 1916'. He wrote:

> With much caution one could even peep over the top and it was lovely to see groups of red poppies . . . Considering the numerous shell holes they were very numerous and made a very brave display – I know they thrilled me intensely.

Edwin Campion Vaughan at Quéant near Cambrai, May 1917:

> The morning was absolutely gorgeous; the sun was frightfully hot but there was a delightful breeze which just caught our heads when we stood on the first earth step. The grass is about a foot long and thousands of poppies are swaying along the lips of the trench, whilst among the stems of grass are multitudinous wild flowers.
>
> It was very pleasant sitting at our dugout door or strolling along the trench chatting to the troops as they carried out their morning duties of shaving and cleaning buttons and rifles.[26]

Private Fred Hodges was eighteen in 1918, one of the very last of his generation to sign for service in the war. The poppies were there for him too:

One day I picked a bunch of red field poppies from the old grassy trench and put them in the metal cup attached to my rifles. They quickly wilted in the hot sun, but in any case I don't think the idea would have appealed to my officer if he had seen them. Most of the boys and men I was with apparently found no pleasure in flowers, but I was acutely conscious of them growing there in the midst of all that man made destruction. Only field poppies and a few other wild flowers, but the persistent charm of nature in such conditions during that period of May, June and July, 1918, was more poignant than it had ever been before in my life, or since.[27]

Hodges was surely wrong to suggest his comrades lacked fondness for flowers. Love of flowers in the trenches was similar to love of religion. Few British soldiers declared it, almost everyone had it. Admiring wild flowers or picking them is a constant bright thread in soldiers' letters and diaries. Into a filthy dugout in Flanders Sapper Jack Martin brought a little homely comfort. On a makeshift table:

> we have a vase of small marguerites and flaming poppies . . . The vase is an old 18-pdr shell case that we have polished up and made to look very smart.

In the trenches at Thiepval Charles Douie remarked that 'flowers were often to be found growing in the side of the trenches . . . The flowers found their way into dug-outs'.[28]

Wild flowers were more than pretty decoration; they suggested the war's goal of freedom and proved the inevitability of regeneration. And there was always succour in nature's redemptive healing of a mutilated countryside. Captain George Stringer was struggling through the ruins of Bucquoy south of Arras in the winter of 1916 when he chanced on a mass of snowdrops:

> It really was the most pathetic thing I have ever experienced. My groom, who was following me closely, absolutely wept, when I

drew his attention to them, and I had a big lump in my throat myself. We did not gather them up as it seemed like sacrilege. The wee white flowers sticking up and out of chaos and desolation.[29]

Wandering near his battalion's camp at Corbie, Captain C.P. Blacker, 4/Coldstream Guards, entered a wood:

The floor was ablaze with white, yellow and blue flowers. The luxuriance was so unexpected as to make me feel that, as in a fairy story, I had inadvertently broken into some secret and privileged place where I had no business to be. The white flowers, pinkily nodding in the sunlight, as in timid recognition, were of course wood anemones; the yellow flowers were lesser celandines and primroses ... As I picked my way through the trees I came to a concealed clearing thick with wild daffodils, mostly in bud but a few in flower ... What a revelation![30]

Blacker took several friends to see the wood, among them Overton-Jones and Philimore, the padre, who talked of a 'theophany'. This was a period of sensitivity and spirituality for Blacker himself. Later, he would have his own 'theophany', near the same wood. War heightened awareness of nature, which in turn, accentuated religious feeling, or at least spirituality. The First World War saw a marked rise in religious observance.[31]

There was another keen botanist in 4/Coldstream Guards, Lieutenant E. Overton-Jones, who worked as an artist for Wedgwood, and he and Blacker took nature walks together. When Overton-Jones died in 1963, Blacker looked forward to meeting up with him in the 'Elysian fields' for more nature-watching perambulations. Blacker pictured Heaven as a place with 'sunny chalk-ridges, valley streams, beech woods and plenty of butterflies with bright chalkland flower'. Heaven was the Somme before 1 July 1916, or downland Britain at any time. There was comfort in the companionship of naturalists as well as nature. One of Lieutenant Siegfried Sassoon's main regrets on a return to the trenches after a short course at the Fourth Army School for Officers at Flixecourt was saying goodbye to a fellow officer, Captain Marcus Goodall, also keen on flowers and birds. (Goodall appears in *Memoirs of an Infantry Officer* as Allgood; Goodall, a captain in the Yorks and Lancasters, and like Sassoon an Old Marlburian, was killed in July 1916. He was twenty-one.)

There could be advantage in botanical knowledge. Soldiers foraged for edible plants and berries.[32] Carlos Blacker managed to avert a full-scale military panic at the front by identifying a flower:

> I recall an occasion belonging to this period when a glimmer of botanical knowledge proved useful. I was leading a couple of pla-toons on our way up to the forward area in fading light on a wind-less steamy night with plenty of midges about. We were straggled over a sedgy, churned up field in which we had to pick our way, skirting shell-holes and avoiding wire. A message was passed up: 'Gas. Put on your helmets.' I had noticed no gas, so I halted the uneven column, and went back to investigate. 'Where did the message come from? Who had smelled gas etc?' I was standing in the rear of the by-then halted column, when I was told that, a few yards behind, there was a strong smell of gas. No one knew who had given the warning. I walked back a few yards and true enough a faint but pungent smell was noticeable which seemed to come from underfoot. My Orilux torch showed me that we were stand-ing in a patch of flowers with white rays: these when crushed, were emitting the alarming odour. I recognized the flowers as stinking camomile, over a patch of which we had trampled. The smell from the crushed leaves and flowers did not rise high enough from the ground to be noticed until the party had nearly passed. I picked a bunch and took it back. This was No. 3 nearly 'hoaxed by daisies', as someone later put it.[33]

Sometimes merely to look at flowers, and have the time to do so, was enough. Philip Gosse:

It might be wondered how a grown-up man could sit down in a hayfield and do nothing for a whole hour, but the truth is that after being in or about the line for several months, one was content to sit in the sunshine, and do nothing at all, beyond admire the flowers and listen to the song of the birds and enjoy the quiet. It was medicine for the mind and solace for the soul.[34]

The Somme region had the best of the flowers. At Maresquel in July 1918 Second Lieutenant Arnold Monk-Jones regretted not bringing his floral guide book, such was the diversity of species:

> Unluckily I cannot keep up with flowers, not having my book. Among others I have seen Vipers Bugloss, Forget-me-Knot, Yellow Moneywort (if that is the name of the bright marsh flower, prostrate, with almost round leaflets); and many of the dry soil flowers, such as Thyme, on the hill top where the bombing ground is.[35]

Only the 'obnoxious' horseflies ruined the idyll.

Lieutenant Harold Rayner wrote to his brother Ed, 5 May 1916, from 'the Downs':

> We have been making the banks in the Downs into a sort of lean-to dugouts [sic], meanwhile I have been able to note the flowers of the field, and profuse, if humble, they are welcome and homelike. The not to be despised dandelions, the snowdrifts of daisies, early buttercups, wild mignotte (lacking the pale terra-cotta parts of the flower and the scent of the garden plant), forget-me-knot dwarf, and in places, big, with thick nappy leaves, and white May just bursting into blossom, these and many other humbler specimens including a kind of grass whose flower looks like little catkins, and on examination consists of small bells rather like two-headed columbine.[36]

Three days later Rayner was writing to his mother about a wood the battalion had just moved to:

> ... an oak wood of the Downs on a natural terrace overlooking a smiling valley. We can sit at our ease and watch shells burst on the white line of the trenches in the distance and so relish our silvern retreat all the more. This is the most picturesque bit of France we have struck, a real joy – this wood in May with enormous violets and bluebells, and the variegated floor of undergrowth in an oakwood reminding John and me of Sussex woods. We dub it the Bois de Paradis, in memory of a paradise wood he and I used to frequent in Bordon last year. We have cuckoo-echoes by day and nightingale-song by night and between passing rain clouds, blue and white sky-scapes through the new foliage of the oaks ... Every prospect pleases and only war is vile.[37]

In the same wood he spotted speedwell ('pride of place' in his affection), and enclosed a specimen in a letter to his brother. The 'dog-violets are great too, fine proportions, resembling pansies in form and in prime blossom – see sample'. Also enclosed was white ragwort. (The soldier generation of 1914–18 knew their flowers.) Later, camped in another wood, he made his own 'bivvy' out of a piece of canvas and an oil silk waterproof sheet:

> I own a little clearing in the wood, greenery all round me plus a piece of honeysuckle almost out, and for bathroom I have a priceless little recess surrounded completely with bushes. I have erected a young flagstaff on which I fly the Devon pennant (part of the Devon braces I got at Nice) ... Things are rather jolly in this wood – this out-of-door under-the-greenwood tree life.

Vile war intervened on 1 July 1916, the first day of the Somme. Harold Rayner was killed in action. He is buried in the Devonshire Cemetery at Mametz, which is positioned on the forward trench the 8th and

9th battalions went 'over the top' from on that day. The stele at the entrance reads: 'The Devonshires Held This Trench. The Devonshires Hold It Still.'

Just days before his death he had attended a church parade in evening sunlight next to the wood, writing home:

It was rather picturesque, as the Padre had raised a small Union Jack for the occasion, and a miniature oak screen and two vases of poppies . . .

\*

### Red Poppies in the Corn

I've seen them in the morning light,
When white mists drifted by:
I've seen them in the dusk o' night
Glow 'gainst the starry sky.
The slender waving blossoms red,
Mid yellow fields forlorn:
A glory on the scene they shed,
Red Poppies in the Corn.

I've seen them, too, those blossoms red,
Show 'gainst the Trench lines' screen.
A crimson stream that waved and spread
Thro' all the brown and green:
I've seen them dyed a deeper hue
Than ever nature gave,
Shell-torn from slopes on which they grew
To cover many a grave.
Bright blossoms fair by nature set
Along the dusty ways,

You cheered us, in the battle's fret,
Thro' long and weary days:
You gave us hope: if fate be kind,
We'll see that longed-for morn,
When home again we march and find
Red Poppies in the Corn.

*Lt Col. W. Campbell Galbraith, 1917*

There was no absolute inevitability in the rise to pre-eminence of the poppy as the flower of remembrance. Other flowers of the front were similarly evocative, and rooted themselves in the consciousness of the soldier. The French, after all, chose the startling blue cornflower, the 'bluet', as their floral memento mori.[38]

Britain's adoption of the poppy as the flower of remembrance for the war dead owes much to one man, Lieutenant-Colonel John McCrae.

John McCrae was a man of action. He was a sharpshooter with medals from the Boer War, but he was also a deep thinker, a deeper feeler and a devout Presbyterian. He was a medical doctor, with a penchant for writing. In 1914 he was in the first flush of Canadian volunteers for the war.

In May 1915, during the Second Battle of Ypres, McCrae was working in a dressing station dug into the side of the Yperlee Canal; the Essex Farm Cemetery was opened next to his bunker. His great friend, Lieutenant Alexis Helmer, Canadian Field Artillery, was blown to bits by an artillery bombardment at 8 a.m. on 2 May. Helmer's scattered body parts were gathered, assembled into an approximation of the human form and buried at Essex Farm. At the ad hoc funeral McCrae stood in for the chaplain, and recited from memory extracts from the Order for the Burial of the Dead.

Crouching in the entrance to his dressing station at dawn next day, McCrae looked at the wild corn poppies and the freshly dug graves with their wooden crosses. As soon as he came off duty, he sat on the tail gate of an ambulance, and on a page torn out from his dispatch book wrote the first fifteen lines of 'In Flanders Fields' in almost as many minutes.

'In Flanders Fields' was rejected by *The Spectator* but published by *Punch* on 8 December 1915. The poem was an immediate sensation, in trenches and around the English-speaking world. The corn poppy became the Flanders Poppy became the symbol of the war dead.

In Flanders fields the poppies blow
Between the crosses, row on row . . .

McCrae was an educated man, and his immortalisation of the poppy was never entirely innocent, or at all accidental.

The Romantic poets had celebrated the poppy as the flower of the deepest sleep; John Keats in 'To Autumn' wedded the corn poppy with the opium poppy's timeless tranquillity: 'Or on a half-reaped furrow sound asleep/ Drowned with the fume of poppies'. As a medical man McCrae knew that the corn poppy (*Papaver rhoeas*) was a mild sedative, since the milky sap contains the alkaloid rhoedine. The poppy eases pain. Dioscorides, the physician who accompanied Roman armies and wrote the magisterial *De Materia Medica*, had identified the corn poppy as a tranquiliser as early as *c.* AD 50; on boiling five or six little heads with three cups of wine, then reducing by heat to two, Dioscorides advised 'give it to drink to those whom you would make sleep'.

Similarly, the corn poppy was an emblem of death long before McCrae. Its petals are the colour of blood, its multitudinous seeds the colour of night. The poppy featured in Ancient Greek funerary rituals and Persephone wore the poppy as a symbol of her death-like state when imprisoned in the underworld. When archaeologists entered the 'Cave of Bats' in southern Spain in 1935 they found poppy capsules, alongside locks of hair, tucked in baskets laid beside human remains dating to 4000 BC.[39] The poppy was the funereal flower in Neanderthal times.

What McCrae saw outside his dugout, as grief had its way with him, was history in the making. The Great War itself made the poppy the emblem of the Great War. As Captain J.C. Dunn, Royal Welch Fusiliers, noted, pre-battle the Somme was far poorer for poppies than his native Norfolk. So was Flanders. The soils of Northwest France were too impoverished to grow swathes of the corn poppy, which, as its name suggests, is loving of the richly manured earth of plough-land. What created the conditions for the luxuriant bloom-ing of poppies on the Western Front was artillery shelling: this sowed poppy seeds (by impersonating ploughing), and then fertilised them with the nitrogen in its explosives. Lime in the shattered rubble of buildings was another food aid. Artillery also blasted the blood and bones of men and horses into the earth, as alluded to by Private Isaac Rosenberg – on the Western Front with the bantam (for men under 5′ 3″) battalion, 11/The King's Own Royal Lancaster Regiment – in 'Break of Day in the Trenches': 'Poppies whose roots are in man's veins'. The blood of soldiers is the fertiliser for the poppy.

Thus, the more the war went on, the more poppies there were growing. Rosenberg was among that minority of men irrevocably disenchanted with the war. For Rosenberg war, nature and the Geor-gian poets who hymned it are guilty, and to be cursed:

Down – a shell – O! Christ,
I am choked . . . safe . . . dust blind, I
See trench floor poppies
Strewn. Smashed you lie.[40]

The poppy is an annual. In its brief flowering, most soldiers at the front saw not war-blame but their own lives. Short, brave, brilliant.

When McCrae himself died his fellow officers fruitlessly searched for some winter poppies to lay on his grave (he lapsed into coma on 27 January 1918, and died in the early hours of the next day). Unsuc-cessful in their search McCrae's comrades ordered instead a wreath of artificial poppies from Paris. Quite by chance, John McCrae's

wreath was the first appearance of the millions of manufactured
Remembrance Poppies to come.[41]

There were poppies on the battlefields of other fronts. When the
Anzac forces stormed ashore at Gallipoli on 30 April they were met
with a landscape awash with poppies. According to Australia's official war historian C.E.W. Bean, a valley south of Anzac beach got its
name Poppy Valley 'from the field of brilliant red poppies near its
mouth'.

One of the Britons fighting this latter day siege of Troy was the
young amateur naturalist (and medic) Private Denis Buxton. His
many missives home are full of observations on the peninsula's
plants, and frequently contained specimens of the flora: 'I enclose a
bit of real Greek thyme. It grows in a bush'; 'perhaps you would like
some acorns off a few big Turkey Oaks that I have only seen here &
off the dwarf prickly ilex which makes such a lot of the typical scent';
'seeds of a very pretty kind of Love-in-the-Mist'. He picked figs for
stews.

At night he slept behind the Essex Regimental Aid Post:

> It is a lovely spot, the mound dotted with almonds, figs and olives,
> and covered with purple vetch, poppies, grass, etc, and great big
> white leaves like thistles, like those we had in the garden at Chig-
> well. It was strange to go to sleep, and to wake up, about a mile
> from our trenches, and hear no rifle nor guns and only the birds
> singing in the fig tree over our heads.[42]

The flowers of Gallipoli, concluded Buxton, were 'very beautiful,
with lots of tall purple Irises in the hedges, and poppies'. Only man
is vile, 'and he is very vile'.

# Interstice 5
## Nature and the Ancre battlefield, 30 July 1917

From 'A Correspondent' of *The Times*:

The valley of the Ancre, which was so hideous last year when the trickle of the stream ran from one half-stagnant pool to another through a brown waste of shell-kneaded earth, is now all waving rushes dotted with meadowsweet and hemp, agrimony and purple loosestrife. In Aveluy Wood the riven tree-stumps stand out against a background of acres of red rosebay. And so it is all over the battle-fields of a year ago.

It is an old legend that roses never blow so red as over a hero's grave. I think it must be true of poppies. Norfolk Poppyland itself can show no braver fields of scarlet than these year-old battlegrounds, and though it may be only fancy it seems that the sheets of colour are richer and more unbroken where the fighting was fiercest. Nowhere does the ground flame quite so brilliantly as around the Butte de Warlencourt, on the dreadful expanse above the Bazentins towards

High Wood, and on the face of the Thiepval slope, where the Ulster-men passed on July 1. Elsewhere the scarlet is half veiled in the mist of flowering grasses, and mixed with them are a profusion of other blossoms, yellow ragwort, hawkweed, sow thistles, and ladies' bed-straw, mauve scabious and purple vetch and knapweed, tall campan-ulas, blue chicory, and vipers' bugloss and cornflower, and nearer to the ground pale field convolvulus and pimpernel, with everywhere, white yarrow and camomile.

No yard of all this ground but last year was ploughed up by shells and beaten and ploughed again, so that much of the soil which now lies on the surface must have been thrown up from two or three feet below and then it was churned and churned again. Yet the grass and the flowers are as in any rich meadow at home. There are no villages, no landmarks beyond the occasional patches of sparse tree-stumps which once were woods, but only the wide waving expanse, where there are no human beings, as if it were the heart of some new continent which man had but just discovered. All larger things were destroyed and swept away by war, and only the little things like plant seeds and insects' eggs were able to survive.

Rarely outside the tropics have I seen more butterflies, whites and tortoiseshells and peacocks and skippers and little crambite moths. The kingly swallowtails are here too, but so far I have chanced this summer to see only one, and that was not among the flowers, but on the bare white summit of the Butte de Warlencourt when the King was there. The royal butterfly sailed round and round the little party and, as if recognising kinship, more than once made to settle on the King while he stood looking at the graves of the gallant Durhams.

There are places where crops flourish, patches of an acre or more being covered with oats or barley or wheat, mixed with "weeds" certainly, but hardly less close and even than if they had been truly sown. All three are growing strongly between Longueval and Ginchy, where it seems impossible that they could have been sown last year. More likely, they survive from three summers ago and, self seeded, they have held their own well against the wild things which riot around and among them. In one place I found a solitary potato plant, going strong, sprung presumably from some potato strayed from a German field kitchen.

Next to poppies the most abundant flower is camomile, and it alone seems to have been able to spring up and grow on the roads and beaten paths by which the enemy used to travel to and from his lines; so that, looking over the country, amid the deep green and waving colours, you can often trace the course of an old path where it runs like a pure white ribbon amid the sea of green and waving colours.

The woods remain desolate beyond imagination, even though in most of them grass and flowers have sprung up to cover the ground and shoots have risen from the old roots. Above ground level hardly a tree has put out any new life, but the shattered trunks still stand bare and blackened. Nature finds a use, however, even for the shell scars on the wood, for sparrows have built their nests this year at the points where trees have splintered. In Leuze Wood a pair of crows have nested. Perhaps they thought that later in the year the tree would put forth leaves as usual; but as it is the nest stands absurdly a landmark for long distances round, as exposed as if it were on the top of a flagstaff or bare ship's mast. Near Clery, amid the waste, a single post some 3ft high stood up, and on the top of it I saw a mother warbler feeding a young cuckoo three times her own size.

But the strangest thing of all in nature's haste to hide the ravages of war seems to me the shell holes. As one wades through the deep herbage the lesser shell holes merely make the walking very difficult and uneven, for one's feet blunder among the shell holes, which are concealed by the growth, and trip over strands of barbed wire and unexploded shells and other things scattered everywhere out of sight. Many of the larger holed, however, still remain half filled with water. Around the edges of the water white butterflies, which are thirsty creatures, crowd to drink, and when you disturb them they rise in clouds till the air is full of them, like a snowstorm.

In the water itself a luxuriant pond life has developed. Little whirligig beetles dance mazy dances on the surface, and water boat-men swim about and water scorpions and other things just as in any village pond at home. I have spoken before of frogs in the new shell holes on the Vimy Ridge. But here, on the dry slopes of the Albert Ridge, on the high ground, how has all this teeming life come into the shell holes of last summer?

['Poppies Bloom Red Over the Graves of Heroes',
The Times, *30 July 1917*]

# CHAPTER VI

# The Dogs (and Cats, Rabbits, etc.) of War

*Trench Pets*

'The British soldier cannot exist for long without pets of some
sort, and consequently all sorts of animals lead a precarious
but overfed existence in the trenches.'

*Country Life,* 29 January 1916

When *Country Life*'s correspondent declared that 'all sorts of
animals' were requisitioned as pets he did not lie, although only a
Lieutenant-General like Sir Henry Rawlinson, commander of IV
Corps, was likely to have the space in his billet to keep a pet boar.
The latter was known, like the general, as 'Rawly'. Equally, most
private soldiers in the trenches would have found the lion of
General Sir Tom Bridges, commander of the 19th Division, tricky
to house. The lion, 'Poilu', was given to Bridges while he was on
leave in Paris in 1916. ('Poilu', meaning hairy one, also being the
French nickname for an infantry soldier.) The general took the
beast back to his HQ in a hamper, and his staff, it is said, were

'sobered' when the hamper was opened and a lion cub sprang out.

Poilu became thoroughly tamed and followed Bridges around 'like a dog'. When people superior even to Bridges hinted that Poilu had no place at the front, Bridges responded 'Come and take him'. The troops loved Poilu – he was a real British lion – and he was elevated to mascot of the 19th Division. In a war not lacking in surrealist scenes, Poilu starred in a classic, as Bridges himself recorded:

> My headquarters were then in dugouts in Scherpenberg Hill, a prominent point, where distinguished visitors would come and actually see shells bursting. Such callers were frequent and they very often dropped in for refreshment. Mr. Asquith came one day but his climb to the hill-top was interrupted by meeting Poilu face-to-face. 'I may be wrong,' he said, 'but did I see a lion in the path?'[1]

Bridges was wounded in September 1917, and as his successor had no liking for big cats, Poilu was sent home and placed in Mr Tyrwhitt-Drake's private collection near Maidstone. 'Always the perfect gentleman,' wrote Bridges of Poilu, 'he contrived to die, aged nineteen, on the 19th of June, 1935, the mascot of the 19th Division.'

There were some outsize pets with the enlisted men. One company kept a pet donkey, another a milch cow called Mary. During the day she lived in a dugout; at night she was tethered in a field behind a wood to graze. A guard was kept, in case another unit was overcome by temptation. She lived under fire for nearly twelve months. The 23rd Infantry Brigade's cow, Jane, lasted three years at the front, and provided Devonshire cream.

But generally soldiers' pets were small and portable. Sister Evelyn Luard, Army Nursing Service Reserve, served in a field ambulance post at Ypres. She recorded in her diary an encounter with an armoured train at Ypres, manned by thirty Royal Navy ratings: 'They were very jolly, and showed us their tame rabbit on active service.'[2] Birds were popular pets at the front, as they were at home. One 'Old Contemptible', a BEF veteran of 1914 vintage, set up a bird hostel in his Brixton house so that soldiers posted abroad could leave their feathered friends in safe care.[3] The terraced house had cages stacked floor to ceiling, with cuttlefish stuck into the bars. Also in need of housing were some doves adopted by a front line unit in Flanders. On leaving the trenches the men erected a large noticeboard which read: 'To our successors – Kindly feed these doves, they are homeless.'

Soldiers have had their pets for centuries. Cavalier Prince Rupert's dog, 'Boye', was killed at Marston Moor in 1644. Just as danger and death heighten sensitivity to 'wild' nature, they increase appreciation of 'tamed' nature. It is sometimes suggested that the British love of pets derives solely from national emotional stuntedness, with pets being substitutes for children. (An argument demolished by one bite from a 'family dog'.) While pets in the trenches could be stand-ins for human relationships, soldiers discovered that the species barrier between man and animals is thin and permeable. They are more like Us than we suppose. Pets have 'personhood', a degree of free will, the capability of choice.

In the trenches, pets gave soldiers elements of friendship, affection and psychological support comparable to those received from humans. Often pets were communal property; a pet for a platoon enabled comradeship among men by giving them something to talk about, bond over, forge identity through. A motor-cycle dispatch rider at the front wrote home about 'Ration', a baby rabbit with a broken leg found by the men:

He has now grown up to quite a size, and although he cannot use one leg he gets about a lot. He goes into the cookhouse every day for his tea. We shall take him with us when we move, of course, as he is quite a favourite, and the pet of the section.[4]

A sense of identity with the orphaned and the homeless, connected to a feeling of guilt in having had a hand in the catastrophe which has engulfed the animal, is also discernible in pet-keeping. In Italy a pigeon chick, blown out of its nest, was hand-reared by British Royal

Artillery gunners and became so attached to the battery it would not leave and accompanied the guns through Asiago and Montello. A British infantry officer in Salonika had a pet eagle, again having found it newly hatched,[5] while one AVC officer in Salonika adopted a wolf cub. The same AVC officer also possessed two jackdaws, a wild goose and an Alsatian dog. Veterinary officers tended to be managers of menageries, because they received a steady stream of large-hearted soldiers bearing wounded wild animals for treatment.

'Talking' birds were much sought after, which in the Colony meant magpies, and for their 'gift' of speech their association with bad luck was overlooked or brazenly accepted. While acknowledging the ill fortune attached to *Pica pica*, No. 13 Squadron RFC (a numbering, one might suppose, to strike dread in the heart of a fatalist) decided, with some chutzpah, to make a magpie their pet. Apparently he was 'a very friendly chatty fellow', as he would be: English names for the bird were Chatterpie, Chatternag and Haggister, the last derived from Old German Agalstra = chatterer. Their previous mascot, a barn owl, had escaped.[6]

Cats and dogs topped the popularity chart of trench pets. Since cats tend to be highly territorial, they came literally with the turf as Douglas Gillespie discovered. His attempt to write home, he informed his parents, was made difficult because Sonia, the trench cat, was 'making herself into a living sporran':

She has come from the ruined farm behind, I suppose, but she takes the change very philosophically, and is a sort of permanent housekeeper, who never leaves company headquarters in this dug-out, but is handed over to each relieving regiment, along with other fixtures, appearing in the official indent, after the ammunition – spades, fascines, R.E. material, &c. – as 'Cat and box I.' She has no real affections, but prefers kilts, because they give more accommodation in the lap than breeches; on the other hand, she has an unpleasant habit of using bare knees as a ladder to reach the desired spot.[7]

Asleep at night in his Givenchy dugout, Philip Gosse was struck by something heavy. After quelling his panic that the object was a rat, he realised from the 'kneading with alternate paws' it was 'Landlady' (a significant nomenclature), a cat that was passed on from battalion to battalion, along with precise instructions on feeding as loving as a 'mother's over her baby's first bottle'.[8]

Cats, with their tendency to stay with place rather than person, were owned by many, albeit fleetingly. Major Ronald Schweder's cats went treacherously back and forth between the German and British lines. His cats paid no price for their treason, though others did. Time of war is time of paranoia; in the 12th Division's tranche of Flanders at least one cat plus two dogs were arrested by military authorities because they 'have been in the habit of crossing our trenches at night'.[9]

Cats were always in generous supply. In the trenches at The Keep, Wailly, Private Norman Ellison noted: 'This place is simply overrun with cats. There are literally dozens of them. The originals, the fireside tabbie left behind when the inhabitants fled, are semi-wild, but their offspring are as wild and ferocious as young tigers.'[10] Additionally, stray cats in Britain were rounded up by contractors commissioned with the 'supply of pussy to the army', as one newspaper phrased it less than felicitously for modern ears, which were dispatched to the Western Front as vermin-hunters and gas detectors.[11] (According to Major-General C.H. Foulkes, the gas expert, cats 'complain at once' about gas.) French fireside tabby, wild cat, British ex-pat cat, they all got fed and petted.

*

There is a photograph of battle-wearied British soldiers sitting in the ruins of the French town of Athies in 1917. They give off the air of veterans. One holds on his lap, as though it were a loved child, a terrier dog. The comfort given by the dog to the soldier is visible down the century.

The British on the march along the *pavé* of France and Flanders, or resting on waysides, were always easy to distinguish. Aside from the plume of tobacco smoke which arose from the khaki column, like steam from a green liveried locomotive, courtesy of all the 'gaspers' and the pipes, there were the dogs. 'Almost every British battalion was accompanied by a small pack of mongrel mascots wherever it went', recalled Captain Philip Gosse.[12]

It is the fancy of the British that they know and love dogs better than anyone. The British were early to adopt dogs as pets, meaning companions with names, rather than living instruments. On the fourteenth century funerary brass of Dame Alice Cassey in the Saxon church at Deerhurst in Gloucestershire, there is a little dog. The dog is not placed on the brass as a nameless symbol of loyalty; it has a name, 'Tirri', which is engraved on the collar. Reel forward five hundred years and the British relationship with dogs has become so profound that canines are regarded as family members. Solicitor and 'Saturday Night Soldier' Captain Lionel Crouch was no emotional incontinent, and went to France with the desire to have 'bagged at least one German' before coming home. He wrote to his mother from the trenches, 'Love to all the family, Winkle, Dick . . .' Winkle was a Pekinese, Dick a terrier. Lionel Crouch was twenty-eight.

When the British man was at war it was perhaps inevitable that his best friend was there too. The dog was as much a part of the front line experience on the Western Front as German snipers, Maconochie stew, mud and lice.

Where did all the dogs come from? Initially, there were few injunctions against taking dogs abroad (bringing them home was another affair altogether), although the journey could be fraught for masters and canines alike. On one Channel crossing on an over-packed steamer, Lionel Crouch was below deck with some officers who had their greyhounds with them. The sea turned rough, and men puked everywhere. So did the dogs.

The greyhounds were doubtless for some downtime hare-coursing. There might be a war on, and the German guns yards away, but the British upper class would still a-hunting go (see p. 278). Julian Grenfell took his greyhounds with him to France, as he had taken his greyhounds with him to South Africa when the Royal Dragoons were there in 1911. He had owned greyhounds since boyhood, and they were the subject of one of his first poems: 'To a Black Greyhound', of which this is part:

Shining black in the shining light,
Inky black in the golden sun,
Graceful as the swallow's flight,
Light as swallow, winged one,
Swift as driven hurricane,
Double-sinewed stretch and spring,
Muffled thud of flying feet
See the black dog galloping,
Hear his wild foot-beat.

Julian Grenfell thought that 'greyhounds are the most beautiful things on earth; they have got all the really jolly things, affection, and courage unspeakable, and speed like nothing else, and sensitiveness and dash and grace and gentleness, and enthusiasm.'

He never cared to be parted from his dogs. In one of his last letters he wrote:

The long dogs were very good when I got back here [to his billet]. A kind woman at the farm had kept and fed them for me. One had been run over by a motor-bus, but was none the worse. We arrived in the middle of the night, and when they heard my voice they came out of the yard like shrapnel bursting. 'Comrade' jumped up on to my horse's shoulder, and when he fell back they all started fighting like hell from sheer joy![13]

His joy too.

The *Daily Sketch* raised a laugh with the witticism that hunting hares made 'a change from herr-shooting!' on the Western Front. This was in relation to the pack of beagles loaned to thirty-year-old Captain Charles Romer Williams, 4th (Royal Irish) Dragoon Guards, and taken out with him to France. Like Grenfell, Williams had been master of the school beagles at Eton. He was the mainstay of the busy 2nd Cavalry Brigade Beagles out in France. Their hunt-meet card for January 1915 read:

THE 2ND CAVALRY BRIGADE BEAGLES WILL MEET –

SUNDAY Jan. 3rd, C Squadron 4th Dragoon Guards.
TUESDAY Jan. 5th, St-Jans-Cappel, Berthen, Cross Roads.
THURSDAY Jan. 7th, Headquarters 9th Lancers.
SATURDAY Jan. 9th, Berthen.
MONDAY Jan. 11th, II Battery.
WEDNESDAY Jan. 13th, Headquarters 18th Hussars.
FRIDAY Jan. 15th, St-Jans-Cappel Church.
SUNDAY Jan. 17th, Headquarters 4th Dragoon Guards.
Each day at One o'clock.[14]

Alas for *la chasse* an order came along one day in January 1915 from GHQ which stated that 'the Commander-in-Chief regrets that it is necessary to prohibit any more hunting, coursing, shooting, or paper-chasing. This order comes into effect at once.'

Among the 2nd Cavalry Beagles' most enthusiastic supporters was Edward, Prince of Wales, then a lieutenant in 1/Grenadier Guards, who described his day hunting with them as 'the only day I have felt really fit out here. I did enjoy that afternoon's run, and it did me worlds of good! It was very bad luck on poor R[omer] Williams who took all the trouble to bring out that fine pack; and then to get so little fun out of it'.[15]

The prince blamed the 'bloody French' for stopping the sport of kings and princes, although in fact the War Office was wholly in accord with the Gallic ruling. A steady stream of officers was being injured pursuing Reynard and Brer Hare. Better, considered the War Office, that men died hunting Fritz instead, and most of the 2nd Cavalry Beagles were returned to Britain. The remainder, reported

*Country Life*, stayed on in the trenches as pets, 'living a life of inglorious ease'.[16]

The majority of soldiers' dogs in the Colony were adopted waifs and strays of war. Aside from the dogs lost or abandoned by French and Belgian civilians, the French and British armies sent many terriers to the front as ratters, numerous of which went AWOL. On being introduced to trench life at Le Touret, Second Lieutenant Edmund Blunden saw that 'some of the men were amusing themselves in digging out a colony of rats, for which sport they had enlisted a stray terrier'.[17] The callow subaltern himself caught a 'stray mongrel' at Auchonvillers (or 'Ocean Villas' as Blunden's batman insisted on spelling it) in September 1916. Cleaned up with a sandbag, dug a small recess and given a couch of fresh new sandbags, the dog was attached to an old bayonet driven into the chalk. It went in the night. Blunden attributed the disappearance to the dog fleeing its diet: 'I think I gave him W.H. Davies' Corned Beef by mistake, an unpopular brand; he may have thought me an agent.'

A dog-napper, rather than Davies' Corned Beef, may have been responsible for the disappearance of Blunden's dog, since the stealing of dogs from other units was rife. Sitting in the officer's mess of 182nd Labour Company, Lieutenant Andrew McCormick suddenly saw the door open and one of his corporals fling a puppy inside, 'remarking in the most casual sort of way – "a souvenir for you, sir".' The puppy was a 'dear wee Manchester terrier, black with brown points'. An NCO from another regiment tried to claim the dog as his, but McCormick paid him off with ten francs:

> And I gladly paid him the filthy lucre, for I thought that anybody who could part with that dog for 7/6 should never have the privilege of keeping a dog.

The puppy was christened Teddie because she loved to dance around on her back legs when 'Are you there little Teddy Bear?' played on the gramophone. The dog captivated the mess. McCormick was so cheered by Teddie, 'I could scarcely do enough for her in repayment. Chocolate at 5/- a packet was entirely consumed by Teddie.'[18]

When the Irish pointer of Major Neil Fraser-Tytler, RFA, was stolen 'the many professional and unprofessional dog stealers in the battery set to work to effect his recovery' from captivity half a mile away. One gang tried with 'Red Indian stealth' to get into the dugout where the pointer was tied up, while another gang started a tunnel. The enthusiasm of Fraser-Tytler's men was motivated by more than sentiment or dented regimental pride. There was a rumour that Fraser-Tytler was prepared to pay a 'Large Sum' for the dog's return. Eventually, Fraser-Tytler's battery was relocated and 'it was only our move out of the locality that brought to an end these pious efforts'.[19] The pointer's name was Mehal-Shahal-Hash-Baz, Hebrew for plunderer, and right well, wrote Fraser-Tytler, 'did he earn his name if ever he was left in a dug-out alone!' There was some consolation for Fraser-Tytler in the thought that Mehal-Shahal-Hash-Baz would live up to his name in his new accommodation.

Dogs needed to be guarded. When Private Albert Lowy, an ambulance driver with the Army Service Corps, developed the flu ('that many army men caught: some died of it') he knew he should admit himself to hospital but worried what would become of his wire-haired terrier. So he decided not to report sick:

> I managed those two awful days and then gradually recovered. My dog was saved.[20]

Men were sometimes buried with their dogs, in recognition of their mutual bond. Lieutenant-Colonel Charlie Duncombe, 2nd Earl of Feversham, was killed in action at the Battle of Flers-Courcelette, while commanding 21st Battalion (Yeoman Rifles) King's Royal Rifle Corps. He had taken his deerhound to war: it too was killed and was interred with him.[21]

Dogs were often gifts. The dismal march of 1/Royal Welch Fusiliers to the Somme's front line, remembered Lieutenant Bernard Adams, was accompanied by 'the plum-pudding dog' who belonged to one of the men, 'a gift from a daughter of France'. It was a fifteen mile march, and when Adams stopped to give the men half an hour to eat their bread and cheese, there appeared 'a sort of Newfoundland collie'. He joined 'plum-pudding hound for the rich harvest of crusts and cheeses'.

The dog that adopted Rowland Feilding was also hungry. In the fire-trench at Guildford Alley in October 1915, it was getting colder and colder at night. Feilding wrote to his wife:

> Last night a half-starved dog crawled into the trench and slept beside me, and I was glad of his company for the warmth it gave.[22]

That warmth was likely as much spiritual as physical.

Dogs could be bought. When Second Lieutenant Edmund Fisher, RFA, told his parents he had 'adopted' a French foxhound belonging to some road navvies, francs passed hands. To Fisher's delight, the dog proved to be 'the most accomplished ratter I have ever met ... Though he is a great lumbering fellow he is about 6 times quicker than any terrier I have met and quite often catches them in the air. He caught 27 yesterday, today about 15.'[23]

A good ratter was a treasure. Fisher's dog slept in his bed, thus doubling up as companion and anti-rodent device. Fisher wondered whether he should 'try him on a hare later on'.

Of course, the most obvious way of obtaining a dog was the most natural one. Dogs begat dogs. Second Lieutenant George Atkinson recorded in his diary:

> Beryl, our terrier bitch, presented us with seven puppies of every breed and colour – the little harlot![24]

The harlot's puppies would need homes.

Philip Gosse, RAMC, won his dog playing cards, though medics with dogs usually gained them because they had treated them as patients. There was always a stream of animals going through the Casualty Clearing System for humans. Lieutenant Reginald Dixon, 251st Siege Battery, RGA, recalled:

> Soldiers love animals and will make pets of any strays they find. After the Vimy Ridge battle, the battery I was serving with at the time found in the battered village of Thelus a small mongrel dog that had had its front paw shot away by a shell splinter. The brigade MO had treated it, the wound had healed, and the MO had actually made and fitted a little artificial wooden leg for the little beast. We named him Thelus, because that was where he was found, and he became the battery pet, running around among the guns as if the business of war was his natural milieu.[25]

Lieutenant-Colonel John McCrae was a notably soft touch. When on one occasion McCrae treated a wounded English soldier who arrived with his dog, Windy, whose leg had been shattered in battle, McCrae treated both and kept Windy in his personal quarters. The soldier was evacuated to England and because he was not allowed to take Windy, McCrae added him to his collection of dogs.

Private James Brown of the 1/North Staffordshire Regiment had no need to take his dog to war, or buy, steal or be gifted one. Prince went anyway, all by himself.

When Brown was posted to France in September 1914 he left his dog, Prince, behind with his wife in Hammersmith, London. To Mrs Brown's dismay Prince soon went missing; after days spent looking for the half Irish terrier-half collie she wrote to her husband with the bad news.

Her husband wrote back in reply: 'I am sorry you have not found Prince and you are not likely to – he is over here with me. A man brought him to me from the front trenches. I could not believe my eyes till I got off my horse and he made a great fuss of me.' Prince, inconsolable at his master's parting, had travelled independently to Armentières, a distance of 300 miles from Hammersmith, in two weeks. There were disbelievers. How could a dog make such a journey? In all likelihood the dog tagged along with some Tommies to make the Channel crossing and along to the front where he eventually sniffed out his owner. The RSPCA investigated the story and were said to 'establish its authenticity beyond doubt'. Private Brown provided Prince with his own British Warm, fashioned from some old greatcoats. He used to wear his master's identification disc. 'He is now the pet of the regiment,' Brown wrote.

Many regiments had mascots, with dogs featuring prominently among them. A mascot, strictly speaking, was a symbol of military virtue. Unofficially, mascots were good luck charms and collective pets. There were mascots who went to war, such as Leitrim Boy, the Irish wolfhound mascot of the Irish Guards, and Jack, the old black Labrador of the Royal Dublin Fusiliers. Both dogs went into the trenches. When Captain R. Macfarlane, 2/Black Watch, was killed in action at Istabulat on 21 April 1917 his loyal dog Jean was then adopted as the regimental pet of the battalion and stayed with them through the rest of the campaign. When in July 1916 Billy the bulldog, regimental pet to the Royal Inniskilling Fusiliers, died at Dawlish in South Devon, he was sufficiently highly regarded to be given an honours funeral.

*

Along with ceiling-high prices in *estaminets*, where Tommy went for egg and chips, dogs were one of the bones of contention with the French. Almost to a man, the British soldiery complained of the way dogs were worked by the locals. Trooper Benjamin Clouting, 4th (Royal Irish) Dragoon Guards, observed:

In France, the dog was an integral part of village and farm life and was not a luxury . . . On the Mont des Cats, as with many villages we came to during the war, it was common to see the local milkman going round not with a pony but with a large dog as his main mode of transport. This dog would plod along, harnessed to a cart, on the back of which stood the village's milk churn. When not pulling the milk, the dog worked the butter churn. To the encouragement of '*vite, vite!*' the dog ran on a wheel like a treadmill, the motion of which turned the churn over and over, forming the butter.

Sapper Guy Buckeridge, 37th Division Signal Company, Royal Engineers, stayed at a farm where Great Danes were put on a wheel to churn butter:

> It used to irritate me to see ordinary companionable animals used as beasts of burden and spoiled in temper ... On the whole the French and Belgians were not friendly with their animals, as we are, and their lives seemed pretty miserable in consequence.

All animals seemed to be tied up in France. 'I never saw a horse out to grass,' Buckeridge added. 'Nor a cow.'[26]

Tramping through villages and farmland deserted by fleeing civilians, British soldiers came upon pitiable scenes. Patrick Butler of the 1/ Royal Irish Rangers noted that:

> Pigs and chickens were enjoying a most unwonted degree of freedom, and not being confined within any limits were able to fend for themselves in food. The unfortunate watch-dogs were the most to be pitied, for in a great number of cases they had been left to starve on the chain. Our men often tried to release them, but in many cases they had become so fierce that nobody dared approach them.[27]

The farmyard dogs of France made for an indelible memory; Charles Douie, on the Somme, encountered in every farmyard vast accumulated heaps of manure and 'Mongrel dogs, perpetually chained and half-savage, through lack of exercise, were kennelled within the courtyard, and barked angrily at every passerby.'[28]

Second Lieutenant Andrew Buxton, 3rd Rifle Brigade, considered:

I suppose there is no licence fee for keeping dogs, hence everyone keeps them, and they are most abominably thoughtless. For
the most part dogs are continuously tied up, sometimes in a little
kennel, sometimes just to a wall, sometimes to a little round brick
place; one such place where we were two nights ago had an entrance
at the bottom of a slope in the yard, so that the water ran down
into it, and a poor little shivering dog lying in the sodden bottom
of it . . . I found one tied to a wall, a most charming looking fox
terrier, but so painfully starved, and with claws quite worn down.
I gave it an old box as some shelter, and let it out this afternoon,
such terrific joy at getting a run around.

Another day, another dog to be pitied. 'Yesterday,' wrote Buxton, 'I
gave a little terrier here some dry bread, and a tiny bit of meat – all I
had – and really too awful to see its intense hunger. I may be wrong
in thinking they suffer as I do, but it is very wretched to see this
treatment on every hand. It puts me off *my* good meals badly!'

When Buxton was killed in 1917, a fellow officer wrote to Buxton's
parents describing how their son was forever arguing with civilians
over their treatment of animals. He had once performed a commando
raid over a fence into a garden at night to lengthen a dog's chain.[29]
Throughout the Colony, British soldiers went on missions to improve
the lot of the French dog.

In Flanders, Douglas Gillespie's battalion of the Argyll and Sutherland Highlanders was placed in

the usual farm, with the usual midden in the middle of the courtyard; there is a big dog there too, chained to his barrel, who is
having the feast of his life on scraps of bully beef.[30]

Although the 11/Suffolk's farmhouse billet at Essar was, Edmund
Blunden decided, 'one of the happiest to which my lamented battalion ever went', the 'smelly little farmyard dog' was a cause of anguish;
he was let off his chain in the night by 'our humanitarians', and

walked out into a liberty he could scarcely remember since puppy days. When the Sussex men left the dog 'hung a mournful head'.

Whatever the general feeling of British soldiers, some approved of the French penchant for putting dogs to work, and they included 'Buffalo Bill', the eccentric major of 2/Royal Welch Fusiliers, who, to the chagrin of his men, bought a large dog with the intention of making it pull a cart. Private Frank Richards:

> All over Flanders it was a common sight to see dogs in harness working and pulling little carts about, which in England is against the law. Buffalo Bill calculated that the dog would be able to pull as much trench stores to the front-line trench in one journey as six men could carry, thereby saving six men who could work repairing the trenches.[31]

A man was appointed to take charge of the dog, who went by the exalted title of 'the Dog-Major'.

The experiment was a disaster. Richards went with the dog and the Dog-Major on their first night-time trip to the front line. A shell exploded and 'the dog gave a leap off the track, pulling cart and stores into a shell-hole which was knee-deep in mud and water'. The cart was reloaded and carried off but the dog kept going off track and upsetting the stores cart. Other attempts ended equally dismally. An aggrieved Buffalo Bill made the Dog-Major take up his abode in the kennel with the dog, giving literal truth to 'in the dog-house'. Then the cart got blown to pieces, and the dog spent the rest of the day 'yelping and barking with delight'.

Buffalo Bill left the company, but the dog stayed and became a pet. 'We all got to like the dog, which used to go in and out of the line with us.' He went missing ('I expect a Frenchman pinched him') but nine months later, when 2/Royal Welch Fusiliers were in Béthune, the dog came running up wagging his tail. He was given a permanent home with transport, but was killed in 1917 by a shell splinter in the Ypres sector. As Richards remarked, 'He had survived four or five months in a front-line trench but was killed miles behind one.'[32]

In the paranoia of war, the dog, like the cat, became victim. Packs of dogs roaming the Somme caused the issuing of an order to the effect 'that all [stray] dogs seen in the trenches are at once to be killed as they may be bearers of messages or poison from the Bosche lines, and are extremely dangerous'.

But it is not so easy to kill a dog. When a company sergeant-major in the 22/Manchester Pals was ordered to dispatch one such stray, he fired two shots into the dog's head, yet missed the brain. According to Lieutenant William Gommersall the dog then 'came for our dug-out, where I was sitting in my usual place near the door. It had gone absolutely mad, and was foaming at the mouth, and blood was pouring from its eyes.' Gommersall whipped out his revolver but couldn't fire for fear of hitting the sergeant-major. Finally the sergeant-major seized the dog by its tail, put another bullet through its head and flung it over the parapet, with the intention of burying it at night.

The dog was seen to move, so someone shot it with a rifle. 'Almost immediately,' recalled Gommersall, 'we saw it on the parapet above us . . . It was bleeding and foaming as before, and sprang down over some barbed wire coils into the trench bottom, where three rounds rapid fire from the revolver finished it.'[33] Charlie May, Gommersall's fellow officer in the Manchester Pals, thought shooting dogs 'a dirty trick' but considered the Germans 'quite capable of inoculating the brutes with some beastly disease and then letting them loose on us. I may be wrong but in war one cannot take chances – especially against Fritz.'[34]

Or against the Turks. At Gallipoli there were also orders to shoot dogs, where they were feared to be bait to lure British soldiers out into the open for the convenience of Turkish riflemen. Private Denis Buxton wrote in his diary.

Some nice sandy dogs, small colley [sic] size, mongrels, near the trenches are shot, as they are supposed to belong to snipers. One I met was very affectionate, but I suppose 'it's always safest to be on the safe side'.

One soldier who fraternised with the dogs of Gallipoli, despite the decree, was Geoffrey Dearmer. There is a curious lack of incidence of dogs in First World War poetry. Julian Grenfell's much anthologised 'To a Black Greyhound' is actually pre-war. Only Geoffrey Dearmer's 'The Turkish Trench Dog' stands out:

Night held me as I crawled and scrambled near
The Turkish lines. Above, the mocking stars
Silvered the curving parapet, and clear
Cloud-latticed beams o'erflecked the land with bars;
I, crouching, lay between
Tense-listening armies peering through the night,
Twin giants bound by tentacles unseen
Here in dim-shadowed light
I saw him, as a sudden movement turned
His eyes towards me, glowing eyes that burned
A moment ere his snuffling muzzle found
My trail; and then as serpents mesmerise
He chained me with those unrelenting eyes,
That muscle-sliding rhythm, knit and bound
In spare-limbed symmetry, those perfect jaws
And soft-approaching pitter-patter paws.
Nearer and nearer like a wolf he crept –
That moment had my swift revolver leapt –
But terror seized me, terror born of shame
Brought flooding revelation. For he came
As one who offers comradeship deserved,
An open ally of the human race,
And sniffling at my prostrate form unnerved
He licked my face!

Second Lieutenant Geoffrey Dearmer, Royal Fusiliers, had landed at barren Gallipoli only days after his younger brother had been killed there.

*The Spectator*, in a wartime review of Dearmer's poetry, noted that the 'writer never loses hold of his conviction that love is stronger than hate'. Dearmer was never cynical in the way that Sassoon and Owen were cynical. His religious faith was undimmed by war. Then again, Dearmer's father was the Anglican parson Percy Dearmer, the celebrated compiler of *The English Hymnal*. 'The Turkish Trench Dog' is a parable; it is also a paean to the man–dog bond, a restatement of the traditional relationship despite the exigencies of the Gallipoli campaign.

If real-life dogs failed to inspire the poets, the dread hound of Greek mythology, the dog that guards the portal of Hades, loomed large in Captain Robert Graves's verse account of his serious wounding on the Somme in August 1916. In his own words: 'I must have been at the full stretch of my stride to escape emasculation' – instead the piece of shell went through his left thigh. A shell piece also entered his chest; there was damage to his forehead and his hand. Barely twenty-one, Graves, who had never been to university, displayed the casual facility with myth and metre which came from the study of Classics at an Edwardian English public or grammar school:

> . . . but I was dead, an hour or more.
> I woke when I'd already passed the door
> That Cerberus guards . . .

The poem is indebted to real life. Amusingly, the hellhound is defeated by being diverted by army biscuit and jam, a staple treat for the dogs of the trenches.

*

In their prisoner of war camps, the British still managed to recruit dogs as pets. A privilege accorded officer prisoners was the paroled walk, whereby they were allowed to ramble around outside the camp as long as they promised not to escape. A gentleman's word, in those far away days, was his bond, and an officer was, by definition, a gentleman.[35] Out on a paroled walk from Zorndorf camp, Flossie Hervey, a young second lieutenant in the RFC, encountered a small boy dragging a dachshund pup along. A few Marks and some chocolate were enough to effect a change of ownership. Hervey christened the dog, with linguistic appositeness, 'Kleiner' (from the German for small, 'klein'); she slept in his dorm, and accompanied the PoWs on their extra-mural promenades. Once, when she disappeared in full cry after a red deer and got lost, a kindly sentry returned her.

Dachshunds were the dog of choice for the PoW in Germany, being plentiful in supply (they were, of course, a German breed), petite eaters and small enough to tuck under the low wood and wire barrack bed. There were more ways to secure pets than bribing *Kinder* with chocolate; a dog was an easy purchase on the camp black market. At Crefeld Offizierslager, Douglas Lyall Grant's room purchased two dachshunds, whom they named Anthony and Antoinette. He noted in his diary: 'They have been trained to fraternize with the British and bark at the Boche.' At Schwarmstedt, one British PoW befriended the dog kept to track down escapees. According to Lieutenant Will Harvey, the dog, like most other Germans at Schwarmstedt, 'was open to corruption, and on discovery that the English officers could give him better and more plentiful food than his proper masters, he promptly became good friends with them'.[36] When one of the officers escaped, he took the dog with him. British officer PoWs on the march in Germany, as they transferred camps, staggered under the weight of their possessions and their pets. Of the leaving of Crefeld for Schwarmstedt Harvey recalled:

It was an agonising march; every fifty yards or so the column was compelled to halt, while bags were changed from one hand to the other and bundles readjusted on the shoulders. There goes one bearing a large English ham, two bottles of cold tea, a chair, a hockey stick, and on the end of it a canary in a cage. Another staggers onward beneath a cage of live rabbits, a box of tinned meats, and his dirty washing.[37]

Dogs also appeared in camp life in a less favourable aspect. Private Frank MacDonald in his Mannschaftslager:

One day Wallie and I, who had managed to stick together, picked all the bones out of a potful of soup and, sorting them out carefully, managed to piece together the skeleton of a German dachshund.[38]

During a punishment period, at Fort 9 the inmates' pets were banned and collected up. A few days later there was an unexpectedly 'enormous supply of German sausages' on the ration, recalled Captain John Thorn. The prisoners concluded unhappily that their *Wurst* was composed of dog, rabbit, cat, canary and all the other pet fauna in the camp. One British hut had a cat – until the Russians put the cat in the pot. The French trapped small birds, rooks and hooded crows and ate them until the Germans stopped the practice. A young rabbit scampered into camp and was caught by a British officer, who let it go 'to the disappointment of our Allies, who would have liked it for dinner'.

All this was in Germany. In Turkey, the British officer PoWs at Yozgad enjoyed hunting hares and foxes with long dogs in the hills around.[39] 'Our chief problem was how to pass the time,' recalled Lieutenant E.H. Jones, and the Hunt Club was one recreation among many, as well as an evocation of home. Inside the camp someone had painted English landscapes. A homesick Jones thought 'we could sit all day looking at the "village-green" scene.'[40]

The Turks had little reason to guard the Hunt Club members and their excursions, because the camp was 350 miles over mountain, rock and desert from a friendly border. The killing terrain surpassed wire or man as a guard.

*

There were dogs who went to war on active service.

Prior to the Great War, the British army had, with the exception of mascots, one canine on the strength: an Airedale guard dog, which accompanied the 2/Norfolk Regiment to France and was killed by a shell on the Aisne. Other countries had long been experimenting with dogs as instruments of war, and the Germans had even subsidised a network of village clubs to breed and train dogs for army work. The Germans had also gone to Britain and bought up the best British breeds, so when war broke out they had about 6000 dogs ready to serve.[41]

How to explain British reticence about the employment of canines on war work? Essentially, military service was regarded as being unsuitable for dogs, which, aside from rounding up sheep, chasing vermin, retrieving game or guarding homes, had long stopped being tools for human ends. In the British mind, the dog was, foremost, a companion. Herding sheep, pursuing other animals, defending establishments passed the moral muster because they were 'natural' activities.

The eventual establishment of the British War Dog School was due to the indefatigable persistence of one man, Lieutenant-Colonel E.H. Richardson. An ex-Regular soldier turned Scottish farmer, Edwin Hautenville Richardson had been, in a tentative way, training dogs for military purposes since 1900. With the outbreak of war in 1914, he took some ambulance dogs across to Belgium on behalf of the Red Cross, but got no further than Brussels; the use of ambulance dogs was forbidden, largely because the Germans shot them. Richardson tried to persuade the War Office of the usefulness of dogs on the battlefield, to no avail. Then, in winter 1916, an officer in the Royal Artillery sent Richardson a letter 'in which he expressed a great desire for trained dogs to keep up communications between his outpost and the battery'.[42] The first trials of messenger dogs were a great success and the War Office relented. Within a week of being given the nod, Richardson had shut up his house at Carnoustie and moved to Shoeburyness in Essex with his wife (the equally talented and dog mad Blanche). There, on the bleak marshes, within the sound of the bombardments on the Western Front, the British War Dog School was established.

The canines for training came from Battersea Dogs Home, then from similar institutions in Birmingham, Liverpool, Bristol and Manchester. The dogs' homes were full, because of the national shortage of food. Later, the Home Office ordered police forces across the country to send stray dogs to the War Dog School. Thus in Richardson's words:

> many a homeless, deserted 'stray' was saved from the lethal chamber and transformed into a useful member of His Majesty's Forces.[43]

When even these sources were insufficient for Richardson's school the War Office appealed to the public for the gift of their pets. There were many offers, many of them heartbreaking. 'My husband has gone, my son has gone,' wrote one woman to Lieutenant-Colonel Richardson. 'Please, take my dog to bring this cruel war to an end.' A letter from a little girl read: 'We have let daddy go to fight the Kaiser, and now we are sending Jack to do his bit.' Another letter: 'I have given my husband and my sons, and now that he, too, is required, I give my dog.'

The sacrifice was perhaps leavened by the hope that in trying times on the home front, the army would at least feed and care for the donors' pets.

Richardson's speciality was the training of messenger or dispatch dogs. Before being sent to France each dog was tested for weeks, running messages by burning haystacks, through barbed wire, to a soundtrack of shells and small arms fire. 'Coercion is of no avail,' considered Richardson, in the training of dogs. 'The highest appeals of mind – love and duty – have to be appealed to and cultivated.'[44] Each dog was allocated to a handler to whom it became attached. Of course, every dog runs on its stomach; Richardson used chopped liver, as well as human affection, in the reward system.

Almost every dog breed had its day at Shoeburyness. In one period reviewed by Richardson, the War Dog Training School taught: 74 collies, 70 lurchers, 66 Airedales, 36 sheep dogs, 33 retrievers, 18 Irish terriers, 11 spaniels, 6 deerhounds, 4 setters, 5 Welsh terriers, 5 bull terriers, 2 greyhounds, 2 Eskimos, 2 Dalmatians, 2 Bedlingtons, 2 pointers, 1 bulldog, 1 whippet .

On the whole Richardson found Airedales, collies, lurchers and whippets the best messenger dogs. Some breeds defeated him. Hounds were 'too indulgent'; poodles and fox terriers 'too frivolous'.

Lieutenant-Colonel Richardson was not always successful. 'I much regret to say that it was my experience to find occasionally the canine "conscientious objector" among the ranks.' Failures were returned to Battersea or put down.

When Shoeburyness became too congested, the War Dog School moved to Matley Ridge, above Lyndhurst in Hampshire.

Out in the battlefield, dogs were first allotted to battalions, then organised as the independent Messenger Dog Service.

The good work of Richardson's dogs running messages – 200 or so a day – was sometimes undermined by Tommies spoiling the dogs with affection. Keeper Goodway reported to Richardson from France:

The only fault about the big 'Collie' is, that he is rather a good-looking dog and everybody will make a fuss of him if they get the chance, therefore, if any soldier calls he will stop to be made a fuss of . . .[45]

Another keeper, Corporal Taylor, informed Richardson:

I might mention here, that I found one or two of the dogs were losing time, so I went forward to find out the cause, and found them in a trench, on their chains, and a lot of pieces of bully beef put in a tin in front of them.

Very kind, of course, but spoiling the dogs. I at once informed the signal officers of both Brigades, and it was stopped. That was one of our greatest troubles – troops feeding and fussing about the dogs.[46]

Eventually it was made a military offence to interfere with a messenger dog in the performance of its duties.

The keepers learned an ancient pride in working their dogs. Keeper Sergeant Brown was transfigured by the experience:

The old idea was that a dog's life was nothing, but after the experience I have had with them in the field it has taught me to love and respect them as never before.[47]

The messenger dogs achieved great things in action. On the Western Front the dogs were running over very broken ground, of mud, shell holes, barbed wire, amid artillery and small arms fire. At Kemmel Hill, Keeper Dixon's Airedale 'Boxer' went over the top with the Kents at 5 a.m. and was then released to take a message back to his keeper at HQ. Dixon recorded: 'He jumped at me at 5.25' having gone through 'belly deep' mud. Men were taking two hours to do the same journey.

Gas was another difficulty faced, although again dogs seemed to cope better than humans. Keeper Macleod in the Nieppe Forest sector:

At that time, 'Paddy' was badly gassed in the front line, and came right back to the Section Kennel – a distance of 17 kilos. When he came in he was totally blind, but went direct to his own kennel and lay there till I went to his assistance. In three hours he had his eyes open again and was as lively as ever.[48]

The dogs also seemed to be able to detect aircraft and gas raids. According to Keeper Osbourne:

On another occasion while in the first-line trenches little 'Jim' [a 3-year-old crossbred retriever-spaniel] was instrumental in first giving the warning of gas, due no doubt to his highly sensitive nose, thereupon he was immediately released with the warning to Headquarters, arriving there a little more than three-quarters of an hour earlier than the warning given by wire. His worth is beyond value and his services beyond praise, and I feel honoured to take care of such a very serviceable animal.

Dogs ran as well at night as in the day (unlike men). Keeper Davis reported to Richardson:

Joe and Izzard have done some very good work out here both day and night ... I have had them come three miles at night in 20 minutes.

The dog almost always got through quicker than a man, though both the German and British armies brought bitches on to the front line to distract enemy messenger dogs.

The devotion to duty of the messenger dogs affected everyone they encountered. One of Richardson's keepers informed him:

I am sorry to have to tell you that I have lost poor old 'Smiler.' The Staff Capt. had taken him up the line and sent him back with a message which he brought back in 20 mins., – a distance of 3 kilos. The poor old fellow's jaw was hanging down, being fractured by a bullet – I knew there was not much hope for him, but I took him to the A.V.C., after binding him up, and they immediately shot him. He had been going up the line with the General each morning and bringing his messages back in good time always. The General was very fond of him and told me yesterday he was sorry I had lost him.[49]

On occasion dogs were saviours. On 2 May 1918 'Tweed' was re-leased by Queen Victoria's Rifles with the urgent message to send up reinforcements and small round ammunition. According to Keeper Reid, Tweed 'came through a Boche barrage – the three kms in 10 minutes. The French were sent up and filled the gaps, and straightened out the line, otherwise Amiens would be in the hands of the Germans.'

Was Tweed brave or merely well-trained? Lieutenant-Colonel Richardson was utterly convinced that dogs were guided by character as much as instruction:

> If dogs have lived with people of pluck and courage, they will exhibit these qualities. It is quite natural for dogs to be courageous, and if this instinct has become blunted, it is possible to cultivate it and revive it once more.

After the war was over, Richardson wrote *British War Dogs: Their Training and Psychology*, an account of his canines in the conflict. Inside the flyleaf was printed:

> This book is dedicated to the brave Dogs of Britain who helped their country in her hour of need. FAITHFUL UNTIL DEATH.

# *Interstice 6*

## *A Complete List of Soldiers' and Sailors' Pets and Mascots*

### Antelope

Royal Warwickshire Regiment

### Baboon

'Jackie', taken to France by South African Scottish Regiment

### Bear

'Cocky', black bear, mascot, Canadian infantry
'Winnie', female black bear cub, inspiration for Winnie the Pooh,
    the pet of Lieutenant Harry Colebourn, Canadian Royal Army
    Veterinary Corps, later the mascot of the Fort Garry Horse

## Cat

'Hoskyn', HMS *Chester*
'Jimmy', tortoiseshell, HMS *King George V*, transferred to HMS
    *Renown*
'Lyddite', mascot, HMS *Shark*
'Side Boy', lucky black cat, HMS *Neptune*
'Smut', lucky black cat, HMS *Superb*
'Snowy', mascot of the New Zealand Tunnelling Company
'Togo', HMS *Irresistible*
Ship's cat, HMS *Topaze*

## Chicken

## Chimpanzee

## Cow

'Jane', 23rd Infantry Brigade
'Mary', kept in a dugout by enlisted man

## Crow

Fledgeling nursed and adopted by wounded soldiers as mascot at
    Sheffield Base Hospital

## Dog

'Action', Wellington Infantry Battalion

'Billy', bulldog, regimental pet of the Royal Inniskilling Fusiliers

'Buller', HMS *Indomitable* mascot

'Caesar', A Company, 4 Battalion, New Zealand Rifle Brigade

'Floss', a fox terrier, mascot of the New Zealand army rugby team

'Freda', harlequin Great Dane, mascot of the 5 Battalion, New Zealand Rifle Brigade

'Jack', black Labrador, Royal Dublin Fusiliers

'Jack', Jack Russell, mascot attached to the main body of New Zealand Engineers

'Jean', Captain R. Macfarlane, 2nd Battalion, Black Watch

'Joe', mascot of the 1st East Kent Regiment

'Leitrim Boy', Irish wolfhound, Irish Guards

'Nip', brown spaniel, Wellington Regiment

'Paddy', mascot of the Wellington Regiment

'Pelorus Jack', Staffordshire bull terrier, HMS *New Zealand*

'Pip', HMS *Centurion*

'Shanks', mascot, HMS *Patia*

'Tiger', pedigree Great Dane presented to the new Royal Fusiliers battalion

'Tim', a little brown dog, 2nd Prince of Wales' Leinster Regiment

Airedale, sentry dog for the 1st Battalion, the Norfolk Regiment, at start of war

Bulldog, 5th Battalion, the Royal Scots

Bulldog, Herefordshire Regiment

Little white dog, 5th Queen's Own Cameron Highlanders

Sheepdog, belonging to captain of HMS *Chester*

Unnamed breed, Welsh Regiment

## Dogs collecting for charities

'Bob' at Liverpool, 'Brum' at Euston Station, 'Cymro' at Rhyl,
　'Prince' at Crewe (war charities);
'Nancy' the St Bernard, collecting for the British Red Cross
　Society

## Donkey

'Jimmy, the Sergeant', born on the Somme in 1916
'Moses', Egyptian Donkey, mascot of New Zealand Army Service
　Company in France on board HMS *Centurion*

## Doves

Front line unit in Flanders

## Eagle

Golden eagle, pet of subaltern in Balkans

## Fox

Mascot of No. 32 Squadron

## Geese

'Jimmy' and 'Jane', gander and goose, mascots of A Battery, 52nd
   Brigade, Royal Field Artillery
'Squeak', HMS *Centurion*

## Goat

'Billy', a white Welsh goat, mascot of the Royal Welsh Fusiliers
'Billy', served on the battlefield during First World War with the
   5th Canadian Battalion and received stripes for wounds and
   services rendered during battle
'Nan', an Egyptian goat, mascot of the New Zealand Engineers
'Taffy IV', 2nd Battalion, Welsh Regiment: only animal to receive
   formal recognition after the war – awarded the 1914 Star medal
   for service overseas
Billy goat, battery pet, D Battery, 310th Brigade, RFA
Billy goat, Montgomeryshire Yeomanry
Billy goat, mascot of the Sherwood Rangers Yeomanry
Mascot, Coldstream Guards
Mascot, Machine Gun Company
Mascot, Welsh Regiment

## Guinea pigs

Western Front

### Jackdaw

AVC officer, Salonika

### Jerboa

### Kangaroo

Australian regiments

### Koala

'Tommy Brown', mascot of Motor Transport Section, 3rd Division Supply Column of the Australian Field Force

### Lion

'Poilu', pet of General Sir Tom Bridges, and mascot of the 19th Division

### Magpie

No. 13 Squadron, RFC

### Mice

## Mongoose

## Monkeys

Mascot of Third Army Trench Mortar School

## Mules

## Orang-utan

Pair of babies, Warwickshire Yeomanry

## Parrot

'Coco', 468th Field Company

## Pig

'Muriel', 1st Battalion, the Royal Inniskilling Fusiliers
'Tirpitz', HMS *Glasgow*

## Pigeon

Royal Artillery gunners, Italy

## Rabbit

Motorcyclists, Western Front
'Wilfred', HMS *Centurion*

## Sheep

'Derby XII', Notts and Derbyshire regiment

## Skylark

## Springbok

'Nancy', 4/South African Regiment

## Stork

## Tortoise

Kept by regiments in Mesopotamia

## Wallabies

Australian regiments

# Wolf

AVC officer in Salonika

# CHAPTER VII

# A-Hunting and A-Shooting (and A-Fishing) We Will Go

*Field Sports and Poaching at the Front*

In early October 1914 Lieutenant The Honourable Julian Grenfell went shooting on the 1000 acre family estate, Panshanger Park, in Hertfordshire. He had a good time in the grounds, much of which consisted of parkland sculpted by Humphry Repton in the late eighteenth century; other parts were designed by Lancelot 'Capability' Brown, the doyen of landscape architects.

At the end of his day's shooting, Grenfell entered in his game book, '105 partridges'. His next entries read:

November 16th: 1 Pomeranian
November 17th: 2 Pomeranians

The Pomeranians were German soldiers, sniped by Grenfell in the winter trenches of Ypres in escapades that won him the Distinguished Service Order.

The entries were less glib than they appear. For Grenfell game shooting was not a passionless pot, it was a way of getting 'back to real things, bringing the elemental barbaric forces of ourselves into touch with the elemental forces of nature'.[1] Bagging the Pomeranians required the same skills as game shooting: stealth, patience, careful observation of the quarry. To kill the two Pomeranians Grenfell crawled through 'sodden clay and trenches', a yard a minute, for thirty minutes, until he got to a 'Hun' trench:

It was about ten yards from me.

Then I heard some Germans talking, and saw one put his head up over some bushes, about ten yards behind the trench. I could not get a shot at him; I was too low down, and of course I could not get up. So I crawled on again very slowly to the parapet of their trench. It was very exciting. I was not sure that there might not have been someone there, or a little further along the trench. I peered through their loop-hole and saw nobody in the trench. Then the German behind put his head up again. He was laughing and talking. I saw his teeth glistening against my foresight, and I pulled the trigger very slowly. He just grunted, and crumpled up. The others got up and whispered to each other. I do not know which were most frightened, them or me. I think there were four or five of them. They could not trace the shot; I was flat behind their parapet and hidden. I just had the nerve not to move a muscle and stay there.

My heart was fairly hammering. They did not come forward, and I could not see them, as they were behind some bushes and trees, so I crept back inch by inch.[2]

Grenfell's childhood had been filled with tracking, fishing, riding and shooting. On summer holidays in Scotland he had got up at five every morning to go out after roe deer. On his death bed in 1915, Grenfell, who had taken a shrapnel splinter to the skull, is said to have quoted with 'overpowering longing':

Oh for a deep and dewy spring,
With runlets cold to draw and drink!
And a great meadow blossoming,
Long-grassed, and poplars in a ring,
To rest me by the brink!

These lines of longing for countryside are Phaedra's from Gilbert Murray's 1908 rhyming translation of Euripides' *Hippolytus*.[3]

Captain Lionel Crouch was another ardent sniper, telling his mother:

I hope that I shall be able to get at my first German, as I want to secure his helmet like Dad keeps his woodcock and snipe's spikes.[4]

He added: 'I could sit all day waiting for a Bosche's head to appear. It is a far better sport than rabbit-shooting.'

Sniping on the front was a favourite activity of the bored, or those who romantically believed war to be a contest between man and man, rather than man and mechanised killing. Sniping took skill; the verb 'to snipe' originated in the difficulty of shooting the quick, jinking wader of that name.

In the first year of the war the Germans dominated sniping, largely because they dominated the optics industry which produced telescopic sights. By mid 1915, one British officer calculated, the BEF was losing eighteen soldiers per day to sniping. On the open market the War Office could only secure a paltry 1260 telescopic sights. Consequently, Britain's own sniping effort was initially dominated by game shooters with their own weapons, men like Grenfell and Crouch.

The sniper par excellence was Major Hesketh Hesketh-Prichard, a former big game hunter and Hampshire County fast bowler who had been turned away by the army on account of his age – he was born in 1876 – but pestered and persisted until he reached the front as an intelligence officer. In his luggage he packed 'scoped rifles' for a self-proclaimed mission to 'irritate Germans'. After more character-istically tenacious lobbying, Hesketh-Prichard persuaded generals to found 'The First Army School of Sniping, Observing and Scouting'.

Britain's sniping effort received a further boost in 1916, with the formation of the 'Lovat Scout Sharpshooter' unit. Highlanders of Scotland responded to an advertisement in their local newspaper: 'Wanted – 100 Stalkers and Glassmen [men able to use a telescope], between ages of 41 and 45 for stalking Bosches!'[5] Initially an inde-pendent unit, the Lovat Sharpshooters were later assigned across the BEF, so their expertise was widely spread. The Lovats contained many ghillies, or gamekeepers, who used a specialised 'ghillie suit', consisting of strips of brown and green cloth attached to an outer jacket, which was the acme of camouflage clothing. (The ghillie suit concept is still used by snipers today.) What worked for stalking deer in the Scottish glens worked for stalking men on the Western Front. The Lovat Scouts achieved a formidable reputation too as observers. Using nothing but a 20x spotting telescope, a Lovat Scout could ob-serve troop movements in precise detail at a distance of ten or more miles. Hesketh-Prichard said of the Lovat Scouts that 'keener men never lived' and that 'If they reported a thing, the thing was as they reported it.'

To kill a man was the ultimate blood sport on the Western Front. It was not, however, the only one. The traditional country sports of dear old England, from fox hunting to driven partridge shooting, were all transferred to the Colony across the Channel, sometimes to the very lip of the front line. Looking out from his observation post at Arras in February 1917 Second Lieutenant Edward Thomas of the Royal Artillery saw:

A mad captain with several men driving partridges over the open and whistling and crying 'mark over'.[6]

Mad? Maybe. More likely the captain was trying to assert his usual, civilian identity in the madness of war. Game shooting, the traditional pastime of the British classes from middle to upper (and most of the officer corps until 1917 came from this tranche of society), transferred easily to the Western Front, not least because the exigencies of war allowed game birds to multiply: the French stopped all sport at the outbreak of war, while the acres of uncut wheat near the front line provided partridges, quail and, to a lesser extent, pheasants with both cover and food. (One of the few game birds to decrease in the Western war zone, to suffer a negative effect from the conflict, was the woodcock, which apparently re-routed its migration from Scandinavia to fly along the coast of Brittany rather than over the Aisne and Champagne.)

In deference to their French ally and to reduce the possibility of accidents among their own troops, the British forbade 'sport' in the Colony in early 1915. 'Défense de Chasser' signs went up all over France and Flanders. The injunction was largely observed in the breach. Major Patrick Butler, billeted in a country house in the Somme in the autumn, was an early offender:

The nights were bitterly cold now, and it was good to ensconce oneself in one's room, in front of a fire. I read Kenan's 'Souvenirs de la Jeunesse,' and other works which I found on the shelves. In the billiard-room was a game-book, containing the records of many a happy parti de chasse of pre-war days, and the perusal of this brought back memories of great days at home.

I look back to those three weeks which we spent at Courcelles-sous-Moyencourt as being among the pleasantest of the war. In spite of the prohibition which existed in France against the shooting of game in wartime, I managed to wheedle a 16-bore gun and cartridges out of the caretaker, and another officer and I used to go out together of an afternoon on horseback and bag a few hares and partridges.

We used to take it in turns to shoot, while the one who was not shooting held the ponies.[7]

Game shooting close to the front line came with the added frisson that the shooter might be shot by the Germans. Major Neil Fraser-Tytler, D Battery, 149th Brigade, RFA, wrote:

> Yesterday the Germans deigned to turn a machine gun on me. I was out shooting partridges with the new Irish pointer which I have annexed, and must have come a little nearer to the precious line than he quite approved of. Probably he considered pursuing partridges in no-man's land during April contrary to the laws of the Hague Convention! So he splashed some bullets about in an aimless fashion till I removed myself to a quieter spot . . .[8]

In the past, Fraser-Tytler had been over to the colonel's HQ for joint drives, 'utilising the orderlies and spare signallers as beaters, so neither partridge killing (forget the month) nor Hun killing (always in season) has been neglected'.

By Christmas Day 1916 Rowland Feilding was commanding a battalion of the Connaught Rangers and, having done the necessary festival social niceties in the morning, went out 'with my little .45 gun to see if I could kill a pheasant. I got one, which we had for lunch.' His servant, Glover, acted as beater. One of the officers in the battalion, 'a stout Dublin lawyer', spent much of his free time rough shooting, until Feilding realised that his subordinate's favourite hunting ground turned out 'to be no spot to linger in – a medley of unhealthily new shell holes, under full view of the Germans. Certainly a good place for pheasants: but imagine what courts-martial there would be if a casualty took place under such circumstances. I have now put the locality out of bounds, pheasants or no pheasants.'[9]

Colonel Feilding was proof of how high up the command chain the shooting ban was ignored. Likewise Collingwood Ingram, a mere captain, was invited to join 'a little illicit partridge shooting after lunch' in August 1917 by Colonel Pretyman, RFC. Ingram, happily, was the owner of the poacher's favourite, a .410 shotgun disguised as a walking stick, the one he had used in France pre-war to avoid detection by the gendarmes when obtaining birds for his collection. Ingram wrote in his diary:

> Although I failed to make a contribution to the bag, I thoroughly enjoyed the jaunt, for birds were very plentiful. A piquancy was added to the entertainment by the knowledge that we were harmlessly breaking a Military Regulation and from the fact we were poaching in a most bare faced manner. But surely no one should mind our taking toll of the partridge who have been increasing unchecked for the last three years – although perhaps some of the farmers may have had cause to complain of the way we marched boldly through the standing corn.[10]

There was a distinct class division in shooting methods. By and large officers used shotguns, either brought from home or bought from French civilians. Lieutenant Denis Barnett purchased a twelve-bore shotgun locally for 90 francs. However, his resultant pigeon potting, as he informed his parents, failed to follow plan: 'Hit another pigeon yesterday, but he carried on and dropped in the German lines, so we shan't have them starved out for a bit.' Hugh Munro's company of 8/Argyll and Sutherland Highlanders did better. Issued with a company shotgun to shoot German carrier pigeons, the officers used the gun 'surreptitiously for shooting more innocent pigeons, which lent variety to our commissariat'.

Few rankers owned shotguns, the implement being beyond their pocket.[11] The rule was not absolute; Donald Macintyre, a gamekeeper from the Mull of Kintyre who had volunteered at forty-five, was one such exception. After a long stint guarding Greenock docks and Stobhill Hospital in Glasgow, he ended up at Cambrai in 1918, where he purchased a farmer's old shotgun for partridges. For hares and geese he used a souvenir German rifle.

Usually, the Tommy going game shooting used his standard infantry weapon, the Lee Enfield .303 Mark III rifle. Lieutenant Bernard Adams's orderly, Davies, turned up at the reserve trench at Morlancourt 'holding up a large hare, that dripped gore from its mouth into a scrunched up ball of Daily Mail held to its nose like a pocket handkerchief'. Asked how he had bagged the hare, Davies replied:

> 'Oh! easy enough, sir. I'll get another if you like. There's a lot of them sitting out in the snow there. I was only about fifty yards off. He don't get much chance with a rifle, sir.' (Here his voice broke into a laugh.) 'It's not what you call much sport for him, sir! I got this too, sir!' At which point, Davies produced a plump partridge.[12]

Other ranks blasting away at game with Lee Enfields, which were deadly up to 1000 yards, in places thick with men in khaki, was hazardous and eventually prohibited.

Unfortunately Trooper Ben Clouting, 4th (Royal Irish) Dragoon Guards was unaware of the new order:

> At first we shot ducks close to the river's edge, picking them out of the water at arm's length. However, it was clear that richer pickings would be had if we could get out on to the river itself. By this time the ice was too thin to walk on at the edges, so we improvised a canoe out of three barrels scrounged from a farm. Cutting them in two, we placed three halves in a line and, with two planks along the side to keep everything sturdy, nailed the boat together. A lance corporal sat in the front, and I at the back, then with two spades to paddle the craft out into the river, we collected the ducks we had shot, dropping them into the middle compartment.
>
> As we did this, the Military Police turned up and called us in, arresting us as we landed. There had apparently been several casualties from bullets ricocheting off the ice and wounding soldiers. An order banning such actions had been posted, but no one had told us.[13]

No one told the members of the Machine Gun Corps either. As Lieutenant Charles Carrington, stationed near the Somme marshes, recalled, 'Every morning flocks of wild duck rose from their nightly feeding ground, vainly pursued by a rain of machine-gun bullets from both armies.'[14]

Pilots of the RFC, when airborne, were beyond supervision and could vie with game birds in their natural element. Charles Carrington knew of an instance when:

an airman, out on a trial trip one day from Ramsgate, came across some Mallard; he gave chase, opened fire at them with his machine-gun, and killed three, which were picked up by a fisherman and brought to the R.N.A. mess, where they formed a welcome addition to Government rations.[15]

Some officers eschewed the shotgun for less sophisticated means. Anthony Eden and his friends in the King's Royal Rifle Corps pursued coveys of partridges on horseback, and when a bird tired they slipped from the saddle and hit it over the head with a stick. 'By this unorthodox and dubious method we would occasionally add a brace or two of partridges to our fare.'[16]

Captain John Marshall, 468th Field Coy, RE, found a lump of wood a suitable and natural element for wildfowling:

Crawling through the rhododendrons bordering the moat, I disturbed a pair of roosting swans. Remembering the books of the Middle ages which speak of the swan as an edibility, it occurred to me that I might produce one for the menu of the mess, so I went in search of a weapon and found a pick helve. Cautiously approaching one of the gabblers, I caught him two strong blows on the neck, but he seemed none the worse for them, and escaped me. Men: in future hit swans on the top of the head.[17]

Hares, which abounded, frequently fell to revolver shots (and only officers carried side-arms). Douglas Gillespie told his parents that 'hare-stalking is the only sport in the trenches; I have not gone in for it yet, but one fellow has bagged two with his revolver; rather rough on the hares perhaps, for they are all playing about in couples.'[18]

As there were relatively few hedgerows in France, the snaring of game, reported *Country Life*, was 'considerably handicapped'. It could be done, though. George Stringer, who learned about trapping from the company cook, set some night snares at Lindenhoek in the Salient; he and his mates came back with a brace of pheasants and a brace of partridges, though feral cats disappointingly dragged off the pheasants from the dug-out.[19]

Some 'poaching' was robbery, but then the British soldier had a long reputation for judiciously 'liberating' the goods of both friend and foe. Private Norman Ellison 'foraged' pigeon's eggs for breakfast and pigeons for lunch and supper: The day's menu was:

Breakfast: bacon and fried pigeon's eggs, Jam, bread and butter, tea and coffee. Dinner [lunch]: Boiled meat, a stew of two pigeons, carrots, onions, beans and potatoes. Tea: Stewed prunes, stewed rhubarb and stewed greengages, spring onions and lettuce, bread and butter and tea.

Supper: Six boiled pigeons.[20]

He noted, 'I don't think you can beat that for a good day's foraging.' The 'foraging' took place in an abandoned pigeon loft at Méaulte.

Tommy rarely missed the opportunity for improving the menu. Captain Charlie May wrote home:

Major Allrey told me of a little incident which serves to show how quick the men can be if really put to it. The firing line today startled a wild pig which careered down the line at a fine pace. A man saw it coming, whipped out and fixed his bayonet and had pointed [it] in a flash. The major said it was done before you could say knife.[21]

By and large, British soldiers eschewed the French habit of eating passerine birds. Hunger, however, could make men unfastidious. Private Arthur Alexander, 1/14th London Regiment (London Scottish) recalled:

> Corporal King shot a blackbird here and gave it to me. This I plucked and cleaned and then roasted over the fire. Not much of it, but it was tasty nonetheless. Between four of us it only amounted to a taster each, and we wished it had been chicken.[22]

Some animals shot for the menu were fit for royalty. The Somme woods provided roe deer, the Somme marshes snipe (for those, like Brian Lawrence and his party of Grenadier Guards officers, adept enough with a shotgun), and wild boar or *sanglier* were chivvied almost the entire front along. Occasionally, British officers were formally invited on *la chasse au sanglier* in the spirit of the *entente cordiale*; the wild boar, dweller (largely) of woodland was exempted from the hunting ban, together with 'vermin'. At billets in Airaines, Major Poore of 2/Royal Welch Fusiliers was asked along on a boar hunt by the local notary. All Poore bagged was a rabbit and a squirrel.[23] Collingwood Ingram had real luck on a day spent with French boar hunters at Ochey in November 1917. One of the party, a French *poilu* on leave, shot a large female boar:

> With ropes tied to its feet and jaw, four of us hauled the grizzled body to the nearest road – about a kilometre distant. Long before we reached our destination we fully appreciated the great weight of the ponderous body. The tiny eyes, high withers and long and heavy black coat were the most striking features of the beast.[24]

Ingram later dined on the boar with the French family who had organised the hunt:

> Properly cooked and served with a delicious sauce, it proved a

most delectable dish – a tender close-grained viand equal to the best venison, if not better.

*

On first arriving in the Colony, Second Lieutenant Siegfried Sassoon travelled down to the front from Étaples. Looking out of the railway carriage window, his primary concern was that the grey November countryside was 'A hopeless hunting country'.[25]

Nonetheless, the hunting went on. Fox-hunting was the default activity for the squirearchy, men like Siegfried Loraine Sassoon of Weirleigh House, Matfield, in Kent. Organising hunts in the Colony was a confirmation of the continuation of normal life in the place of death. As with the organisation of other traditional blood and field sports in the Colony, fox hunting was a self-aware act of contempt towards the Kaiser. The society magazine *Tatler* wrote across photos of British officers fox hunting in France: 'We Don't Care for the Shells and the Shot, and We'll All Go A-Hunting Today.'[26]

Hunting was also bonding for country people. Siegfried Sassoon was upper class but found some of his easiest hours on enlistment talking to Bob Jenner, the hunting son of a Kentish farmer:

What I should have done without him to talk to I couldn't imagine. I had known him out hunting, so there were a good many simple memories which we could share.[27]

Although the Kaiser failed to deter fox-hunting, the British army was more formidable and banned the sport under the general prohibition of field sports of January 1915.

Something of the loss the hunting fraternity felt about the ruling was captured in the print 'That far, far-away Echo' by *The Graphic* artist 'Snaffles' (properly Charles Johnson Payne, later a lieutenant in the Royal Naval Volunteer Reserve (RNVR), where he designed camouflage for ships at sea). It depicted the dream of a soldier in his shell-torn trench mentally cheering on his hounds. Somewhat pitifully, one of Sassoon's favourite hobbies in reserve was riding around the French countryside 'having an imitation hunt'. Other officers also, contrary to regulations, rode to paper chase hunts; Major Ronald Schweder, RFA, did so at Cayeux-sur-Mer in 1916 and 1917. These paper chase hunts were poor substitutes, though, for pursuing a live Reynard.

On leave in winter back in Britain Sassoon hunted, ardently.[28] Although the Masters of Foxhounds Association had qualms about hunting's continuance in wartime Britain – people dashing around the countryside having fun looked bad form in a national emergency – there were loud voices in favour. One pro case was that if the sport continued it would allow hunting soldiers on leave their familiar winter recreation. And so hunting, the quintessential British country sport, carried on, with one conspicuous change. With the Master away at the war, women sometimes took over the red coat role. The wife of Major Richard Selby-Lowndes acted as Master of the Whaddon Chase Hunt, Mrs Ralph Lubbock headed the North Herefordshire Hunt, while Mrs W.F. Inge took charge of the Atherstone, formerly hunted by her father.[29]

There was a last tally-ho of sorts for the soldier fox-hunters abroad, as Lieutenant Harold Hemming, RFA, witnessed. Hemming was part of the occupation army which marched into Germany in 1918 when:

the horsey members of our army decided that they should start fox-hunting. Unfortunately there were no foxes, so they had to descend to a drag hunt. However, everything else was done in style. They sent to England for their red coats and caps, and managed somehow to collect a pretty comic pack of hounds, appoint a master of Hounds, etc.[30]

\*

There were field sports to be had on other fronts too, though the quarry erred to the fantastic. In Mesopotamia, where sporting opportunities tended to be limited by the extremes of weather (it was either baked or flooded), Lieutenant Mackay enjoyed a fine March hunt, 'finishing up with a four mile gallop after three jackals which, however, all separated and got away. The huntsman always carried a loaded stick to finish off the jacks as they take such a lot of killing.' The dogs used in the chase were Persian greyhounds. More useful on the plate were the plentiful wild boar of the region. There were some ex-Indian army officers in Mackay's regiment, who were old hands at 'pig-sticking' – hunting boar with lances. On a three day 'show' the said officers 'got 29 pigs in all'. The downside was the 'several casualties though to the horses. Horses have to be trained for it as wild boar are very courageous and go for the horse and most horses won't face them.' With a dose of the *noblesse oblige* that helped keep the British army together, two of Mackay's fellow officers, majors Wallis and Lumsden, went out shooting and brought back four fine geese: 'These are big birds and we have sent two across to the Sergeants' mess.'

The hunting of the jackal had an importance beyond entertainment. Mackay's mess kept chickens: 'They go clucking round our tents at each stopping place, laying eggs occasionally – it seems strange taking poultry with one on the warpath.' The chickens numbered over thirty, producing up to twenty-five eggs a day, so many indeed, that the cook was hard pushed to think of ways to use them up, despite omelettes and cakes 'accounting for many'.

But golden jackals threatened the operation. 'We have to batten them [the chickens] down well at night though to protect them from jackals who are always prowling around.' The mess's two sheep also required protection from *Canis aureus*. The jackals and hyenas barked and so disturbed sleep. Pest control, as well as a good night's sleep, required the killing of the jackals.

British troops in Mesopotamia were expected to respect the 'close season' for game birds. Which chafed. To the relief of Lieutenant-Colonel Perreau, constantly tormented by the sight of sandgrouse ('there's quite a lot of game if we were now allowed to shoot it'), 'the glorious Twelfth of August duly came'. 'We get fresh bird meat and the fun of getting it,' he informed the Mater from 'Somewhere in Mesopotamia', though he gave her a clue; it was near 'Immaculatus'.

Cartridges were few, and Perreau, as the self-confessed 'best poacher' in the regiment, did most of the shooting for the pot. The sandgrouse were: 'Very handsome birds and very welcome change.' Perreau was also the best birdwatcher, and was disappointed that 'Bird life is not in great variety out here', adding that, 'an insect man would probably appreciate the fauna more than we do'. 'Hang these flies', he signed off, with uncharacteristic irritation.

Gustavus Perreau, born Burma in 1874, was killed in action in Mesopotamia on 9 March 1917.

Neither did Lieutenant Birkett Barker survive the war; he was one of the malaria victims on the Salonika front, dying in August 1917. He had suffered bout after bout of malaria, despite 'consuming very generous daily doses of quinine'. During his periods of recuperation, he had enjoyed game shooting in the Vardar sector, though he found observing the wonders of nature infinitely more diverting than killing them. When pursuing a brace of partridge in winter snow, he was

> interrupted by the sight of a fine hawk perched within a hundred yards or so and he is so large that we abandon the more edible quarry in order to get closer. These birds are so shy here that at about 50 yards we are not surprised to see him take wing.[31]

On another occasion he and the major went shooting up and down a long ravine, 'with the assistance of two ex-game keepers beating thoroughly, but to no effective purpose'. Three 'very fine eagles' flew above them, and Birkett Barker was on the point of firing at what seemed to be a hare emerging from the undergrowth, when he realised that it was 'that privileged individual, a fox'. Some sort of 'chivalrous instinct' caused Birkett Barker to relax his grip on the trigger. Overall, he thought the ground 'rather overdone' by the shooting enthusiasts in the regiment.

When Birkett Barker died his brother, also on active service, sent their parents a note saying that he hoped to spend 'my leave in my terrestrial arcadia'. The terrestrial arcadia was the garden of the family home, the Croft, in springtime.

*

With the exception of ratting, fishing was the only field sport with no official prohibition by the army. For a place of terranean siege warfare, the Western Front was surprisingly well appointed with places to cast a line. Aside from the major rivers – the Yser, the Somme, the Lys and the Ancre – there was the network of canals on which the industry of the Pas-de-Calais depended. Then the dykes and becks which made Flanders a flooded Hades in winter made it a piscean paradise in summer. In those far off days before chemical farming, fish could be found in the quaintest places. On going out of the old British line at Festubert on the Somme, along 'the joyful path to billets', through the acres of glistening self-sown wheat, Edmund Blunden was struck that:

> Life, life abundant sang here and smiled; the lizard ran warless
> in the warm dust; and the ditches were trembling quick with odd
> tiny fish, in a world as remote as Saturn.[32]

Up in Flanders, Douglas Gillespie wrote to his parents in April 1915 requesting 'a few yards of fishing-line, and some small single hooks; I'm sure I shall find some kind of fish in the moats round these farmhouses'. He added: 'I wish we could hear some more news from the Dardanelles.' The fortunes of the Allied landings at Gallipoli, the possibility of a breakthrough in a war already beginning to drag on, occupied the minds of many men that spring.

A pike in 'a small, shallow pond, just by our dug-out, with low rushes' tormented Second Lieutenant Andrew Buxton, 3/Rifle Brigade. This was just behind the front line trench in the Salient. Buxton estimated the 'ripping' pike to be about five pounds. Dispensing with orthodox fishing methods, he shot at the pike with his revolver, stunned it, then tried another shot but the pike 'only went off with a big rush'. Buxton was sorry not to get him, 'as it would have given the men great joy to have had him for breakfast'. Young Buxton was one of those selfless, caring officers on which the army depended. He was a trier too: a couple of days later he managed to shoot a one pound roach in the pond with his revolver, but when one of the orderlies tried to retrieve the fish from the muddy rushes he drove it away instead.

Something to break the monotony of endless stew brought up in dixies, or corned beef fried by an officer's servant, was a powerful incentive to go fishing on the front. Billeted on the Somme Major Ronald Schweder, RFA, invited two cavalrymen to dinner in the officers' mess; to his delight they arrived carrying a brace of trout they had caught in the Ancre. On being invited to dine at General Maxe's HQ in 1916, Lieutenant-Colonel Rowland Feilding, that most faithful of spousal letter writers, informed his wife:

> We had whitebait for dinner, which is caught by a very persevering mess cook, who sits on the bank of the Somme with a gauze net at the end of a pole. He waits till the minnows and small gudgeon swim over his net; then lifts them out of the water; and it takes several hours to get a plateful. But they are very good, and I shall adopt the idea.[33]

Maxe's cook was, as well as being a paragon of patience, a paragon of virtue. Fishing on the front tended to involve the illicit use of ordnance. At Morlancourt, Private Norman Ellison recalled:

> The river abounded in fish and in peaceful days had supplied eels to the Paris market. All sorts of improvised fishing tackle appeared, whilst those lacking the true patience of your true angler frequently added to their rations by bombing the river. Ducks, in a semi-wild state, did not appear on the menu until an ingenious mind baited a spring rat-trap and floated it down amongst them on a board fastened to a line. This was easy 'fishing' for no duck could resist such an easy meal![34]

The Mills bomb, a fragmentation grenade introduced in 1915, was the impatient fisherman's weapon of choice. Private Frank Richards fished lawfully but fruitlessly with some 'cheap rods and lines' for hours at Givenchy-lès-la-Bassée before chucking Mills bombs into the canal; ten seconds later he and Paddy had 'more fish than what we could carry back'. Soon after 'dereliction took hold' because shelling of the mining district leached impurities from slag into the watercourses. In the right place and at the right time, however, the results of Mills bomb fishing could be spectacular, as Captain Charles McKerrow, RAMC attached 10/Northumberland Fusiliers, attested:

> In the afternoon, Scott of the 12th DLI came in and suggested a fishing expedition in the evening. I was keen on it so he collected some pills [bombs] from the store. At 6.30 we set off with shovels and gumboots. The boat was on the south side of the reservoir, well hidden in rushes. We baled her out and started with some vigorous shoving. We tried some casts [throws of Mills bombs] in the middle with no success. We were rather noisy I'm afraid, and it was fairly light. We tried closer in shore on the north side. One cast gave us about 30 or 40 nice dace and roach, and another nearly as many. We practically filled a sandbag and then paddled home. We hid the boat as far as possible in the rushes. Scott came in and supped with me on fried trout etc. The fish were not all bad, though a trifle bony.[35]

The fish were fried by Mat, the batman, in ration butter. When the bomb subaltern in Douglas Gillespie's company of the Argyll and Sutherland Highlanders threw a Mills into the Lys he secured 'about twenty fish, one big carp, the rest mostly roach and perch … The Frenchmen seem to catch a good many, and our stretcher-bearers fish a lot too.'[36]

For a proper angler a fishless day still offered compensation, an old and familiar one. Captain Philip Gosse RAMC managed a day's fishing on the Somme, away from the cares of doctoring and sanitation:

I caught not a fish, but what did that matter? How better could a long summer's day be spent than sitting alone among tall reeds, watching a red-tipped float, even if it never bobbed?

There were birds in the reed-beds; noisy, suspicious reed-warblers and chuckling sedge-warblers. Dab chicks dived close by, kingfishers hurried up and down the river on urgent business. One, evidently thinking my rod a convenient resting place, perched on it for a while until, unable to keep still any longer, I moved, and the gorgeous bird went off like a flash of blue.

This was one of those rare days of ecstasy whose memory remains but whose charm and mystery are difficult to convey to others.[37]

# Interstice 7
## British and Empire Naturalists Who Died on Active Service 1914–1919

**Private C.J. Alexander**, ornithologist, 2nd Battalion The Queen's (Royal West Kent Regiment) (5 October 1917). His two brothers were also ornithologists. Hooge Crater Cemetery, Belgium.

**Private Charles F. Ball**, botanist, editor of *Irish Gardening*, with a cultivar of the South American shrub *Escallonia* named 'C.F. Ball' in his honour, 7th Battalion Royal Dublin Fusiliers (13 September 1915). Lala Baba Cemetery, Turkey.

**Second Lieutenant C.C. Baring**, educated at Haileybury, winner of the Silver Medal in the RSPB's Public School Essay Competition (*Birds and Notes* described him as 'a capital field naturalist'), died of wounds aged twenty, 8th Battalion Queen's Own (Royal West Kent Regiment) (21 March 1918). His brothers Reginald, Charles and Arthur Baring also fell. Sudbury War Memorial, Suffolk.

**Lieutenant John Bateson MC**, 'A naturalist of exceptional promise', 'A' Battery, 28th Brigade Royal Field Artillery (14 October 1918). Dadizeele New British Cemetery, Belgium.

**Lieutenant Thomas Bentham**, protozoologist at Mtarfa Hospital, Malta, Royal Army Medical Corps (3 March 1919). Croydon Cemetery, Surrey.

**Second Lieutenant John Charles Beswick**, botanist and gardener at Royal Botanic Gardens, Kew, 11th Battalion King's Own (Royal Lancaster Regiment) (22 April 1917). Cambrai East Military Cemetery, France.

**Commander The Hon. Richard Bridgeman DSO,** member of the Avicultural Society, HMS *Hyacinth*, Royal Navy (9 January 1917). Dar es Salaam War Cemetery, Tanzania.

**Captain Sydney F. Brock MC**, ecologist, ornithologist and farmer, Royal Scots, died of wounds (11 November 1918). Kirkliston Burial Ground, Scotland.

**Lieutenant George Wyman Bury**, Arabist and naturalist who gave his name to the Yemen warbler (*Sylvia buryi*), the southern grey shrike (*Lanius meridionalis buryi*), streaked scrub warbler (*Scotocera buryi*), the buff-spotted flufftail (*Sarothrura elegans buryi*) and Bury's worm snake (*Leptotyphlops burii*), Royal Naval Volunteer Reserve (23 September 1920). Cairo New British Protestant Cemetery, Egypt.

**Second Lieutenant Hugh Charlton**, wildlife artist, 7th Battalion Northumberland Fusiliers (24 June 1916). Buried at La Laiterie military cemetery. His brother John also fell.

**Captain John Charlton**, ornithologist, author of *The Birds of Southeast Northumberland* and *Notes on Norwegian Birds* (1 July 1916). Thiepval Memorial, France.

**Gunner James Clarke**, gardener and Sub-Foreman Indoors at Royal Botanic Gardens, Kew, Royal Marine Artillery Howitzer Brigade (26 March 1918). Lijssenthoek Military Cemetery, Belgium.

**Rifleman Sydney Cobbold**, gardener, 8th Battalion Rifle Brigade (3 October 1916). Le Fermont Military Cemetery, France.

**Private David Collins**, poet, botanist, nineteen years old at the time of his death, 1st Battalion Grenadier Guards (11 October 1918). Delsaux Farm Cemetery, France.

**Private Wilfrid Omer Cooper**, Fellow of the Linnean Society, 12th Battalion Middlesex Regiment (26 September 1916). Thiepval Memorial, France.

**Private Lionel Henry de Barri Crawshay**, botanist, torpedoed en route to Egypt, 3rd Battalion Queen's (Royal West Surrey Regiment) (4 May 1917). Savona Town Cemetery, Italy.

**Captain J.C. Crowley**, member of the British Ornithologists' Union, 4th Battalion Queen's (Royal West Surrey Regiment) (11 September 1916). Basra War Cemetery, Iraq.

**Lieutenant Arthur Davidson,** ornithologist, Royal Flying Corps (9 September 1917). Zuydcoote Military Cemetery, France.

**Rifleman John Divers**, gardener at Royal Botanic Gardens, Kew, 9th Battalion London Regiment (Queen Victoria's Rifles) (9 October 1916). Ploegsteert Memorial, Belgium.

**Captain Geoffrey Donaldson**, botanist, educated Oundle and Cambridge, killed in the battle of Fromelles, 7th Battalion Royal Warwickshire Regiment (19 July 1916). Ploegsteert Memorial, Belgium.

**Lance Corporal Arthur Duley MM**, gardener, died as a result of mistreatment while a prisoner of war of the Germans, 7th Battalion Somerset Light Infantry (14 March 1918). Tournai Communal Cemetery Allied Extension, Belgium.

**Second Lieutenant Eric B. Dunlop**, described in *British Birds* as 'one of the most promising young ornithologists of the north of England', 5th Battalion Border Regiment (19 May 1917). Arras Memorial, France.

**Sergeant George Fallow,** gardener at Royal Botanic Gardens, Edinburgh, after whom *Buddleja fallowiana* is named, 5th Battalion Royal Scots (19 August 1915). Port Said War Memorial, Egypt.

**Private Gordon Farries**, gardener at Royal Botanic Gardens, Kew, 11th Battalion Argyll and Sutherland Highlanders (20 April 1918). Feuchy Chapel British Cemetery, France.

**Private Dene Fry,** reptologist, Fellow of the Linnean Society of New South Wales, 3rd Battalion Australian Infantry Force (9 April 1917). His brother Alan also fell. Beaumetz Cross Roads Cemetery, France.

**Second Lieutenant Duncan Hepburn Gotch**, assistant at the Imperial Bureau of Entomology, 1st Battalion Worcestershire Regiment (11 March 1915). Le Touret Memorial, France.

**Captain J. Grafton-Wignall**, ornithologist, who according to his obituarist 'had that perfect sight which enabled him to "pick up" a sitting Woodcock'; also a 'capital cragsman' and Regular soldier, killed in action Shatt-el-Hai. His commanding officer eulogised: 'He died as he lived – a clean and gallant gentleman', 82nd Punjabis (26 January 1917).

**Captain Leonard Gray**, ornithologist, contributor to *British Birds*, 5th Battalion Essex Regiment (31 July 1917). Alexandria (Hadra) War Memorial Cemetery, Egypt.

**Lieutenant-Colonel Herbert H. Harington**, member of the British Ornithologists' Union, author of *Harington's Birds of Burma*, 1909. There are several birds named for him including *Polioneta haringtoni and Oreicola ferrea haringtoni*. Commanding officer of the 62nd Punjabis (8 March 1916). Basra Memorial, Iraq.

**Second Lieutenant Brian Hatton**, portraitist and countryside artist, member of the Chelsea Arts Club, Queen's Own Worcestershire Hussars (Worcester Yeomanry) (23 April 1916). Kantara War Memorial Cemetery, Egypt.

**Private Joseph Hayhurst**, gardener, 6th Battalion Queen's Own (Royal West Kent Regiment) (7 September 1918). Unicorn Cemetery, France.

**Captain Auberon Herbert**, 9th Baron Lucas and 5th Lord Dingwall, member of the British Ornithologists' Union and President of the Board of Agriculture, 22nd Squadron Royal Flying Corps (3 November 1916). HAC Cemetery, France.

**Lieutenant-Colonel Boyd R. Horsburgh**, aviculturalist, ornithologist, author of *The Game-Birds and Water-Fowl of South Africa*. He gave his name to the red-necked falcon (*Falco chicquera horsbrughi*), Army Service Corps (11 July 1916). Tandridge Churchyard, Surrey.

**Private David Hume**, gardener at Royal Botanic Gardens, Edinburgh, after whom *Roscoea humeana* is named, 2nd Battalion Royal Scots (29 August 1914). Bethencourt Communal Cemetery, France.

**Ordinary Seaman John Jackson**, gardener, HMS *Fortune*, Royal Navy (1 June 1916). Farsund Cemetery, Norway.

**Private Edward Kensit,** gardener, known to his friends as 'Pansy' because of his devotion to his work at the Bolus Herbarium, Cape Town, South African Infantry (18 July 1916). Thiepval Memorial, France.

**Lieutenant Wyndham Knatchbull-Hugessen**, 3rd Baron Brabourne, member of the British Ornithologists' Union, co-author of *Birds of South America*. He gave his name to Brabourne's Emerald (*Agyrtrina versicolor brabourniib*). Special Reserve attached 1st Battalion Grenadier Guards (11 March 1915). Le Touret Memorial, France.

**Lieutenant Ernest Lee**, lecturer in the Department of Agricultural Botany, University of Leeds and Fellow of the Linnean Society, 4th Battalion Duke of Wellington's (West Riding) Regiment (11 July 1915). Artillery Wood Cemetery, Belgium.

**Captain The Hon. Gerald Legge**, ornithologist, breeder of wildfowl, explorer (with R.B. Woosnam) of the Ruwenzori and Kalahari; gave his name to short-tailed pipit (*Anthus brachyurus leggei*), 7th Battalion South Staffordshire Regiment (9 August 1915). Helles Memorial, Turkey.

**Rifleman Henry Longhurst**, gardener, 2nd Battalion King's Royal Rifle Corps (25 September 1915). Loos Memorial, France.

**Second Lieutenant Donald Macpherson**, botanist and agriculturalist, died in Leith War Hospital of wounds, Royal Field Artillery (11 November 1917). Edinburgh Cemetery, Scotland.

**Colonel Neville Manders**, AMS, FZS, FES, the most senior entomologist to fall (his obituary in *The Entomologist's Monthly* declared 'no name is better known to, or has been more highly esteemed by entomologists than that of Neville Manders, long time a Fellow of the Entomological Society of London, and recognised also as an expert in our Science as well as the best of good comrades.'). He carried out observations on the butterflies and birds of the Gallipoli

Peninsula, where he served as an RAMC medical officer attached to the New Zealand and Australian Division, until the time of his death from a chance bullet. He was the author of numerous papers and books, chief among them his catalogue of the butterflies of Mauritius and Bourbon (1907). He added, inter alia, the species *Nacaduba mandersi Druce* and subspecies *Antanartia mauritiana Manders* to the list of lepidoptera, both of which are named for him. At the start of the First World War he was stationed in Egypt, which furnished the material for 'The Butterflies of Lower Egypt', *The Entomologist's Record*, XXVII (9 August 1915). New Zealand No. 2 Outpost Cemetery, Turkey.

**Captain Alfred Marsh**, author of *The Maritime Ecology of Holme-next-the-Sea, Norfolk*, shot by a sniper at Armentières, 8th Battalion Somerset Light Infantry (5 January 1916). Cite Bonjean Military Cemetery, France.

**Lieutenant-Colonel Aymer Maxwell**, ornithologist and father of novelist Gavin Maxwell, Collingwood Battalion Royal Naval Division (8 October 1914). Schoonselhof Cemetery, Belgium.

**Rifleman Arthur Meads**, gardener, 16th Battalion London Regiment (Queen's Westminster Rifles) (1 December 1917). Ramleh War Cemetery, Israel.

**Lieutenant Francis Monckton**, ornithologist, who from the age of fifteen contributed notes on the birds of Staffordshire to *The Transactions of the North Staffordshire Field Club*; his obituary in *British Birds* observed that 'the study of Staffordshire Ornithology will suffer much by his having given his life so nobly for his country'. Killed in action, his brother, Geoffrey, also killed in the war, 1st Battalion Scots Guards (8 November, 1914). Menin Gate Memorial, Belgium.

**Private Walter Morland**, rose specialist on the staff of the Royal Botanic Gardens, Edinburgh, 5th Battalion Royal Scots (7 May 1915). Helles Memorial, Turkey.

**Second Lieutenant Henry Otto Murray-Dixon**, wildlife artist, contributor to J.G. Millais' *British Diving Ducks*, 1913, 4th Battalion

Seaforth Highlanders (10 April 1917). Aubigny Communal Cemetery Extension, France.

**Lieutenant Cuthbert St. John Nevill**, Fellow of the Linnean Society, 'C' Battery, 251st Brigade, Royal Field Artillery (18 April 1918). Chocques Military Cemetery, France.

**Private H.G.L. Peavot**, Librarian of the Zoological Society of London, 1st Battalion Honourable Artillery Company (21 April 1917). Arras Memorial, France.

**Second Lieutenant Wallis Penn Gaskell**, member of the South London Entomological Society, London Regiment (25–26 June 1916). Le Touret Memorial, France.

**Lieutenant-Colonel Gustavus Arthur Perreau,** aviculturalist, a frequent contributor to *Bird Notes* (which eulogised him as a man with 'a charming personality which drew all to him and the writer mourns the loss of a dear friend') killed in action in Mesopotamia, 4th Battalion Gurkha Rifles (9 March 1917). Basra Memorial, Iraq.

**Second Lieutenant L.N.G. Ramsay**, Fellow Imperial College of Science, co-author of *Ornithology of the Scottish National Antarctic Expedition*, 3rd Battalion Gordon Highlanders (21 March 1916). Estaires Communal Cemetery and Extension, France.

**Rifleman Edwin Riseley**, Librarian of the Linnean Society, 3rd Battalion Rifle Brigade (1 August 1917). Menin Gate Memorial, Belgium.

**Sir Marc Armand Ruffer,** bacteriologist, Fellow of the Linnean Society, served with the Red Cross, torpedoed while aboard SS *Arcadian* (27 August 1917).

**Second Lieutenant Munro Scott**, on the Herbarium staff at Royal Botanic Gardens, Kew, 12th Battalion Royal Scots (12 April 1917). Arras Memorial, France.

**Second Lieutenant Colin Mackenzie Selbie**, Assistant Naturalist at the National Museum, Dublin, 11th Battalion Cameronians (Scottish Rifles) (14 July 1916). Thiepval Memorial, France.

**Captain Frederick C. Selous DSO**, big game hunter and conservationist, the inspiration for H. Rider Haggard's Allan Quatermain, shot by a German sniper, Tanzania, aged sixty-five, 25th Battalion Royal Fusiliers (4 January 1917). His son also fell. He was the older brother of writer and ornithologist Edmund Selous. Beho Beho, Selous Game Reserve, Tanzania.

**Private Edward Frank Southgate**, wildlife artist, member of the Royal Society of British Artists, aged forty-three at the time of his death, 24th Battalion Royal Fusiliers (23 February 1916). Lillers Communal Cemetery, France.

**Sergeant Herbert Southgate**, orchid specialist and contributor to *The Gardener's Magazine*, 5th Battalion Norfolk Regiment (19 April 1917). Gaza War Cemetery, Palestine.

**Corporal F.H. Stallman**, entomologist with 'a keenness that boded useful future work', died of wounds sustained in the Battle of the Somme, London Regiment (London Rifle Brigade) (8 April 1917). Étaples Military Cemetery, France.

**Colonel Charles Stonham CMG, TD**, physician, member of the British Ornithologists' Union, author of the illustrated *British Birds of the British Isles*, London Mounted Brigade Field Ambulance RAMC (31 January 1916). Golders Green Crematorium, London.

**Private George Stout**, son of a crofter, ornithologist at the Fair Isle Bird Observatory, taxidermist, 'the means of adding the Red-rumped swallow and the Eastern short-toed lark to the British avifauna', 93rd Field Ambulance RAMC (13 November 1916). Couin British Cemetery, France.

**Second Lieutenant Edward Thomas**, poet, essayist, lover of the English countryside, 244th Siege Battery Royal Garrison Artillery (9 April 1917). Agny Military Cemetery, France.

**Captain Harry Toppin,** plant collector and winner of the Croix de Chevalier of the Legion of Honour, 1st Battalion Northumberland Fusiliers (14 September 1914). La Ferté-sous-Jouarre Memorial, France.

**Major Sidney Toppin MC**, botanist, plant collector, brother of Harry Toppin, 151st Heavy Battery Royal Garrison Artillery (27 September 1917). Lijssenthoek Military Cemetery, Belgium.

**Major John Veitch MC**, horticulturalist, 1st Battalion Devonshire Regiment (21 May 1918). Thiennes British Cemetery, France.

**Private Frederick Wallington**, worked for taxidermists Rowland Ward of Piccadilly, 6th Battalion Northamptonshire Regiment (14 July 1916). Thiepval Memorial, France.

**Lieutenant Godfrey Vassal Webster**, ornithologist, winner of the Silver Medal in the RSPB's Public School Essay Competition, 1915, 3rd Battalion Grenadier Guards (3 August 1917). Menin Gate Memorial, Belgium.

**Major C.H.T. Whitehead**, ornithologist with a particular interest in the birds of Northwest India having a thrush, *Zoothera mollissima whiteheadi*, named for him; the author of *On the Birds of Kohat and Kurram, Northern India*, 56th Punjab Rifles (26 September 1915). Neuve Chapelle Memorial, France.

**Lieutenant Edward Woodhouse**, economic botanist and Principal of Sabour Agricultural College, Indian Army Reserve of Officers attached 38th King George's Own Central India Horse (18 December 1917). Tincourt New British Cemetery, France.

**Corporal Herbert Woolley**, horticulturalist, 5th Battalion London Regiment (London Rifle Brigade) (9 October 1916). Brother of archaeologist Lieutenant-Colonel Sir Charles Woolley and Major George Woolley VC. Thiepval Memorial, France.

**Lieutenant R.B. Woosnam**, leader of the 1906 Ruwenzori natural history expedition and explorer of the Elburz Mountains and Kalahari Desert, member of the British Ornithologists' Union, silver medallist of the Zoological Society of London, who gave his name to the trilling cisticola (*Cisticola woosnami*), fire-crested alethe (*Alethe castanea woosnami*), red-tailed bristlebill (*Bleda syndactylus woosnami*), two mammals and a reptile, 6th Battalion Worcestershire Regiment (4 June 1915). Helles Memorial, Turkey.

**Private Albert Wright**, gardener, 7th Battalion Royal Warwickshire Regiment (25 February 1919). Birmingham (Lodge Hill) Cemetery, Britain.

# CHAPTER VIII

# And Quiet Flowed the Somme

*War's End*

**Telling the Bees**
*(An Old Gloucestershire Superstition)*

They dug no grave for our soldier lad, who fought and who died
out there:
Bugle and drum for him were dumb, and the padre said no prayer;
The passing bell gave never a peal to warn that a soul was fled,
And we laid him not in the quiet spot where cluster his kin that
are dead.

But I hear a foot on the pathway, above the low hum of the hive,
That at edge of dark, with the song of the lark, tells that the world
is alive:
The master starts on his errand, his tread is heavy and slow,
Yet he cannot choose but tell the news – the bees have a right to
know.

Bound by the ties of a happier day, they are one with us now in
　　our worst;
On the very morn that my boy was born they were told the tidings
　　the first:
With what pride they will hear of the end he made, and the ordeal
　　that he trod –
Of the scream of shell, and the venom of hell, and the flame of the
　　sword of God.

Wise little heralds, tell of my boy; in your golden tabard coats
Tell the bank where he slept, and the stream he leapt, where the
　　spangled lily floats:
The tree he climbed shall lift her head, and the torrent he swam
　　shall thrill,
And the tempest that bore his shouts before shall cry his message
　　still.

*G.E. Rees, father of a fallen soldier*

When all quiet came to the Western Front on 11 November 1918, men looked at what they had done to the landscape and feared that it would never recover. Even such a sensitive and time-served soldier as Lieutenant Charles Douie, who knew the ability of nature to turn war's wasteland into floral summer wonderland, believed there were areas of the Somme beyond salvation:

> so heavy was the fighting here that the scars will remain till the end of time ... the forest of graves above the Ancre will remain to tell the tale of that island race whose sons were lords of these woods and fields.[1]

The earth was bone white because it consisted purely of chalk brought up by shelling. The top soil had been vaporised. At Delville Wood only one tree was said to be standing. So complete was the devastation along parts of the front line that the French government considered leaving them as a *voie sacrée* that would be lined with monuments.[2] According to the statistics of the French government a total of 1,923,479 hectares of shell-pitted farmland needed to be levelled at the time of the Armistice. The French peasantry, however, had a different idea to their government and drifted back to their farms. Neither had nature given up on the Western Front.

Private Stephen Graham made a pilgrimage to the Western Front in the early 1920s, and was witness to its transformation:

> After a mile or so farmhouses and cultivation cease and one enters the terrible battle area of Passchendaele, all pits, all tangled with corroded wire – but now as if it were in tumultuous conflict with Nature . . . The stagnancy has not dried up, but festers still in black rot below the rushes. Double shell-holes, treble shell-holes, charred ground, great pits, bashed-in dug-outs, all overgrown with the highest of wild flowers . . .[3]

There was also a rebuilding plan. One reason that so many houses in Northwest France look alike is that they were erected in a single reconstruction phase, and this included the 'gaunt hotels' for the increasing numbers of veterans and bereaved Britons on pilgrimage. One such pilgrim was Nurse Vera Brittain:

> Nature herself conspires with time to cheat our recollections; grass has grown over the shell-holes at Ypres, and the cultivated meadows of industrious peasants have replaced the hut-scarred fields of Etaples and Camiers where once I nursed the wounded in their great retreat of 1918.[4]

Like time-lapse photography, the memoirs of visiting veterans show the old Western Front re-natured. Captain Graham S. Hutchinson, ex-Machine Gun Company, a participant in the battle for High Wood, toured the battlefield in 1935:

Except in topographical outline the battlefields have changed. The rebuilded [sic] towns and villages and the re-sown fields, yielding their crop, bear no resemblance to the crumbling ruins, shattered woods and shell-pitted wastes, which marked the War years. And as for the pilgrim, revisiting the scene, it may even be difficult to rediscover villages and scenes whose every stone and contour in former years were so familiar as the palm of the hand.[5]

In time, the Somme would recover almost completely. Even the giant mine crater at Lochnagar near La Boisselle has been reclaimed by nature. Stand on its vertiginous edge today and it is like looking down at the ground from the window of a plane. Then one notices that the only tunnelling being done is by rabbits. Real *lapins*, as opposed to scared, burrowing soldiers.

Compare the photographic panorama of the Somme taken by the British army when they moved into the zone in July 1915 and the present vista – they are virtually identical. (The panorama may be purchased from the visitor centre at the Thiepval Memorial to the British 'missing' on the Somme.) Mametz and High Wood, then and now, are indistinguishable.

Ironically, veterans became worried that insufficient traces would remain of what had taken place on the Western Front, that the earth would lose its memory.

There are no cemeteries for those who fell at Waterloo, at Blenheim, at Agincourt. Dead soldiers used to be, to borrow the indignant words of the Victorian novelist William Makepeace Thackeray, 'shovelled into a hole . . . and forgotten'.

The First World War brought a revolution in the treatment of Britain's war dead. Every soldier, no matter how low his birth, received a headstone and interment in specially created, intensely beautiful cemeteries – nearly a thousand of them in a necklace of death along the old Western Front. There are pearls of necropolises too in Greece, Gallipoli, Palestine – wherever British and Empire men fought and fell. It was, after all, a world war. For the half million soldiers who were missing there were magnificent memorial monuments, such as the Thiepval arches, on which their names were carved in stone.

One man was largely responsible for the new way of honouring the military dead. This was Sir Fabian Ware, a most unlikely revolutionary.

When the shooting started in 1914 Ware, at the age of forty-five, was too old to fight, too young to do nothing. So the Tory former editor of the *Morning Post* packed himself off to France to become the commander of the Mobile Ambulance Unit of the Red Cross. Ware's unit, though, did more than transport the wounded away from the battlefield; at his urging it searched for the graves of the killed.

In fighting for its life, the British army had little time to deal with its dead. Fallen soldiers lay in hasty shallow graves, often dug by their mates, identified with nothing but a cross whittled from branches, or a Huntley & Palmers' biscuit lid with some scrawled words, and a bunch of flowers which wilted, then decayed away.

Finding soldiers' graves and marking them with a proper wooden cross and a metal identification plate soon became the sole job of Ware's unit, whose name was duly changed to the Graves Registration Commission. Marching through the old Somme country in 1918, Private Stephen Graham's eyes constantly flicked to the groves of Ware's white crosses where the dead lay buried, many of them with the date 21 March 1918, the first day of the German Spring Offensive:

> Such crosses, without particulars, are generally called 'Lonely Soldiers', and much love is always lavished on them by the private soldier bringing wild flowers to them, making formal gardens round them of glass and chalk.[6]

Just as British soldiers had made unofficial gardens at the front to celebrate life they made unofficial gardens to commemorate death.

Registering the graves was not enough for Ware, who became pre-occupied with finding a permanent solution for the commemoration of the fallen. The ultimate backroom boy, Ware won friends in powerful places. In 1917 the Imperial War Graves Commission (IWGC) was founded by Royal Charter, with Ware as vice-chair. Lord Derby acted as figurehead.

For a body with an aristocrat at its head, the IWGC, at Ware's cajoling, committed itself to utterly radical policies. The IWGC determined that all war graves should be uniform, because 'private initiative' would lead to the well-to-do erecting 'costly monuments' which would 'contrast unkindly with those humbler ones which would be all that poorer folk could afford'. Some families, notably that of the former prime minister Gladstone, had already disinterred the bodies of relatives, and repatriated them. Ware stopped the practice because it smacked of privilege. Soldiers were to be buried in the foreign fields where they fell.

In no mood to skimp in honouring the war dead, Ware insisted that the cemeteries and the monuments to the missing, wherever they were on the globe, were constructed from the finest materials and designed by the greatest architects of the day. Sir Edwin Lutyens, Sir Reginald Blomfield and Sir Herbert Baker led the list of distinguished architects employed by the IWGC. As Rudyard Kipling observed, the building of the British war cemeteries was 'The biggest single bit of work since any of the pharaohs – and they only worked in their own country'.

By 1927 the IWGC had overseen the construction of more than 500 permanent cemeteries, in which 400,000 headstones had been laid down. As one admirer told Ware: 'You have created a new Empire within and without the British Empire, an Empire of the Silent Dead.'

From the outset there was a strong feeling that the cemeteries should be more than cemeteries. They should be *gardens* or *small parks* of remembrance, rather than depositories for the deceased.

So, the cemeteries were planted with trees and flowers, and to preserve a special British feeling snowdrops and crocuses were allowed to push up through the grass. In the cemeteries, where memory was planted, the French countryside was sequestered and remodelled to become little bits of Britain. Unambiguously, the cemeteries are corners of foreign fields 'for ever England'. The dead are not buried in France; they lie in English scenes. They are interred at home.

*The Times* noticed the absolute Englishness of the war cemetery at Forceville, the first cemetery completed by the IWGC:

> Picture this strangely stirring place. A lawn enclosed of close clipped turf, banded across with lines of flowers, and linked by these bands of flowers, uncrowded, at stately intervals stand in soldierly ranks the white headstones. And while they form as perfect, as orderly a whole as any regiment on parade, yet they do shoulder each other. Each one is set apart in flowers, every one casts its shade upon a gracious space of green. It is the simplest, it is the grandest place I ever saw.[7]

The cemeteries continue to be gardens, with headstones set in narrow flower borders between grass paths.

The gardeners and nature lovers who went to war in 1914 are among flowers still. Flowers for the soldiers, in death and in life. Roots into earth, blooms into the sky, flowers connect the living and the dead. In the cemeteries, Remembrance is linked to the cycle of nature, just as war service was. The flowers bloom and die in accordance with the passing of the seasons.

Nowhere is the connection between nature, England and Remembrance more stark than Le Trou Aid Post Cemetery, designed by Sir Herbert Baker, the gentlest of the IWGC's principal architects.

Le Trou is a place of peaceful reflection, overhung with weeping willows, ringed by a moat, reached through a cottage gate.

It is an English country garden. Abroad.

There are memorials for the animals too. The first was the RSPCA's Animals War Memorial plaque at the dispensary in Kilburn, which remembers the 484,143 horses, mules, camels and bullocks and many hundreds of dogs, carrier pigeons and other creatures killed by enemy action, disease or accident in the Great War.

Perhaps the most striking memorial is The Animals in War Memorial at Park Lane, which was unveiled in November 2004. The inscription on the memorial reads:

This memorial is dedicated to all the animals that served and died alongside British and Allied forces in wars and campaigns throughout time.

They had no choice.

*

Lieutenant Edward Thomas and Britain's soldiers fought for a landscape that was no longer theirs. While the shell-torn Western Front, with its iconic charred trees, muddy mires and asphyxiating gases consumed the imagination of participants and public, the real and lasting ecological destruction occurred at home, in Britain. Whereas the Western Front reverted, by and large, to its pre-war state, the British countryside did not.

Before 1914, Britain imported most of its timber from Scandinavia, Canada and Russia, but when Germany's U-boat campaign began the deliberate sinking of merchantmen the nation suffered an acute lumber crisis: over 450,000 acres of woodland was felled. In order to compensate for food imports lost to the U-boats, ancient pasture land began to be ploughed up. A climactic round of unrestricted, shoot-on-sight U-boat warfare over the winter of 1916–17 sank as much as 860,000 tons of Britain-bound shipping per month. In April 1917, Britain's food reserves were down to six weeks' worth. The Board of Agriculture began a 'plough up' campaign, and more ancient pastureland, some of it half a millennium old, went under the plough. By November 1918 two and a half million acres of pastureland had been ploughed up, and countless water meadows drained (one of the favourite environments for Thomas's meadowsweet). When Thomas watches the ploughman at work in 'As the Team's Head Brass' (see p. 4), he is quite likely witnessing meadow going under the plough.

There was also great destruction of farmland birdlife during the war. The silence of Britain's fields – birdsong in the countryside has

declined by about 60 per cent since 1914 – began with the government
and farming industry's war against birds they deemed to be grain-
eating, human-starving pests. War Agricultural Committees were
advised to destroy rookeries and, by stretching the interpretation of
the law, previously protected species such as house sparrows were
categorised as 'vermin' which could be destroyed by poison. Soldiers
in training in England were sent off on official bird's-nest destroying
expeditions.[8] There was a clamour in the papers for 'Sparrow Clubs',
meaning extermination squads. 'Shoot the birds' urged the *Daily
Mail*. Under the Defence of the Realm Act (DORA), in February and
March 1917 orders were issued allowing local Boards of Agriculture
to deputise bodies to kill game outside the season where necessary,
while the pheasant and grouse shooting seasons were extended. The
number of game birds had grown significantly over the course of the
war, as sportsmen went off to that other shooting party, the one in
Flanders and France. The gamekeepers went too. There were 22,000
gamekeepers in 1911; after the war there were 12,000.

The country house lifestyle did not revert to its pre-war pattern.
Returns from land were small, death duties were weighty and so the
already established trend for the break-up of the great estates continued. The scions of the aristocracy and gentry were prominent among
the fallen. There was a rush to sell land, with tenant farmers the
major buyers; by 1927 36 per cent of farmland in England was owned
by its farmers, compared with 12 per cent before the war.

With fewer shoots, some species of birds and animals bucked the
trend towards decline. Before 1914 gamekeepers in some areas had
been so zealous in maintaining ideal habitats for game that they
had shot and trapped creatures to local extinction. Sparrowhawks,
hen harriers and other raptors recovered numbers in game shooting
areas.[9] Likewise the wildcats crept out of the corner of the Highlands
to which they had been confined in 1914.

But generally countryside fauna and flora entered into decline.
Oddly, the shortage of rural housing exacerbated the loss of nature.
The housing stock was insufficient, and rents tended to be more

than agricultural workers could afford. Farmers complained of a shortage of workers, which led to more mechanisation (frequently lethal for field-nesting birds and mammals), fewer horses, fewer people.

Britain's landscape, and its value to the war's soldiers and civilians, was understood by some, however.

There was concern for forests following widespread felling during the war. The government founded the Forestry Commission in 1919 to make good some of the losses. The Commission became one of the greatest landowners in Britain and its vast plantations such as Thetford Heath, Norfolk were among the lasting legacies of the war.

Two preservation societies were founded in 1915: the National Trust (NT) and the Council for the Protection of Rural England. Canon Rawnsley, a founder of the NT, bought some land at High Rigg Fields, Derwent Water, which he gave to the NT. He wanted to preserve 'this fair land' (Rawnsley's words) as a memorial to the war, and provide land for all to enjoy. He called it 'Peace Howe'. Lord Leconfield likewise gave the NT the summit at Scafell Pike.

Some of the more perceptive – or cynical – politicians realised that nature might be a prophylactic against Bolshevism. The government's 'Homes for Heroes' campaign sought to provide improved housing for returning soldiers. Before the war local authorities were responsible for the building of 2 per cent of new dwellings erected; during the years 1919–23 this figure rose to more than 60 per cent. Domestic betterment had a nature-aspect, as E.G. Pretyman, MP for Chelmsford, elucidated in the debate over the Housing and Town Planning Bill (passed in 1919):

If there is one part of these proposals that appeals to me ... it is that houses shall be provided in semi-rural conditions with good garden plots and good transport access to the work in which the man is engaged, so that he can do his work in the factory while his family can live in fresh air ... and where, when he gets home at night, he will find not only a healthy family, but healthy occupation outside where they can go and work together in the garden.[10]

Noel Pemberton Billing, MP for Hertford, averred: 'If a man is comfortably housed . . . you will not find much unrest there.'

'England is the country, and the country is England', ventured Stanley Baldwin in 1924. The middle classes took him at his word, and began the flight to the new ruralist leafy suburbs of Metroland. The cosy semi-detached Metroland villa, with its faux Tudor black-and-white timbering, ornamented with herbaceous borders and shaded by laurel hedges, was urban England's symbolic version of the rural cottage. Back to nature, but by commuter train.

*

To assist in the control of soldiers' dogs on demobilisation, arrangements were made with the Royal Society for the Prevention of Cruelty to Animals and the authorities of the Dogs' Home at Hackbridge, to quarantine for a nominal fee some 500 dogs, the property of officers and soldiers returning from the Expeditionary Forces, who could not pay the usual quarantine fee for dogs imported into Great Britain.

War Office, *Statistics of the Military Effort of the British Empire During the Great War 1914–1920*

With the Armistice of November 1918 the men looked forward to coming home. The future was less certain for their animals.

At the end of the war there came a strict law that any animal to be imported into Britain needed to spend four months in quarantine to ensure it was not carrying rabies; the period of quarantine was lengthened to six months and the cost of care was set at £14 – an amount far beyond the pocket of the vast majority of the soldiery.

The government's concern over rabies was well founded; the Royal Foxhound Show was cancelled from 1915 to 1919 because of a limited outbreak of rabies, caused by servicemen smuggling dogs home.

In time organisations such as the RSPCA and the Blue Cross Society heard of the soldiers' plight and approached the government in order to take over the care and cost of these animals during their months under supervision. The soldiers deposited £2 with the charity to ensure that they would collect animals after the quarantine period. One of the dogs cared for by the RSPCA was Prince, Private Brown's terrier, quarantined at Hackbridge kennels in May 1919.[11] Even so, £2 was a stretch for many a soldier, and the quarantine system was imperfect, if not chaotic.

Private Albert Lowy wrote to the proper authority for papers 'but perhaps due to my being a mere private, I got no reply'. He therefore determined to smuggle his 'darling dog' back to England.

At the railway station for the Channel port a staff officer offered to lend him the money for quarantine; Lowy explained he had failed to get the necessary papers and was intending to smuggle the dog back. 'He wished me good luck.' Lowy hid the terrier in his kitbag through the rail journey and the wait at Cherbourg camp: 'We men going to England, were warned against trying to take dogs with us, and the tents were watched by officers looking for dogs.'

Several men with dogs hidden under their greatcoats were rumbled. Lowy, however, managed to get the dog across the Channel without detection, and on disembarkation the staff officer who had wished him luck said: 'Well done, I am glad that you have succeeded in bringing her with you.'

The danger was not quite over. To avoid tell-tales, Lowy took the dog along the platform and gave her a drink from a fire bucket and some railway biscuits. His demob train took him to Wimbledon – where man and dog became separated in the crowd of milling soldiers anxious to get home and those welcoming them.

Lowy gave up the dog as lost. 'I had to stay in the column and march up to the demobilisation camp, which occupied dozens of army huts. After an hour and half she found me – to our great joy.' The 'long rigmarole' of discharge from the army done, Lowy took the dog home. 'She and our fox terrier, Spot, produced a litter of half-pedigree pups; their father was not at all thoroughbred, but she didn't mind anything after what she had been through in the war and had come back.'

Boulogne was the only crossing permitted for those wishing to return with pets, and Lieutenant Andrew McCormick, 182nd Labour Company, was one of many soldiers who fell foul of the ruling. He was ordered to cross via Calais, and was refused permission to divert to Boulogne, or take his dog, despite all his arguments. 'I had to turn away sick at heart when I saw Teddie being taken away on the shoulder of an NCO who had promised to look after her for me.' He believed Teddie 'the dearest and best of soldiers' doggie chums ... the dog of my heart'. He never saw Teddie again, though his 'soul cry' was slightly salved when a retired army colonel came to live near him in England. 'When I paid my first call I received joyous greeting at the doorway from a little doggie, the living image of Teddie.'[12]

\*

On 11 November 1918 there were 735,409 horses and mules serving with the British army, and these were regarded by many soldiers as comrades in arms. (There were also 56,287 camels, bullocks and donkeys in the various theatres.) In the words of Private Massie:

> The warhorse is honest, reliable, strong. He is a soldier. And I have written this eulogy of his merits as one soldier might write of another. I want someone to take his case up and see that he falls 'cushy' after the war. It is only fair. He is a mate of ours – one of us. A Tommy. Don't ring a lot of bells and forget him. A field of clover, a bundle of hay, a Sussex meadow, a bushel of apples, a loaf of bread, a sack of carrots, sunshine and blue hills, clean stables, and trusses of straw, may they all be his, he has earned them! It is only fair.[13]

Sadly, the effort made by the government to find homes fit for the animal heroes was conspicuous only in its parvanimity. Twenty-five thousand younger, healthier horses stayed in the army and 62,000 were sold to British farmers at an average of £37.[14] A lower grade of horse was flogged off to foreign farmers. Within eighteen months of the end of the war nearly 200,000 horses branded with the British army arrow had been sold.

The remainder, lame and blind because of service faithfully given, went to the butchers of Belgium and France; tens of thousands of horses, sold by the pound. Private Fred Lloyd, AVC:

> We used to go right up to Paris with horses, each man leading four to sell to the French for food. In the slaughterhouses, we led them on to scales four at a time and weighed them up. We sold them by weight. It was a bit upsetting.[15]

During the period of demobilisation, from 11 November 1918 to 31 March 1920, the Royal Army Veterinary Corps disposed of 49,751 animals for human food, which realised the sum of £1,009,243, being an average of £20 5s 9d per carcass sold.

In addition to this, by-products from animal carcasses realised £33,573. The Army Salvage Branch wasted nothing. Items sold included: hoof parings, horseshoes, horsehair, horse clippings.

Trooper Ben Clouting looked after Colonel Carton de Wiart's horse, Nancy. Her party trick was to kiss Clouting in a cafe for a lump of sugar. They were very close:

> At night, if we were in a barn, she would lie down and place her head on my legs and I'd put my arm round her neck . . . She was killed at the end of the war when a shell burst almost underneath her, but, though it seems hard, I was glad. So many of the regiment's horses were handed over to local farmers at the end of the war, and there was no knowing what might have happened to her.[16]

Some soldiers killed their horses rather than have them end up on a plate. All twenty thousand of the Palestine horses were cast aside. There was uproar in the ranks. The official line of the War Office was that because Britain had pressed Egyptian camels into military service it was only fair to sell our horses to them. The real truth was cash. The Egyptians would pay £11 1s 6d for a horse; if it was destroyed it would fetch £1. Major-General Sir George Borrow, the GOC of the Yeomanry (and no fan of the War Office's diktat), looked the other way when officers of the Desert Mounted Corps took their favourite chargers out into the desert and shot them.

There were, however, a few happy endings. Thanks to the animal charities and some persistent soldiers a few lucky horses were able to see out their final years in the quiet green fields of Britain: the land they had helped save. Captain Guy Chapman MC, 13/Royal Fusiliers:

> We stopped in the market square. It was the day of condemnation for our horses. They were to be examined by the A.D.V.S., and those which he cast were to be sold to the Belgians. Knowing the manner in which the natives treat their animals, we were as angry at this as at every other scheme which a vile administration was putting into practice. Hallam met me with a gap-toothed grin more distended than ever. 'It's all right, sir. She's going home. Aren't you my beauty?' Ginger took her congratulations coldly. She was quite aware of her value. Home too was the sentence for Polly and the quarter-master's Bob. Something had been saved.[17]

Chapman noted that quartermasters' hair turned grey during these last days, as every battalion was required to hand in full equipment, not more, not less. Chapman's battalion had a spare pair of mules. What did Quartermaster Keeble do?

> He decided to lose them. They were ridden out six miles at midnight and left beyond a wood through which the abductors fled. At 5 a.m., they were braying outside the stables. The ruse was repeated. Back they came. In the end, the Babes in the Wood were surrendered to the Veterinary section as two strays.

The whole of our world was crumbling . . . England was said to be a country fit only for profiteers to live in . . . Many of us were growing bitter. It was an island we did not know.[18]

Chapman, twenty-nine, decided to volunteer for the Army of Occupation. He said goodbye to the contingent going home. 'They stood on the steps of the mess and grinned, English fashion. We grinned back. It was the end.'

He passed into Germany at Herbesthal. No trumpets sounded.

Warrior went home. After injury in 1918 Jack Seely's steed recovered sufficiently to join the victory parade in Hyde Park and three years later won the race at the Isle of Wight point-to-point. The date? The anniversary of Moreuil Wood, 30 March.

He also went fox hunting with Seely (now Lord Mottistone) on his back, then Seely's son Patrick; Warrior was usually at the head of the hunt. Warrior died in 1941, aged thirty-three. Seely wrote: 'I do not believe, to quote Byron on his dog Boatswain, that he is "denied in Heaven, the soul he had on earth".' Warrior was awarded a posthumous PDSA Dickin medal, the 'Victoria Cross for Animals', in 2014.

Four officers on the Western Front clubbed together to purchase and then ensure a peaceful retirement for a horse called David. This extraordinary animal had served in the Boer War when a youngster. As a veteran on the Western Front, David served every day without fail (except for the one occasion he was wounded).

Other survivors were a gun team of beautiful black horses which were later given the great honour of transporting the coffin of the Unknown Soldier to Westminster Abbey. The team, affectionately known as the 'Old Blacks', were finally retired in 1926. The Sikh, the steed of Lieutenant-Colonel A.C. Vicary DSO MC of the Gloucestershire Regiment, was on active service in Russia at the war's end; Vicary walked her back across Europe, and home. She died in peaceful retirement at Vicary's home in Devon.[19] Sergeant George Thompson, who had taken charge of two requisitioned horses back in a drill hall in Northumberland in 1914, managed to bring one of them home. Bevil Quiller-Couch MC, the son of the writer Sir

Arthur, survived the war but succumbed to Spanish Flu in 1919. Sir Arthur, known famously as 'Q', acquired his son's warhorse, Peggy, and took her home to Fowey. On first meeting her, Q felt the bond:

> Whether or not she detected something familiar in my footstep when I went into the loose box, she was waiting for me. Took no notice of the stableman, but came straight to me, snuffled me all over the chest and then bent down her neck like 'Royal Egypt'. While I stroked her, she nuzzled my wrist and back of my other hand ... It sounds silly, but it seemed as if the creature really did know something and was trying to say it.[20]

Bevil's fiancée, May Wedderburn, remained close to the man who would have been her father-in-law and rode Peggy on her visits to Fowey. She wrote a poem called 'Riding', which included the lines:

> He must have ridden her often, felt the lilt
> Of the sure swift strength moving between his knees
> And I came near him a second, riding so,
> Dreams, but Love lives by these.[21]

Once again, the animal charities did their bit. Our Dumb Friends League rescued 4000 ex-war horses from Belgium. Then in 1930 Dorothy Brooke, the wife of a brigadier, travelled to Cairo, where she discovered many former warhorses still alive, the distinctive arrow brand-mark of the British army just visible on their emaciated bodies as they pulled carts through the streets. She wrote in her diary:

> Out here in Egypt, there are still many hundreds of old army horses sold of necessity at the cessation of the war. They are all over 20 years of age by now, and to say that the majority of them have fallen on hard times is to express it very mildly.

These old war horses were, many of them, born and bred in the green fields of England – how many years since they have seen a field, heard a stream of water or a kind word in English.

Within three years, she had set up a committee and bought 5000 former warhorses, and then she founded the Brooke Hospital for Animals in Cairo. It remains in operation to this day.

*

Will you at least, if I am killed, try not to let the things I have loved cause you pain, but rather to get increased enjoyment from the Sussex Downs or from J singing folk songs, because I have such joy in them, and in that way the joy I have found can continue to live.

> *Lieutenant Arthur Heath, 6/Queen's Own (Royal West Kent*
> *Regiment), to his mother, July 1915, Flanders.*
> *He was killed at Loos three months later.*

On return to Britain, soldiers took to nature as a cure for the wounds of the mind. Private Henry Williamson locked himself away in a Devon cottage to write *Tarka the Otter,* a keystone of British twentieth-century nature writing; Lieutenant Arnold Monk-Jones continued his nature diary when he went up to Oxford, and became active in the League Against Cruel Sports; Lieutenant Edmund Blunden MC, who served two years on the front line, also went up to Oxford, and during research work discovered a hoard of missing poems by his hero John Clare, the peasant poet, in a cupboard in Peterborough Library.

Captain Carlos Paton Blacker wrote a memoir entitled *Have You Forgotten Yet?* He never forgot the comfort nature had given him on active service:

I became aware of a sense of awe and gratitude to the trees, to the forest, but above all to the rooks. The feeling of gratitude to the

rooks has often come back since. Indeed it comes back every time
I hear these birds contentedly calling to each other round their
rookeries in spring. It comes back now as I type these lines.[22]

The lines were written in 1963.

Lieutenant Will Harvey's overwhelming emotion on being back
'in my own country and my own county' was relief. And his desire
was never to leave either again:

> For I am come to Gloucestershire, which is my very home.
> Tired out with wandering and sick of wars beyond the foam.
> I have starved enough in foreign parts, and no more care to
>     roam.
> Quietly I will bide here in the place where I be,
> Which knew my father and his grandfather,
> and my dead brothers and me.
> And bred us and fed us, and gave us pride of yeoman ancestry
> Men with sap of Earth in their blood, and the wisdom of weather
>     and wind.
> Who ploughed the land to leave it better than they did find,
> And lie stretched out down Westbury way, where the blossom is
>     kind;
> And lie covered with petals from orchards that do shed
> Their bloom to be a light white coverlet over the dead
> Who ploughed the land in the daytime, and went well pleased to
>     bed.[23]

Having tasted life inside nature, thousands of soldiers on return to
Blighty wanted a life as a small farmer out in the country.

This coincided with a political feeling that soldiers should be re-
warded, and so the post-war smallholding movement was born.

There were precursors. Between 1819 and 1914 a series of Smallholdings Acts had authorised overseers of the poor and county
councils to acquire blocks of land for rent or purchase. Between 1908

and 1914 alone 205,103 acres were acquired in England and 14,045 smallholders settled on land.

Alongside the official smallholding movement, there was the English tradition of agrarian communes and cottage farms dating back to the Diggers of the English Revolution. Cottage settlements were quite the vogue in late Victorian and Edwardian Britain. The Methwold Fruit Colony in the Norfolk fens, set up in 1889–90 by Robert Goodrich, had about fifty settlers on two- and three-acre plots within a decade, all managed by vegetarians, the majority of them from London. A women's smallholding colony at Lingfield in Surrey was promoted by the Women's Farm and Garden Association. The Salvation Army set up a company called Land for the People Ltd with the aim of buying land to let as smallholdings. When the poet Lascelles Abercrombie had gone to Dymock to be self-sufficient in 1912 he had done so as flotsam in a social current.

For the soldiers coming home in 1918–19 legislation was enacted to provide funds to establish them on allotments or smallholdings. By the time the scheme was wound down in the mid 1920s, 24,000 ex-servicemen had been resettled in England and Wales. The number of smallholdings had more than doubled. Unfortunately, the supply of smallholdings did not meet demand, and few ex-servicemen found life as a smallholder easy in a time of agricultural depression. So many demobbed soldiers opted for poultry farming, having taken courses with ex-servicemen's training centres, that there was a crisis of over-production. Not for the first time, soldier–novelist Ford Madox Ford voiced the tribulations of his generation. In *Parade's End* Ford has Captain Tietjens escape into the life of a West Sussex smallholder. It is an escape into nature. The surroundings are idyllic, he has down-sized from Groby Hall to a cottage and there is romance in nature. But none in humankind. Christopher Tietjens is not much good as a smallholder, or as an antiques dealer. His pregnant girlfriend Valentine rebukes him for stupidly leaving some coloured prints in an unwanted jar which he has given away to another dealer. Valentine sobs: 'How are we to live? How are we ever to live?'[24]

That question was asked by tens of thousands, millions even, in the post-war years. Still, Christopher and Valentine would not have lacked company out in the country. For decades after the war British society, from low to noble, became obsessed with nature and 'Country Life' as it sought to heal the wounds of four years of conflict. If the land of 1918 was less perfect than that of 1914, it was still green and pleasant; the countryside was still worthy of devotion. And so, socialists cycled to the countryside with the Clarion Club, factory workers rambled over dales, and conservative car owners pootled along lanes spotting birds and country houses. There was a mass movement towards the open air.[25]

But, then, going to nature was always the British way.

# NOTES

## CHAPTER I

1 Quoted Matthew Hollis, *Now All Roads Lead to France,* p. 139.

2 Edward Thomas, *Collected Poems*, p. 92.

3 Rupert Brooke, *Collected Poems*, 1916, p. 152. The first verse begins:
Just now the lilac is in bloom,
All before my little room,
And in my flower-beds, I think,
Smile the carnation and the pink;
And down the borders, well I know,
The poppy and the pansy blow . . .

4 Quoted Hollis, p. 139.

5 See Hollis, pp. 151–239, for an extensive account of Thomas's volunteering for service in the Great War.

6 David Wright (ed.), *Edward Thomas Selected Poems and Prose*, p. 164.

7 Thomas, *Collected Poems*, p. 115.

8 The pastoral landscape was inspiration in the Second World War too. One PoW, Thomas Smithson, wrote on a postcard from Japan, sent to his wife, 'ALL I ASK OF THIS WORLD IS MY OWN LITTLE COTTAGE AND THE REMAINDER OF MY LIFE IN YOUR SWEET COMPANIONSHIP COTTAGE'. See Jon E. Lewis, *War Diaries and Letters*, p. 407. In 1950 Britain's pre-eminent nature writer of the twentieth century, Denys Watkins-Pitchford (aka 'B.B.'), sympathized with a young National Serviceman over his 'almost *painful* affection for English fields' in *Letters from Compton Deverell*.

9 F.W. Harvey, 'In Flanders', from E.B. Osborn (ed.), *The Muse in Arms*, 1917, p. 238.

10 Ivor Gurney, 'Strange Service', Osborn, *The Muse in Arms*, p. 14.

11 Ivor Gurney, 'Song', from *Severn & Somme*, p. 42.

12  David Elliston Allen, *The Naturalist in Britain*, p. 210. There is also a thread within the Judaeo-Christian tradition which values nature and kindness towards other animals; this is associated with, amongst others, Francis of Assisi. The first British man known to have fed wild birds was the sixth-century monk, St Serfe of Fife.

13  The misconception that nature-love is intrinsically modern and metropolitan is persistent. George Orwell felt obliged to dish out a rejoinder in 'Some Thoughts on the Common Toad', *Tribune*, 12 April 1946:

'This is often backed up by the statement that a love of Nature is a foible of urbanised people who have no notion what Nature is really like. Those who really have to deal with the soil, so it is argued, do not love the soil, and do not take the faintest interest in birds or flowers, except from a strictly utilitarian point of view. To love the country one must live in the town, merely taking an occasional week-end ramble at the warmer times of year.

'This last idea is demonstrably false. Medieval literature, for instance, including the popular ballads, is full of an almost Georgian enthusiasm for Nature, and the art of agricultural peoples such as the Chinese and Japanese centre always round trees, birds, flowers, rivers, mountains.'

14  Ford Madox Hueffer, 'Footsloggers', from *On Heaven, and Poems Written on Active Service*, pp. 73–4.

15  Quoted in Grieves, 'The propinquity of place: home, landscape and soldier poets of the Great War', from, Jessica Meyer (ed.), *British Popular Culture and the First World War*, p. 29.

16  Grieves, p. 28.

17  Hollis, p. 47. If a greater contrast between an Edwardian childhood and a twenty-first-century one is needed, it comes with the case of the *Oxford Junior Dictionary*: the OUP has now deleted entries no longer felt to be relevant to modern-day childhood. The cull included acorn, adder, ash, beech, bluebell, buttercup, catkin, conker, cowslip, dandelion, hazel, heron, ivy, kingfisher, mistletoe, newt, otter, pasture and willow. In went broadband, bullet-point, MP-3 player, voice-mail.

18  Thomas Traherne, *Centuries of Meditations*, 1908, p. 90.

19  Housman, *War Letters of Fallen Englishmen*, p. 68.

20  See Grieves *passim*.

21  Robert Nichols, 'At the Wars', Osborn, *The Muse in Arms*, p. 4.

22  Charles Douie, *The Weary Road*, p. 89.

23  See Garth, *Tolkien and the Great War*, *passim*.

24  Housman, p. 60.

25  Quoted in Andrew Roberts, *Elegy*, p. 78.

26  Sidney Rogerson, *Twelve Days*, p. 88.

27 Francis Cox, 'The First World War: Disease the Only
   Victor', http://www.gresham.ac.uk/lectures-and-events.
   the-first-world-war-disease-the-only-victor.

28 Douie, p. 158.

29 Edward Grey (Viscount Grey of Fallodon), *Recreation*, pp. 42–3.

30 David Lewis (ed.), *Remembrances of Hell: The Great War Diary of Writer,
   Broadcaster and Naturalist – Norman Ellison*, p. 90.

31 Max Plowman, *A Subaltern on the Somme in 1916*, p. 45.

32 Douie, p. 152.

33 Gillespie, p. 142.

34 F. Hitchcock, *Stand To: A Diary of the Trenches 1915–1918*, p. 38. His brother
   was the Hollywood director Rex Ingram.

35 Stephen Graham, *A Private in the Guards*, p. 206.

36 Quoted in Richard Holmes, *Acts of War*, p. 273.

37 J.W. Graystone IWM 91/3/1.

38 Hugh S. Gladstone, *Birds and the War*, p. 137.

39 Richard Holmes, *Tommy*, p. 527.

40 Housman, *War Letters of Fallen Englishmen*, p. 138.

41 Gillespie, p. 19.

42 Douie, p. 62.

43 G. Atkinson (aka Ralph Scott), *A Soldier's Diary*, pp. 47–8.

44 R.B. Talbot Kelly, *A Subaltern's Odyssey*, p. 104.

45 E.W. Parker, *Into Battle*, p. 48. His genius for the book trade was spotted
   by Longman Green & Co. and after the war he became the most successful
   educational publisher in London.

46 Quoted Anne Powell (ed.), *The Fierce Light: The Battle of the Somme in Prose
   & Poetry*, p. 44.

47 Harold Leslie Rayner, *Letters from France, July 26, 1915 to June 30, 1916*, p. 193.

48 See 'The Woods and Copses: Nature's Fortresses of the Somme on the
   Western Front', http://www.westernfrontassociation.com/great-war-on-
   land/61-battlefields/422-woods.html

49 Housman, pp. 69–70.

50 Richard Devonald-Lewis, *From the Somme to the Armistice: The Memoirs of
   Captain Stormont Gibbs MC*, p. 94.

51 noglory.org/index.php/articles/164-richard-mabey-poppies-and-skylarks-
   among-the-horrors-of-world-war-one.

52 Edward Thomas, *Collected Poems*, p.171.

## CHAPTER II

1  Quoted Richard Holmes, *Tommy*, p. 527.

2  18/West Yorkshire Regiment was formed on 22 January 1915 by the Lord Mayor of Bradford.

3  G.W. Broadhead IWM 85/32/1.

4  A. Monk-Jones IWM 01/50/1.

5  L. Housman (ed.), *War Letters of Fallen Englishmen*, p. 154.

6  Arthur de C. Sowerby, 'Birds of the Battlefields', *British Birds*, Vol. 12, No. 12, May 1919.

7  Gerry Harrison (ed.), *To Fight Alongside Friends: The First World War Diaries of Charlie May*, pp. 121–2.

8  W.S. Medlicott, 'Bird-Notes from the Western front (Pas-de-Calais), *British Birds*, Vol. 12, No. 12, May 1919. Medlicott became an estate agent after the war. He was a prominent fox hunter and judge in retriever trials.

9  *Daily Express*, 27/9/18.

10  Rowland Feilding, *War Letters to a Wife*, p. 123.

11  On British soldiers' superstitions in the Great War see J. Lewis-Stempel, *Six Weeks*, pp. 193–4.

12  The episode figures in Graves's poem 'Bazentin'.

13  Quoted in Matthew Hollis, *Now All Roads Lead to France*, p. 323.

14  Quoted in *Bird Notes & News*, Spring, 1916, No. 1.

15  *Country Life*, 7/10/16, p. 399.

16  Ford Madox Ford, *Parade's End*, p. 631.

17  Sowerby, 'Birds in the North of France, 1917–18', *Ibis*, 1919; A.W. Boyd MC, MBOU 'Birds in the North of France 1917–18, *Ibis*, 1919; W. Maitland Congreve, 'Ornithological and Oological Notes from the River Somme Valley at its Mouth and Near Peronne', *Ibis*, 1918.

18  Arnold Whitworth Boyd MC, MA, FZS, FRES, MBOU (20 January 1885–16 October 1959) was an ornithologist and naturalist from Cheshire. Educated at Rugby and Oxford. He was twice wounded in the First World War, including losing an eye. In spite of this, he managed to rejoin the army and became a Major in the Second World War. http://britishbirds.co.uk/article/obituary-arnold-whitworth-boyd-1885-1959/.

19  C.C. Baring, 'Random Notes from France and Belgium', *Birds and Notes*, Vol. II, No. 7, 1917.

20  Quoted Stephen Moss, *A Bird in the Bush*, p. 114.

21  Rupert Hart-Davis (ed.), *Siegfried Sassoon: Diaries, 1915–18*, p. 59.

22  David Lewis (ed.), *Remembrances of Hell: The Great War Diary of Writer, Broadcaster and Naturalist – Norman Ellison*, pp. 88–9.

23  Talbot Kelly, p. 78.

24  A.D. Gillespie, *Letters from Flanders*, pp. 132–3.

25  Philip Gosse, *Memoirs of a Camp-Follower*, pp. 67–8.

26  Gosse, p. xiv.

27  *The Times* 2/3/1916.

28  CWRK, 'Wild life in the Trenches', *Country Life*, 18/12/1915. 'CWRK' was Captain C.W.R. Knight, 1/Honourable Artillery Company.

29  H.H. Munro, 'Birds on the Western Front', *The Square Egg, and Other Sketches*, p. 116.

30  Hart-Davis, p. 83.

31  *The Times* 2/7/1916.

32  Leslie Coulson, 'The Rainbow', *From an Outpost*.

33  Quoted Richard van Emden, *Tommy's Ark*, p. 28.

34  Quoted van Emden, p. 274.

35  Quoted van Emden, pp. 84–5.

36  *Daily News and Leader*, 22/4/1916.

37  Rayner, p. 195.

38  A young Scout, seeing Vaughan Williams scribbling notes on a south-coast clifftop, assumed he was a spy gathering information for the enemy, and made a citizen's arrest. Although the essential tune of 'Lark Ascending' came to Vaughan Williams in August 1914, the full orchestral version was only played in June 1921. The piece frequently tops polls for Britain's favourite classical tune.

39  Isaac Rosenberg, 'Returning, We Hear the Larks', http://www.poetryarchive.org/poem/returning-we-hear-larks.

40  J.W. Streets, 'Shelley in the Trenches', from *Undying Splendour*, p. 49.

41  Gurney, *Letters*, p. 57.

42  Hart-Davis, p. 71.

43  Quoted Stephen Moss, *A Bird in the Bush*, pp. 114–15.

44  Ford Madox Ford, *Parade's End*, p. 631.

45  Quoted Moss, p. 116.

46  *London Mail*, 28/8/15. Captain A. Boyd observed green woodpeckers give their 'loud laugh' during the battle, 'a cry that was greeted on one hazardous occasion with the caustic comment: "Aye, you can . . . laugh"', Martin Wainwright (ed.) *Wartime Country Diaries*, p. 9.

47  J.B. Foulis IWM 85/15/1.

48  Gillespie, pp. 49–50.

49  Gillespie, p. 143.

50  Gillespie, p. 85.

51  Gladstone, p. 108.

52  http://www.exeter.ac.uk/news/featurednews/title_467063_en.html.

53  *The Times*, 2/3/1916.

54  Munro, p. 114.

55  Ibid.

56  Tawney wrote a poem 'To G', published in *The Nation*, probably inspired by the death of Gresty. 'He has left this world of beautiful things/The hawk that hovers, the lark that sings'. See Gerry Harrison, *To Fight Alongside Friends*, p. 149.

57  G.W. Durham IWM 90/7/1.

58  W. Maitland Congreve, 'Ornithological and Oological Notes from the River Somme Valley at its Mouth and Near Peronne', *Ibis*, Vol. VI, No. 3, July 1918, p. 359.

59  A. Monk-Jones IWM 01/50/1.

60  Quoted Stephen Moss, *A Bird in the Bush*, p. 111.

61  Ernest Pollard and Hazel Strouts (eds), *Wings over the Western Front: The First World War Diaries of Collingwood Ingram*, p. 112.

62  L. Housman, (ed.) *War Letters of Fallen Englishmen*, p. 69.

63  Housman, p. 263.

64  John Buxton, who was taken PoW in Norway 1914 and imprisoned in Bavaria, observed a pair of redstarts for 850 hours in 1943. 'No pair of birds has ever been watched so continuously.' A team of fellows helped, and he wrote a definitive guide to redstarts. Part of their appeal in Bavaria was that they 'inhabited another world . . . they lived only in the moment . . . they lived wholly and enviably to themselves'.

65  Thomas Tiplady, *The Cross at the Front*, p. 86.

66  http://christstreasures.blogspot.co.uk/2014/10/treasures-in-focus-14-faith-and-reason.html.

67  Moss, p. 181.

68  Quoted in Sebastian Faulks and Hope Wolf (eds), *A Broken World*, p. 80.

69  Hueffer, *On Heaven*, p. 35.

70  At the start of the Italo-Turkish War in 1911, the Italian Royal Army Air Services shipped its entire aircraft fleet to the battleground of Tripoli, where Captain Carlo Piazza climbed into his spindly Blériot XI – and made history by spying on the enemy below – and Lieutenant Giolio Gavotti, in a Taube, flew the first ever bombing raid.

71  Churchill even took to the skies himself as a passenger in Hamel's Morane-Saulnier monoplane. Churchill was as passionate about technology, in particular aviation, as he was about nature. Fortunately for Churchill he was

not accompanying Hamel on 23 May 1914 when Britain's 24-year-old darling of aviation crashed his Morane-Saulnier monoplane somewhere in the misty Channel. Hamel's fatal dive into the drink was a prefiguring of the slaughter of the pilots to come. Of the 14,166 RFC pilots who died in the Great War, 8000 perished in accidents. Gravity would always be more deadly than the Germans.

72  Gladstone, p. 151.
73  Ralph Barker, *The Royal Flying Corps in World War 1*, p. 278.
74  Pollard and Strouts, p. 11.
75  Pollard and Strouts, pp. 153–4.
76  C. Ingram, 'Notes on the Height at which Birds Migrate', *Ibis*, No. 2, 1919.
77  He later decided they were shearwaters.
78  P.A. Buxton IWM 99/4/1.
79  Claud B. Ticehurst, P.A. Buxton, R.G. Cheesman, 'The Birds of Mesopotamia' (in 3 parts), *Journal of the Bombay Natural History Society*, Vol. XXVII, Nos 1, 2, 3, 1922–1923.
80  The complete list of birds seen by Sladen, condensed from Sladen's article, is:
    *Corvus umbrinus*. Brown-necked raven
    *Corvus corone*. Carrion-crow
    *Corvus cornix*. Hooded crow
    *Corvus frugilegus*. Rook
    *Garrulus [species?]*. Jay
    *Sturnus vulgaris*. Starling
    *Pastor roseus*. Rose-coloured pastor
    *Oriolus oriolus*. Golden oriole
    *Cliloris chloris chlorotica*. Palestine greenfinch
    *Carduelis carduelis carduelis*. Continental goldfinch
    *Passer domesticus biblicus*. Palestine sparrow
    *Passer hispaniolensis transcaspicus*. Spanish sparrow
    *Fringilla ccelebs*. Chaffinch
    *Acanthis cannabina fringillirostris*. Linnet
    *[Erythrospiza githaginea?]*. Desert bullfinch
    *Emberiza calandra calandra*. Corn-bunting
    *Emberiza csesia*. Cretzschmar's bunting
    *Emberiza cia*. Meadow-bunting
    *Emberiza melanocephala*. Black-headed bunting
    *Emberiza hortulana*. Ortolan bunting
    *Alauda arvensis*. Sky-lark
    (Possibly this is the eastern form of *A. arvensis cinerascens*.)
    *Calandrella brachydactyla brachydactyla*. Short-toed lark

*Galerida cristata cinnamomea.* Crested lark
*Melanocorypha calandra calandra.* Calandra lark
*Lullula arborea.* Wood-lark
*Ammomanes deserti fraterciilus.* Desert-lark
*Motacilla alba.* White wagtail
*Motacilla feldeggi.* Black-headed wagtail
*Motacilla flava flava.* Blue-headed wagtail
*Motacilla flava beema.* Sykes's wagtail
*Cinnyris osea.* Palestine sunbird
*Anthus trivialis.* Tree-pipit
*Anthus cervinus.* Red-throated pipit
*Anthus campestris.* Tawny pipit
*Anthoscopus pendulinus.* Penduline titmouse
*Parus major blanfordi.* Blanford's great titmouse
*Lanius collurio.* Red-backed shrike
*Lanius minor.* Lesser grey shrike
*Lanius elegans.* Pallid shrike
*Lanius nubicus.* Masked shrike
*Lanius senator.* Woodchat
*Sylvia communis.* Whitethroat
*Sylvia curruca.* Lesser Whitethroat
*Motacilla atricapilla.* Blackcap
*Sylvia melanocepliala.* Sardinian warbler
*Sylvia ruppeli.* Ruppell's warbler
*Sylvia orphea.* Orphean warbler
*Phylloscopus trochilus.* Willow-warbler
*Agrobates galactodes.* Rufous warbler
*Acrocephalus schcenobaenus.* Sedge-warbler
*Cisticola cisticola.* Fantail warbler
*Prinia gracilis.* Graceful wren-warbler
*Hippolais pallida.* Olivaceous warbler
*Turdus musicus.* Continental song-thrush
*Turdus merula.* Blackbird
*Turdus pilaris.* Fieldfare
*Monticola cyanus.* Blue rock-thrush
*Phoenicurus phcenicurus.* Redstart
*Phoenicurus titys.* Black redstart
*Luscinia luscinia.* Eastern nightingale or sprosser
*Cyanosylvia suecica suecica.* Red-spotted bluethroat
*Cyanosylvia suecica cyanecula.* White-spotted bluethroat

*Saxicola rubicola.* Stonechat
*Saxicola rubetra.* Whinchat
*Enanthe cenanthe.* Common wheatear
*Enanthe isabellina.* Isabelliue wheatear
*Enanthe deserti.* Desert wheatear
*Enanthe leucomela.* Pied wheatear
*Enanthe hispanica xanthomelaena.* Eastern black-throated and black-eared wheatear
*Pycnonotus xanthopygius.* Palestine bulbul
*Muscicapa grisola.* Spotted flycatcher
*Hirundo rustica transitiva.* Palestine swallow
*Hirundo rufula.* Red-rumped swallow
*Delichon urbica.* House martin
*Riparia riparia.* Sand martin
*Dryobates syriacus.* Syrian pied woodpecker
*Lynx torquilla.* Wryneck
*Cuculus canorus.* Cuckoo
*Clamator glandarius.* Great spotted cuckoo
*Micropus apus.* Swift
*Micropus melba.* Alpine swift
*Caprimulgus segyptius.* Egyptian nightjar
*Merops apiaster.* Bee-eater
*Upupa epops.* Hoopoe
*Alcedo ispida pallida.* Kingfisher
*Ceryle rudis.* Pied or black-and-white kingfisher
*Halcyon smyrnensis.* Smyrna kingfisher
*Coracias garrulus.* Roller
*Flammea flammea.* Barn owl
*Athene noctua glaux.* Little owl
*Asio accipitrinus.* Short-eared owl
*Neophron percnopterus.* Egyptian vulture
*Gyps fulvus.* Griffon vulture
*Circus seruginosus.* Marsh harrier
*Circus cyaneus.* Hen harrier
*Buteo ferox.* Long-legged buzzard
*Buteo riifiventer (B. desertorum anct.)* Steppe buzzard
*Accipiter nisus.* Sparrow hawk
*Milvus aegyptius.* Yellow-billed kite
*Falco peregrinus, [subsp.?]* Peregrine falcon
*Falco subbuteo.* Hobby

*Falco barbarus.* Barbary falcon
*Falco cherrug.* Saker falcon
*Falco aesalon.* Merlin
*Falco tinnunculus.* Kestrel
*Tadorna tadorna.* Common sheld-duck
*Tadorna casarca.* Ruddy sheld-duck
*Anas boscas.* Mallard
*Duerquedula crecca.* Common teal
*Duerquedula querquedula.* Garganey
*Mareca penelope.* Widgeon
*Spatula clypeata.* Shoveler
*Nyroca ferina.* Pochard
*Nyroca nyroca.* White-eyed pochard
*Glaucion clangula.* Golden-eye
*Ardea cinerea.* Heron
*Ardea purpurea.* Purple heron
*Ardeola ralloides.* Squacco heron
*Ardeola ibis.* Buff-backed heron
*Nycticorax nycticorax.* Night-heron
*Botaurus stellaris.* Bittern
*Ixobrychus minutus.* Little bittern
*Ciconia ciconia.* White stork
*Ciconia nigra.* Black stork
*Plegadis falcinellus.* Glossy ibis
*Grus grus.* Crane
*Chlamydotis macqueenii?* Macqueen's bustard
*Edicnemus cedicnemiis.* Stone-curlew
*Cursorius gallicus.* Cream-coloured courser
*Glareola pratincola.* Collared pratincole
*Glareola nordmanni.* Black-winged pratincole
*Scolopax rusticola.* Woodcock
*Gallinago gallinago.* Common snipe
*Limnocryptes gallinnla.* Jack snipe
*Tringa minuta.* Little stint
*Tringa alpina.* Dunlin
*Tringa ferruginea.* Curlew sandpiper
*Calidris arenaria.* Sanderling
*Machetes pugnax.* Ruff
*Totanus totamis.* Common redshank
*Totanus nebularius.* Greenshank

*Totanus hypoleucus*. Common sandpiper
*Totanus glareola*. Wood-sandpiper
*Limosa limosa*. Black-tailed godwit
*Numenius tenuirostris*. Slender-billed curlew
*Himantopus himantopus*. Black-winged stilt
*Charadrius apricarius*. Golden plover
*[ffigialitis?] hiaticula*. Ringed plover
*[iEgialitis?] alexandrina*. Kentish plover
*[igialitis?] geoffroyi*. Geoffrey's plover
*Hoplopterus spinosus*. Spur-winged plover
*Vanellus vanellus*. Lapwing
*Lams ridibundus*. Black-headed gull
*Larus cacliiunans*. Herring gull (probably yellow-legged)
*Hydrochelidon nigra*. Black tern
*Hydrochelidon hyltrida*. Whiskered tern
*Puffimis puffinus yelkouan*. Levantine shearwater
*Porzana porzana*. Spotted crake
*Crex crex*. Corn crake
*Gallinula chloropus*. Moorhen
*Fulica atra*. Coot
*Columba oenas*. Stock dove
*Streptopelia turtur*. Turtle dove
*Pterocles alchata*. Pintailed sandgrouse
*Pterocles senegallus*. Senegal sandgrouse
*Pterocles arenarius*. Black-bellied sandgrouse
*Caccabis chukar*. Chukar partridge
*Coturnix coturnix*. Common quail

81  Gladstone, p. 139.
82  Harrison (ed.), p. 39.
83  H. Birkett Barker IWM 73/140/1.
84  Gladstone, p. 25.
85  Gladstone, p. 85.
86  *Daily Mail*, 1/2/1918.
87  *The Field*, 2/2/1918.
88  Gladstone, p. 9.
89  Martin Wainwright (ed.), *Wartime Country Diaries*, p.9.

## CHAPTER III

1 Siegfried Sassoon, *Memoirs of a Fox-hunting Man*, p. 252.

2 Quoted in Max Arthur, *Forgotten Voices of the Great War*, p. 15.

3 F.W. Harvey, 'The Horses', from *Gloucestershire Friends*, p. 46.

4 John Sadler and Rosie Serdiville, *Tommy at War*, p. 264.

5 Quoted Jilly Cooper, *Animals in War*, p. 40.

6 Ibid.

7 Michael Clayton, 'From British ditches to foreign trenches', *The Field*, August 2014.

8 Quoted Chris Ward, *Living on the Western Front*, p. 60.

9 Specifically, equine influenza is an acute respiratory infection of horses, donkeys and mules caused by two distinct subtypes (H7N7, formerly equi-1, and H3N8, formerly equi-2) of influenza A virus within the genus *Influenzavirus A* of the family *Orthomyxoviridae*. The disease is endemic in many countries with substantial equine populations. The disease has struck war horses from the time of Charlemagne.

10 E. Crawshay-Williams, *Leaves from an Officer's Notebook*, p. 114.

11 Quoted Richard van Emden, *Tommy's Ark*, p. 22.

12 Patrick Butler, *A Galloper at Ypres*, pp.23-4.

13 Rowland Myrddyn Luther IWM 87/8/1.

14 Michael Clayton, 'From British ditches to foreign trenches'.

15 Aldin lost his only son in the war. Second Lieutenant Dudley Aldin of the Royal Engineers was just nineteen when he died at Mont St Eloi, Arras, in May 1916.

16 See Luci Gosling, 'Aldin's War – the Sporting Artist and the Army Remount Service', http://blog.maryevans.com/2014/07.

17 Jack Seely, 'The Real War Horse', *The Field*, January 2012.

18 Robert Graves, *Goodbye to All That*, p. 110.

19 Edmund Blunden, *Undertones of War*, p. 145.

20 A.E. Bundy IWM p. 371.

21 Quoted Sadler and Serdiville, p. 265.

22 Richard Devonald-Lewis, *From the Somme to the Armistice*, p. 131.

23 Richard Devonald-Lewis, p. 68.

24 Quoted Max Arthur, p. 31.

25 Quoted van Emden, pp. 35-6.

26 G. Atkinson (aka Ralph Scott), *A Soldier's Diary*, pp. 70-72.

27 R. G. Dixon IWM Sound Archive 737.

28 F. Hitchcock, *Stand To*, p. 94.

29  J. Reynolds IWM 99/13/1.

30  Cooper, p. 77.

31  Sadler and Serdiville, p. 268.

32  R.M. Luther IWM 87/8/1.

33  Ralph G.A. Hamilton, *The War Diary of The Master of Belhaven, 1914–18*, p. 191.

34  Quoted Sadler and Serdiville, p. 272.

35  Quoted van Emden, p. 190.

36  Devonald-Lewis, p. 92.

37  Quoted van Emden, pp. 240–1.

38  http://www.bbc.co.uk/history/worldwars/wwone/humanfaceofwar_gallery_05.shtml.

39  Quoted van Emden, p. 239.

40  Jack Seely, 'The Real War Horse'.

41  The battle of Moreuil Wood was fought on the banks of the Arve River, 30 March 1918. [See pp. 115–16].

42  Jack Seely, 'The Real War Horse'.

43  See Elizabeth Vandiver, *Stand in the Trench, Achilles*, p. 191.

44  Quoted van Emden, p. 32.

45  At the end of the war General Douglas Haig wrongly believed that horses would continue to be used in warfare: 'I believe that the value of the horse and the opportunity for the horse in the future are likely to be as great as ever. Aeroplanes and tanks are only accessories to the men and the horse, and I feel sure that as time goes on you will find just as much use for the horse – the well-bred horse – as you have ever done in the past.'

46  In September 1914 cavalry comprised 9.28 per cent of the total manpower of the British Expeditionary Force in France. By July 1918 this proportion had fallen to 1.65 per cent.

47  See Lewis-Stempel, *Six Weeks*, p. 34; J.M. Winter, *The Great War*, pp. 92–8.

48  Dennis Wheatley, *The Time Has Come*, pp. 57–9.

49  Richard Holmes, *Tommy*, p. 436.

50  'Epic of the War: Courage which made history', *Western Argus*, January 10 1933, http://trove.nla.gov.au/article/34610461/4264812.

51  Unable to hunt foxes, the colonialists hunted coyotes. https://legionmagazine.com/en/2009/06/the-short-season-of-high-society/

52  Cooper, p. 59.

53  Cooper, p. 61.

54  Van Emden, pp. 239–40.

55  Van Emden, p. 245.

56  Hitchcock, p. 271.

57 J.M. Brereton, *The Horse in War*, p. 130.

58 Brereton, *passim*.

59 Dennis Wheatley, *The Time Has Come*, pp. 53–9.

60 Harrison, p. 88.

61 *Biology Letters*, Vol. XX, 2014, p. 119.

62 A.J.J.P. Aquis IWM 99/70/1.

63 Atkinson, p. 16.

64 W.H. Bloor IWM 99/22/1.

65 Hamilton, p. 342.

66 Quoted Cooper, p. 61.

67 Bernard Adams, *Nothing of Importance*, p. 254.

68 Adams, pp. 255–6.

69 Atkinson, p. 16.

70 Crawshay-Williams, p. 158.

71 Sidney Galtrey, *The Horse and the War*, p. 35.

72 Thomas Tiplady, *The Cross at the Front*, pp. 18–19.

73 C.G. Mackay IWM 09/49/1.

74 Frederic Manning, 'Transport', from G.H. Clarke (ed.), *A Treasury of War Poetry*, 1917, p. 271. Manning was commissioned into the Royal Irish Rifles in 1917. He is Private Bourne in his 1929 autobiographical novel about the War, *The Middle Parts of Fortune* (expurgated as *Her Privates We*).

75 E. Miles IWM 83/6/1.

76 http://defence-honours-tribunal.gov.au/inquiries/completed-inquiries/valour/private-john-simpson-kirkpatrick/.

77 http://nsw.rspca.org.au/get-involved/rspca-awards/rspca-purple-cross-award.

78 Cooper, pp. 199–200.

79 'Mange' is generic for several skin conditions caused by microscopic mites that invade the skin of otherwise healthy animals. The main types of mange affecting horses are sarcoptic mange (equine scabies), psoroptic mange (mane mange), demodectic mange, harvest mites (chiggers, trombiculids) and straw itch mites (forage mites).

80 Quoted Max Arthur, *The Road Home*, pp. 95–6.

81 *The Animal World*, December 1932, p. 178.

**CHAPTER IV**

1 Graves, *Goodbye to All That*, p. 86.

2 Graves, p. 157.

3 T. Kettle, *The Ways of War*, p. 181.

4   David Lewis (ed.), *Remembrances of Hell*, p. 82.

5   F. Hitchcock, *Stand To*, p. 206.

6   Atkinson, pp. 118–19.

7   Philip Gosse, *Memoirs of a Camp-Follower*, p. 127.

8   Quoted John Lewis-Stempel, *Six Weeks*, p. 126.

9   Quoted Max Arthur, *Forgotten Voices of the Great War*, p. 97.

10  David Lewis (ed.), *Remembrances of Hell*, p. 69.

11  Guy Chapman, *A Passionate Prodigality*, pp. 28–9.

12  Patrick Butler, *A Galloper at Ypres*, p. 255.

13  Quoted Richard van Emden, *Tommy's Ark*, p. 166.

14  Cameron Stewart (ed.), *A Very Unimportant Officer*, p. 85.

15  Quoted van Emden, p. 166.

16  Quoted Richard Holmes, *Tommy*, p. 286.

17  Quoted Hew Strachan, *The First World War: A New History*, p. 189.

18  Gerry Harrison, *To Fight Alongside Friends*, p. 26.

19  R.B. Talbot Kelly, *A Subaltern's Odyssey*, p. 108.

20  Quoted van Emden, pp. 167–8.

21  Quoted Malcolm Brown, *Tommy Goes to War*, p. 82.

22  Quoted Lewis-Stempel, *Six Weeks*, p. 126.

23  Quoted van Emden p. 106.

24  A.E. Bundy IWM p. 371.

25  Holmes, *Tommy*, p. 287.

26  Ibid.

27  Butler, pp. 255–6.

28  Atkinson, pp. 62–4.

29  Butler, p. 256.

30  See David John Davis, 'Bacteriology and the War', *The Scientific Monthly*, Vol. 5, No. 5, Nov 1917.

31  The French also issued terriers for ratting.

32  The rodent problem in the UK was such that the Rats and Mice Destruction Act was passed, along with, in November 1919, a national Rat Week, when people were encouraged to kill as many rats as possible.

33  Quoted van Emden, p. 256.

34  J. Reynolds IWM 99/13/1.

35  Quoted van Emden, pp. 222–3.

36  Bernard Adams, *Nothing of Importance*, p. 207.

37  Quoted van Emden, p. 93.

38  Arthur Empey, *Over the Top*, p. 189.

39  Gosse, p. 168.

40  Atkinson, p. 114.

41  Holmes, *Tommy*, p. 287.

42  http://projects.oucs.ox.ac.uk/jtap/rose/hyppoem.html.

43  Quoted van Emden, pp. 225–6.

44  Charles Douie, *The Weary Road*, p. 265.

45  R. Feilding, *War Letters to a Wife*, p. 34.

46  C.P. Blacker, *Have You Forgotten Yet?*, p. 64.

47  Munro, p. 113.

48  The psychologist F.C. Bartlett emphasised the connection between fatigue and psychiatric breakdown: 'In war there is perhaps no general condition which is likely to produce a large crop of nervous and mental disorders than a state of prolonged and great fatigue.'

49  Francis Cox, 'The First World War: Disease, The Only Victor'.

50  http://spartacus-educational.com/FWWlice.htm.

51  See *And We Go On* by Will R. Bird. The 16th battalion CEF scrapbook contained a photograph of soldiers doing some personal delousing captioned 'Looking for an enemy worse than the Germans'.

52  http://ww1lit.nsms.ox.ac.uk/ww1lit/db/object/ww1/3275.

53  Empey, *Over the Top*, p. 21.

54  Quoted van Emden, p. 63.

55  The US Army's *Notes for Medical Officers* observed that 'Keating's powder, "pyrethrum", is not very efficacious, although better than nothing'.

56  Holmes, *Tommy*, p. 590.

57  Empey, p. 20.

58  Stuart Cloete, *A Victorian Son*, p. 67.

59  George Ashurst, *My Bit: A Lancashire Fusilier at War*, p. 118.

60  W.H. Harris IWM 78/4/1.

61  Holmes, *Tommy*, p. 589.

62  Frederic Hodges, *Men of 18 in 1918*, p. 282.

63  From *Aussie: The Australian Soldiers' Magazine*, No. 3, 8 March 1918.

64  L/Cpl T.A. Saxon AIF, 'A Dug-Out Lament', from C.E.W. Bean (ed.), *The Anzac Book*, 1916.

65  See R.L. Atenstaedt, 'Trench Fever: The British Medical Response in the Great War', *Journal of the Royal Society of Medicine*, Nov 2006, 99 (11).

66  Government Committee on Treatment by the Enemy of British Prisoners of War, *The Horrors of Wittenberg: Official Report to the British Government*, 1916, p. 44.

67  Georges Monvoisin, a French doctor held in Wittenberg, claimed a total of 3500 cases, with 400 deaths, the average death rate being 11 per cent, being 4 per cent for Russians, and 17–18 per cent for French PoWs. See H. Jones, *Prisoners of Violence*, pp. 96–7. Russian immunity, however, was far from

absolute. The typhus epidemic that broke out at the end of 1918 invaded Russia along three fronts – Petrograd, the Romanian front and the Volga region – and raged for four years, with 20 million cases, 10 million of which died. The October Revolution looked to be at the mercy of *pediculus humanus*. Lenin, surveying the situation in 1919, put it pithily: 'Either socialism will defeat the louse, or the louse will defeat socialism.'

68 Government Committee on Treatment by the Enemy of British Prisoners of War: *The Horrors of Wittenberg*, p. 44.

69 Crawshay-Williams, *Leaves from an Officer's Notebook*, p. 84.

70 Van Emden, p. 158.

71 Quoted van Emden, p. 159.

72 I.L. Idriess, *Desert Column*, p. 8.

73 Crawshay-Williams, p. 137.

74 G.A. Perreau IWM 12/36/1.

75 David Lewis, *Remembrances of Hell*, p. 69.

76 G.W. Broadhead IWM 85/32/1.

77 Atkinson, pp. 101–2.

78 Atkinson, pp. 101–2.

79 Douie, p. 194.

80 War Office, *Statistics of the Military Effort of the British Empire during the Great War 1914–1920*, p. 744.

81 http://www.westernfrontassociation.com/the-great-war/great-war-on-land/casualties-medcal/693-malaria-in-the-war.html#sthash.Yp9Xzj20.dpbs.

82 In the jungle of East Africa black troops were particularly heavily committed, and in this 'side-show' disease was diabolical. The troop returns of the Gold Coast Regiment make sobering reading. From a force of 3,800 strong 215 died in action, whereas 270 perished from disease. A further 567 men were invalided out of service because of disease. Of the 105,000 who died in East Africa the majority did so from disease.

83 http://www.africaresearchinstitute.org/publications/counterpoints/how-the-great-war-razed-east-africa.

84 Quoted van Emden, p. 158.

85 H. Birkett Barker IWM 73/140/1.

86 Quoted Roberts, *Elegy*, p. 96.

87 Edmund Blunden, *Undertones of War*, p. 93.

88 K.G. Blair, 'Notes from the Trenches', *The Entomologist's Record and Journal of Variation*, Vol XXVII, No 9, September 1915.

89 H. Birkett Barker IWM 73/140/1.

90 http://www.alchemywebsite.com/war_diary/kirke_war_diary.html, transcribed by Adam McLean, 2004.

91 Wainwright, Martin (ed.), *Wartime Country Diaries*, p. 69.

92 W. Bowater, 'Random Notes from France', *The Entomologist's Record and Journal of Variation*, Vol. XXVIII, 1916.

93 Ibid.

94 Other butterflies seen by Buxton at Gallipoli included: 'A nice Burnet'; *C. pamphilus*; *Hyale*; *Megaera*; *Maera*; *Semele*; *Papilio Podalirius*; *C. phloeas*; *Siapsis* (wood white); *Macro stellatarum*; *V. Atalanta*; *C. Pamphilus*; '2 *Pierids brassica* and *belia*?'; *Plusia gamma*; Female *edusa* in camp – marbled white; '*Brassiccae cardui* common'; '*Limenitis* apparently *Sibylla*'.

## CHAPTER V

1 Lionel Crouch, *Duty and Service*, p. 102.

2 Crouch, p. 48.

3 Crouch, p. 47.

4 See *Citizen Soldiers of Buckinghamshire 1795–1926*, by Major General J.C. Swann.

5 Quoted in Kenneth Helphand, *Defiant Gardens*, pp. 37–8.

6 A.D. Gillespie, *Letters from Flanders*, p. 126.

7 Gillespie, p. 223.

8 Feilding, p. 43.

9 Stephen Graham, *A Private in the Guards*, pp. 172–8.

10 Edwin Campion Vaughan, *Some Desperate Glory*, p. 110.

11 Edward Tennant, 'Home Thoughts in Laventie', from Pamela Glenconner, *Edward Wyndham Tennant*.

12 Bernard Adams, *Nothing of Importance*, pp. 253–4.

13 Charlotte Zeepvat, *Before Action*, p. 175.

14 G.W. Durham IWM 90/7/1.

15 G.A. Perreau IWM 12/36/1.

16 War Office, *Statistics of the Military Effort of the British Empire During the Great War 1914–1920*, pp. 582–3.

17 C.G. Mackay IWM 09/49/1.

18 F. Hitchcock, *Stand To*, p. 197.

19 Elgin Strub-Ronayne, '"Cabbage soup again" – the hardships & resilience of men held in Germany's Ruhleben prison camp', centenarynews.com on 10 February 2014, http://www.centenarynews.com/article?id=1446.

20 Brent Elliott, 'A tale of two societies: the Royal Horticultural Society and the Ruhleben Horticultural Society'.

21 Quoted Helphand, p. 130.

22  Quoted Helphand, p. 129.

23  J. Powell and F. Gribble, *The History of Ruhleben*, p. 195.

24  Conrad Hoffman, *In the Prison Camps of Germany*, p. 127.

25  F.W. Harvey, *Gloucestershire Friends*, p. 20.

26  Edwin Campion Vaughan, *Some Desperate Glory*, p. 139.

27  Frederick James Hodges, *Men of 18 in 1918*, p. 84.

28  Charles Douie, *The Weary Road*, p. 138.

29  Chris Ward, *Living on the Western Front*, p. 39.

30  C.P. Blacker, *Have You Forgotten Yet?*, pp. 159–60.

31  See Michael Snape, *God and the British Soldier*, 2005.

32  British PoWs in Germany foraged out of necessity. Corporal Arthur Speight,
    7/DLI, taken prisoner and put to work by his German captors gathered nettle
    and snails in a bid to supplement his starvation rations. IWM 76/206/1.

33  Blacker, pp. 114–15.

34  Philip Gosse, *Memoirs of a Camp-Follower*, p. 83.

35  A. Monk-Jones IWM 01/50/1.

36  Rayner, p. 196.

37  Rayner, p. 198.

38  The cornflower: the colour of the *ciel*, and the hue of the uniform worn by
    French soldiers after 1915; from 1935, after early patronage by presidents, the
    Republic made *bleuet* the official Remembrance Day symbol for France.

39  Nicholas J. Saunders, *The Poppy*, pp. 5–6.

40  Isaac Rosenberg, 'In the Trenches', http://hellesdon.org/documents/
    isaac_rosenberg_2004_9.pdf.

41  In 1921 Anna E. Guerin, who independently began making silk poppies in
    Paris after the war, took samples to Colonel E.C. Heath the general secretary
    of the newly founded British Legion. Guerin enquired whether the Legion
    might want to use the poppy to raise funds for its service. The red poppy
    touched the heart of Haig, one of the Legion's founders. Nine million
    poppies were ordered for the first Poppy Day to be held in Britain on 11
    November 1921. Britain's first Poppy Appeal raised £106,000 – the equivalent
    of £3.1 million today.

42  P.A.J. Buxton IWM 99/4/1-2.

**CHAPTER VI**

1  http://regimentalrogue.tripod.com/blog/index.blog/2318266/poilu-a-lion-for-
   a-mascot/.

2  Quoted John Sadler and Rosie Serdiville, *Tommy at War*, p. 302.

3 Richard Holmes, *Tommy*, p. 302.

4 Tweeted copy of 'Rabbit as "Emergency Ration"' by @roadtowar1914, 16 April 2015.

5 IWM photograph Q32300.

6 Ernest Pollard and Hazel Strouts (eds), *Wings over the Western Front*, p. 45.

7 A.D. Gillespie, *Letters from Flanders*, p. 67.

8 Philip Gosse, *Memoirs of a Camp-Follower*, p. 74.

9 R. Schweder IWM 86/65/1.

10 David Lewis, *Remembrances of Hell*, p. 82.

11 *Llais Llafur*, 1/3/19.

12 Quoted Richard van Emden, *Tommy's Ark*, p. 220.

13 Viola Meynell, *Julian Grenfell*, p. 6.

14 Frederic Coleman, *With Cavalry in 1915*, p. 35.

15 Quoted van Emden, p. 71.

16 'Birds and Beasts at the Fighting Front', *Country Life*, 21 September 1916.

17 Edmund Blunden, *Undertones of War*, p. 26.

18 Quoted van Emden, p. 216.

19 Quoted van Emden, p. 214.

20 Quoted van Emden, pp. 297–300.

21 See Holmes, *Tommy*, p. 627

22 R. Feilding, *War Letters to a Wife*, p. 35.

23 Quoted van Emden, p. 223.

24 Quoted van Emden, p. 73.

25 R. Dixon IWM Sound Archive 737.

26 Quoted van Emden, p. 132.

27 Patrick Butler, *A Galloper at Ypres*, pp. 154–5.

28 Charles Douie, *The Weary Road*, p. 47.

29 Quoted van Emden, pp. 132–3.

30 Gillespie, pp. 71–2.

31 Quoted van Emden, pp. 78–80.

32 Quoted van Emden, pp. 79–81.

33 Gerry Harrison (ed.), *To Fight Alongside Friends*, p. 115.

34 Harrison, p. 118.

35 Lewis-Stempel, *The War Behind the Wire*, pp. 152–4.

36 F.W. Harvey, *Comrades in Captivity*, pp. 150–1.

37 Harvey, *Comrades in Captivity*, p. 129.

38 Lewis-Stempel, *The War Behind the Wire*, p. 87.

39 E.H. Jones, *The Road to En-Dor*, p. 123.

40 Ibid.

41 Jilly Cooper, *Animals in War*, p. 88.

42  E.H. Richardson, *British War Dogs: Their Training and Psychology*, pp. 55–6.

43  Richardson, pp. 60–1.

44  Richardson, p. 70.

45  Richardson, pp. 83–4.

46  Richardson, pp. 123–4.

47  Richardson, p. 120.

48  Richardson, p. 90.

49  Richardson, p. 94.

**CHAPTER VII**

1   Lewis-Stempel, *Six Weeks*, p. 105.

2   Viola Meynell, *Julian Grenfell*, pp. 11–12.

3   Gilbert Murray, *The Hippolytus of Euripides*, 1908.

4   Lionel Crouch, *Duty and Service*, p. 30.

5   Matt Limb, 'From tweed to khaki for king and country', *The Field*, 13 August 2013.

6   George Thomas (ed.), *Edward Thomas*, p. 150.

7   Patrick Butler, *A Galloper at Ypres*, p. 275.

8   Quoted Richard van Emden, *Tommy's Ark*, pp. 272–3.

9   R. Feilding, *War Letters to a Wife*, p. 85.

10  Ernest Pollard and Hazel Strouts, *Wings over the Western Front*, p. 123.

11  Game shooting was, nonetheless, one of the principal recreations of all the occupying Allied armies after the armistice of 11 November 1918. The German civilian population had to surrender its firearms of every description when the occupying troops arrived, so that large stocks of sporting guns and cartridges were available in every town and village.

12  Bernard Adams, *Nothing of Importance*, p. 211.

13  Quoted van Emden, p. 192.

14  Charles Carrington, *Soldier from the Wars Returning*, p. 122.

15  Carrington, p. 145.

16  Quoted Lewis-Stempel, *Six Weeks*, p. 253.

17  Quoted van Emden, p. 279.

18  A.D. Gillespie, *Letters from Flanders*, p. 98.

19  Quoted Chris Ward, *Living on the Western Front*, p. 89.

20  David Lewis, *Remembrances of Hell*, p. 66.

21  Gerry Harrison (ed.), *To Fight Alongside Friends*, p. 87.

22  Quoted van Emden, p. 193.

23  Quoted Lewis-Stempel, *Six Weeks*, p. 253.

24  Pollard and Strouts, p. 141.

25  Siegfried Sassoon, *Memoirs of an Infantry Officer*, p. 272.

26  Lucinda Gosling, *Great War Britain: The First World War at Home*, p. 215.

27  Sassoon, p. 251.

28  Sassoon, p. 27.

29  See Gosling, p. 215.

30  Quoted van Emden, p. 303.

31  H. Birkett Barker 73/140/1.

32  Blunden, p. 37.

33  Feilding, p. 46.

34  Lewis, p. 68.

35  Quoted van Emden, pp. 110–11.

36  Gillespie, p. 269.

37  Philip Gosse, *Memoirs of a Camp-Follower*, p. 85.


**CHAPTER VIII**


1  Charles Douie, *The Weary Road*, p. 176.

2  Hugh Clout, *After the Ruins*, p. 28.

3  Quoted Clout, p. 299.

4  Quoted Clout, ibid.

5  Quoted Clout, p. 300.

6  Stephen Graham, *A Private in the Guards*, p. 346.

7  Philip Longworth, *Unending Vigil*, p. 67.

8  *Daily Mail*, 26/7/17.

9  See Roger Lovegrove's *Silent Fields*, 2008, for the state of nature in Great Britain in the twentieth century.

10  See Brent Elliot, 'Bolshevism in the Garden', *Occasional Papers from the RHS Lindley Library*, Vol. 12, September 2014.

11  Prince died in July 1921.

12  Quoted Richard van Emden, *Tommy's Ark*, pp. 299–301.

13  Quoted van Emden, p. 302.

14  Of the 18,000 New Zealand horses which went to war, only two returned home: one belonged to Lt Col. Thomas Porter, the other to Colonel G.G. Powles.

15  Quoted van Emden, pp. 302–3.

16  Quoted van Emden, p. 301.

17  Guy Chapman, *A Passionate Prodigality*, p. 280.

18  Chapman, pp. 280–1.

19  Geoffrey Maynard, 'Real-life War Horse uncovered: Animal's bravery helped our soldiers in the trenches', *Daily Express*, 22/1/2015. The Sikh, the horse of Lt Col. Vicary, was regarded by all in the regiment as a lucky omen; the Sikh served throughout the war.

20  Charlotte Fyfe (ed.), *Tears of War*, p. 76.

21  Ibid.

22  C.P. Blacker, *Have You Forgotten Yet?*, p. 88.

23  F.W. Harvey, *Gloucestershire Friends*, p. 9.

24  Ford, Ford Madox, *Parade's End*, p. 835.

25  There was a cultural echo of this rural tourism in modish back-to-the-land literature, exemplified by Vita Sackville-West's long narrative poem *The Land*.

# BIBLIOGRAPHY

## PRIMARY SOURCES

**Imperial War Museum:**
A.J.J.P. Aquis 99/70/1; H. Birkett Barker 73/140/1; R.J. Blackadder 88/11/1; W.H. Bloor 99/22/1; G.W. Broadhead 85/32/1; A.E. Bundy P.371; P.A.J. Buxton 99/4/1–2; G.W. Durham 90/7/1; H.N. Edwards 66/144/1; J.B. Foulis 85/15/1; J.W. Graystone 91/3/1; W.H. Harris 78/4/1; S.M. Ironside P.97; R.M. Luther 87/8/1; C.G. Mackay 09/49/1; E. Miles 83/6/1; A. Monk-Jones 01/50/1; G.A. Perreau 12/36/1; J. Reynolds 99/13/1; A.H. Roberts 97/37/1; R. Schweder 86/65/1; A. Speight 76/206/1

**The National Archives:**
J.R.R. Tolkien WO 339/34423

## NEWSPAPERS, MAGAZINES AND JOURNALS

Alexander, H.G., 'C.J. Alexander: Obituary', *British Birds*, Vol. 11, No. 9, 1 February 1918

Anon., 'Torpedoed seaman saved by canary', *Daily Telegraph*, 23 July 2014

Anon., 'Nature and the battlefield. A reading of earth', *The Times*, 30 July 1917

Atenstaedt, R.L., 'Trench fever: the British medical response in the Great War', *Journal of the Royal Society of Medicine*, Vol. 99, No. 11, November 2006

Baker, Godfrey, 'The artistic front', *The Field*, August 2014

Blair, K.G., 'Notes from the trenches', *The Entomologist's Record and Journal of Variation*, Vol. XXVII, No. 9, September 1915

Bowater, W., 'Random Notes from France', *The Entomologist's Record and Journal of Variation*, Vol. XXVIII, 1916

Boyd, A.W., 'Birds in the North of France, 1917–18', *The Ibis*, Vol. 1, No. 1, 1919

Brown, Jonathan, 'After the storm', *BBC Countryfile*, November 2014

Charles, Nickie and Aull Davies, Charlotte, 'My Family and other animals: pets as kin', *Sociological Research Online*, Vol. 13, No. 5, 30 September 2008

Clayton, Michael, 'From British ditches to foreign trenches', *The Field*, August 2014

Congreve, W. Maitland, 'Ornithological and Oological Notes from the River Somme Valley at its Mouth and Near Peronne', *The Ibis*, Vol. VI, No. 3, July 1918

Copping, Jasper, 'The Western Front's dogs of war revealed', *Daily Telegraph*, 28 November 2013

— 'Honoured: The WW1 pigeons who earned their wings', *Daily Telegraph*, 12 January 2014

— 'Cats of war: Animals suspected by British of spying on WW1 trenches', *Daily Telegraph*, 13 March 2014

Cotterell, Laurence, 'Obituary: Geoffrey Dearmer', *The Independent*, 20 August 1996

Cumming, Ed, 'Ruhleben: The WW1 camp where gardening blossomed', *Daily Telegraph*, 1 February 2014

C.W.R.K., 'Wild life in the trenches', *Country Life*, 18 December 1915

Davis, David John, 'Bacteriology and the war', *The Scientific Monthly*, Vol. 5, No. 5, November 1917

Eagle Clarke, William, 'George Stout', *The Scottish Naturalist*, No. 61, January 1917

Edwards, T.J., 'Regimental Mascots', *The Army Quarterly*, Vol. LXVI, April–June, 1953

Elliott, B., 'A tale of two societies: the Royal Horticultural Society and the Ruhleben Horticultural Society', *Occasional Papers from the RHS Lindley Library*, Vol. 12, September 2014

— 'Bolshevism in the garden', ibid.

Grieves, Keith, 'The propinquity of place: home, landscape and soldier poets of the Great War,' in Meyer, Jessica (ed.), *British Popular Culture and the First World War* (Leiden, 2008)

Henton, Ali, 'United Artists', *The Field*, August 2010

Howat, T., 'Gardening at Ruhleben Camp' (letter), *Gardeners' Chronicle*, 20 January 1917

Limb, Matt, 'From tweed to khaki for king and country', *The Field*, August 2013

Lowry, C.A. et al., 'Identification of an immune-responsive mesolimbocortical serotonergic system: Potential role in regulation of emotional behaviour', *Neuroscience*, Vol. 46, No. 2, 11 May 2007

Martins, Susanna Wade, 'Smallholdings in Norfolk, 1890–1950: A social and farming experiment', *Agricultural History Review*, Vol. 54, No. 2, 2006

# Bibliography

Medlicott, W.S., 'Bird-notes from the Western Front (Pas-de-Calais), *British Birds*, Vol. 12, No. 12, May 1919

Milewski, Kevin, 'The flight of the nightingale: from Romans to Romantics', *Vanderbilt Undergraduate Research Journal*, Vol. 9, Summer 2013

Morris, Mandy, 'Gardens "for ever England": Landscape, identity and the First World War British cemeteries of the Western Front', *Ecumene*, Vol. 4, No. 4, 1997

Mount, Harry, 'Surviving the war was the easy part', *Daily Telegraph*, 22 March 2014

Nicholls, Henry, 'A pig's tale: the porker that jumped ship in the First World War', *Guardian*, 14 August 2013

Potter, Bernard E., 'Birds in Macedonia', *The Avicultural Magazine*, Vol. VII, No. 9, 1916

Roper, Michael, 'Nostalgia as an emotional experience in the Great War', *The Historical Journal*, Vol. 54, No. 2, June 2011

Sanborn, Colin Campbell, 'List of birds made during eighteen months' service in France and Germany', *The Wilson Bulletin*, Vol. XXXII, No. 111, 1920

Sladen, A.G.L., 'Notes on birds observed in Palestine', *The Ibis*, XI, Vol. 1, No. 2, 1919

Smith, Amy Victoria, Proops, Leanne, Grounds, Kate, Wathan, Jennifer and McComb, Karen, 'Functionally relevant responses to human facial expressions of emotion in the domestic horse (*Equus caballus*)', *Biology Letters*, Vol. 12, No. 2, 10 February 2016

Sowerby, Arthur de C., 'Birds of the battlefields', *British Birds*, Vol. 12, No. 12, 1 May 1919

Ticehurst, Claud B., Buxton, P.A. and Cheesman, R.G., 'The birds of Mesopotamia' (in 3 parts), *Journal of the Bombay Natural History Society*, Vol. XXVII, Nos 1, 2, 3, 1922–23

Ticehurst, Claud B., Cox, Percy and Cheesman, R.G., 'Additional notes on the avifauna of Iraq', *Journal of the Bombay Natural History Society*, Vol. XXXI, 1926

Tweedie, W., 'Birds in Flanders during the war', *The Avicultural Magazine*, Vol. VII, No. 5, March 1916

**WEBSITES**

www.bbc.co.uk/history/worldwars/wwone

http://www.gresham.ac.uk/lectures-and-events/
the-first-world-war-disease-the-only-victor

www.noglory.org

http://www.warcomposers.co.uk/butterworthbio.html

http://www.westernfrontassociation.com

https://worldwarzoogardener1939.wordpress.com/2013/07/19/
such-is-the-price-of-empire-the-lost-gardeners-of-kew-in-the-first-world-war/

https://worldwarzoogardener1939.wordpress.com/2013/09/11/
lost-fellows-the-linnean-society-roll-of-honour-1914–1918/

https://worldwarzoogardener1939.wordpress.com/2014/03/04/
lost-ecologists-of-the-first-world-war/

## BOOKS

Adams, Bernard, *Nothing of Importance* (New York, 1918)

Allen, David Elliston, *The Naturalist in Britain* (New Jersey, 1976)

Andrews, C.E., *From the Front* (New York, 1918)

Anonymous, *A Book of Poems for the Blue Cross Fund (To Help Horses in War
Time)* (London, 1917)

Armstrong, Patrick, *The English Parson–Naturalist* (Leominster, 2000)

Arthur, Max, *Forgotten Voices of the Great War* (London, 2003)

Austin, L.J., *My Experience as a German Prisoner* (London, 1915)

Baker, Peter Shaw, *Animal War Heroes* (London, 1933)

Barnett, Denis O., *In Happy Memory* (n.p., 1915)

Bird, Will R., *And We Go On* (Montreal, 2014)

Blacker, C.P., *Have You Forgotten Yet?* (Barnsley, 2000)

Blunden, Edmund, *Undertones of War* (New York, 1929)

Boden, Anthony, *F.W. Harvey: Soldier, Poet* (Stroud, 1998)

Brereton, J.M., *The Horse in War* (London, 1976)

Brown, Malcolm, *Tommy Goes to War* (London, 2009)

Butler, Patrick, *A Galloper at Ypres* (London, 1920)

Campbell, James, *Shepherd's War* (London, 2015)

Chapman, Guy, *A Passionate Prodigality* (London, 1933)

Clout, Hugh, *After the Ruins* (Exeter, 1999)

Coleman, Frederic, *With Cavalry in 1915* (London, 1916)

Cook, Tim, *No Place to Run* (Seattle, 2000)

Cooper, Jilly, *Animals in War* (London, 2000)

Coulson, Leslie, *From an Outpost* (London, 1917)

Crawshay-Williams, Eliot, *Leaves from an Officer's Notebook* (London,
1918)

Crouch, Lionel, *Duty and Service* (n.p., 1917)

Devonald-Lewis, Richard, *From the Somme to the Armistice: The Memoirs of Captain Stormont Gibbs MC* (London, 1986)

Douie, Charles, *The Weary Road* (London, 1929)

Drout, Michael D.C., *J.R.R. Tolkien Encyclopedia* (Abingdon, 2007)

Dunn, J.C., *The War the Infantry Knew* (London, 1988)

Empey, Arthur, *Over the Top* (New York, 1917)

Feilding, R., *War Letters to a Wife* (London, 2001)

Ford, Ford Madox, *Parade's End* (London, 2012)

Frankau, Gilbert, *The Poetical Works of Gilbert Frankau*, Vol. I (London, 1923)

Fussell, Paul, *The Great War and Modern Memory* (Oxford, 1975)

Fyfe, Charlotte, *The Tears of War: The Love Story of a Young Poet and a War Hero* (Pewsey, 2002)

Galtrey, Sidney, *The Horse and the War* (London, 1918)

Gillespie, A.D., *Letters from Flanders* (London, 1916)

Gladstone, Hugh S., *Birds and the War* (London, 1919)

Gosling, Lucinda, *Great War Britain: The First World War at Home* (Stroud, 2014)

Gosse, Philip, *Memoirs of a Camp-Follower* (Uckfield, 2014)

Graham, Stephen, *A Private in the Guards* (London, 1919)

Graves, Robert, *Goodbye to All That* (Harmondsworth, 1960)

Grey, Edward (Viscount Grey of Fallodon), *Recreation* (Cambridge, Massachusetts, 1920)

Groom, W.H.A., *Poor Bloody Infantry* (London, 1976)

Hamilton, Ralph G.A., *The War Diary of The Master of Belhaven, 1914–18* (London, 1924)

Harrison, Gerry (ed.), *To Fight Alongside Friends: The First World War Diaries of Charlie May* (London, 2014)

Hart-Davis, Rupert (ed.), *Siegfried Sassoon: Diaries, 1915–18* (London, 1983)

Harvey, F.W., *Comrades in Captivity* (London, 1920)

— *Gloucestershire Friends: Poems from a German Prison Camp* (London, 1917)

Helphand, Kenneth I., *Defiant Gardens: Making Gardens in Wartime* (San Antonio, Texas, 2006)

Hepper, E. Raymond and Hepper, F. Nigel, *Captain Hepper's Great War Diary* (Kirkby Stephen, 2011)

Hervey, H.E., *Cage-Birds* (London, 1940)

Hesketh-Prichard, H., *Sniping in France* (London, 1920)

Hitchcock, F., *Stand To: A Diary of the Trenches 1915–1918* (London, 1988)

Hodges, Frederick James, *Men of 18 in 1918* (Ilfracombe, 1988)

Hollis, Matthew, *Now All Roads Lead to France: The Last Years of Edward Thomas* (London, 2012)

Holmes, Richard, *Acts of War* (London, 1985)

— *Tommy* (London, 2004)

Holmes, W. Kersley, *More Ballads of Field and Billet* (Paisley, 1915)

Housman, L. (ed.), *War Letters of Fallen Englishmen* (London, 1930)

Hueffer, Ford Madox, *On Heaven, and Poems Written on Active Service* (London, 1918)

Hughes, Michael, *Beyond Holy Russia: The Life and Times of Stephen Graham* (Cambridge, 2014)

Hurd, Michael, *The Ordeal of Ivor Gurney* (London, 1978)

Jones, E.H., *The Road to En-Dor* (London, 1920)

Junger, Ernst, *Storm of Steel* (London, 2003)

Kavanagh, P.J. (ed.), *Collected Poems of Ivor Gurney* (Oxford, 1982)

Kean, Hilda, *Animal Rights* (London, 1998)

Kendall, Tim (ed.), *Poetry of the First World War: An Anthology* (Oxford, 2013)

Kettle, Tom, *The Ways of War* (New York, 1918)

Laurie, Martin, *Cupid's War* (Cirencester, 2014)

Lee, Joseph, *A Captive in Karlsruhe and other German Prison Camps* (London, 1920)

Lewis, David (ed.), *Remembrances of Hell: The Great War Diary of Writer, Broadcaster and Naturalist – Norman Ellison* (Shrewsbury, 1997)

Lewis-Stempel, John, *Six Weeks* (London, 2010)

— *The War Behind the Wire* (London, 2014)

Lloyd, L.L. (with W. Byam), *Lice and Their Menace to Man* (Oxford, 1919)

Longworth, Philip, *The Unending Vigil* (Barnsley, 2010)

MacArthur, Brian (ed.), *Voices from the First World War* (London, 2008)

Macdonald, Lyn, *The Roses of No Man's Land* (Harmondsworth, 1993)

MacPherson, W.G. et al., *Medical Services. Diseases of the War, Vol. 2. History of the Great War Based on Official Documents* (London, 1923)

Meyer, Jessica (ed.), *British Popular Culture and the First World War* (Leiden, 2008)

Meynell, Viola, *Julian Grenfell* (London, 1917)

Moore, Jerrold Northrop, *Edward Elgar: A Creative Life* (Oxford, 1999)

Mosley, Nicholas, *Julian Grenfell: his Life and the Times of His Death* (London, 1976)

Moss, Stephen, *A Bird in the Bush* (London, 2013)

Moynihan, Michael, *Black Bread and Barbed Wire* ( London, 1978)

Munro, H.H. ('Saki'), *The Square Egg, and Other Sketches* (London, 1929)

Mynott, Jeremy, *Birdscapes* (Princeton, 2009)

Noakes, Vivian, *Voices of Silence* (Stroud, 2006)

Osborn, E.B. (ed.), *The Muse in Arms* (London, 1917)

— *The New Elizabethans* (New York, 1919)

Paice, Edward, *Tip & Run: The Untold Tragedy of the Great War in Africa* (London, 2007)

Parker, E.W., *Into Battle* (Barnsley, 2013)

Pollard, Ernest and Strouts, Hazel, *Wings over the Western Front: The First World War Diaries of Collingwood Ingram* (Eynsham, 2014)

Powell, Anne (ed.), *The Fierce Light: The Battle of the Somme* (Stroud, 2006)

Richardson, E.H., *British War Dogs: Their Training and Psychology* (London, 1920)

Rogerson, Sidney, *Twelve Days* (London 1933)

Sadler, John and Serdiville, Rosie, *Tommy at War* (London, 2013)

Saunders, Nicholas J., *The Poppy* (London, 2013)

Scott, Ralph, *A Soldier's Diary* ( London, 1923)

Sherriff, R.C., *Journey's End* (London, 2000)

Smith, Wayne (ed.), *George Butterworth Memorial Volume* (Oxford, 2015)

Springer, Shaun and Humphreys, Stuart (eds), *Private Beaston's War* (Barnsley, 2009)

Stallworthy, Jon, *Anthem for Doomed Youth* (London, 2002)

Storey, Neil R., *Animals in the First World War* (Botley, 2014)

Talbot Kelly, R.B., *A Subaltern's Odyssey* (London, 1980)

Thomas, George (ed.), *Edward Thomas, The Collected Poems and War Diary* (London, 2004)

Thornton, R.K.R. (ed.), *Ivor Gurney: War Letters* (Ashington, 1983)

Tiplady, Thomas, *The Cross at the Front* (New York, 1917)

— *The Soul of the Soldier* (London, 1918)

Tombs, Robert, *The English and Their History* (London, 2014)

Van Emden, Richard, *Tommy's Ark* (London, 2011)

Vandiver, Elizabeth, *Stand in the Trench, Achilles* (Oxford, 2010)

Vaughan, Edwin Campion, *Some Desperate Glory* (London, 1981)

Voigt, F.A., *Combed Out* (London, 1920)

Wainwright, Martin (ed.), *Wartime Country Diaries* (London, 2007)

Waller, Michael L., *The Conservatism of the British Cavalry and Its Effect on the British Army of WWII* (Ann Arbor, 2009)

War Office, *Statistics of the Military Effort of the British Empire during the Great War 1914–1920* (London, 1922)

Ward, Chris, *Living on the Western Front* (London, 2013)

Wheatley, Dennis, *The Time Has Come* (London, 1977)

Williamson, Anne, *Henry Williamson and the First World War* (Stroud, 2004)

Wright, David (ed.), *Edward Thomas Selected Poems and Prose* (Harmonds-
    worth, 1981)
Zeepvat, Charlotte, *Before Action: William Noel Hodgson and the 9th Devons*
    (Barnsley, 2014)
Zinsser, H., *Rats, Lice and History* (Boston, 1935)

# INDEX